ONE ARM
BOWLS A LITTLE

ONE ARM
BOWLS A LITTLE

100 Years of the Stragglers
of Asia Cricket Club

WILLY BOULTER

First published in 2025 by Willy Boulter,
in partnership with Whitefox Publishing

www.stragglersofasia.co.uk
www.wearewhitefox.com

Copyright © Willy Boulter, 2025

ISBN 978-1-916797-89-5
Also available as an eBook
ISBN 978-1-916797-91-8

Willy Boulter asserts the moral right to be identified as the author of this work.

All rights reserved. No part of this publication may be reproduced, stored in a retrieval system or transmitted in any form or by any means, electronic, mechanical, photocopying, recording or otherwise, without prior written permission of the author.

While every effort has been made to trace the owners of copyright material reproduced herein, the author would like to apologise for any omissions and will be pleased to incorporate missing acknowledgements in any future editions.

All photographs and illustrations in this book © The Stragglers of Asia CC

Edited by Jenni Davis and Peter Salmon
Designed and typeset by Typo•glyphix
Cover design by Tom Cabot/ketchup
Project management by Whitefox Publishing

For Caterina

FOREWORD

CRICKET ARRIVED IN INDIA with the British in the early eighteenth century and the game has thrived there ever since. It would be another two centuries before the Stragglers of Asia Cricket Club was formed, and the club has since provided some wonderful cricket in the UK, in Asia and on tour. I joined the Stragglers on a tour myself, in 1977, to Germany, where the British forces hosted us.

Willy Boulter brings an historian's instincts to the book. And a great mix of detail, anecdote and cricket lore. The Stragglers of Asia have always attracted some wonderful characters, and they fill the pages.

Later, Willy and I were keen to keep the Club's energy alive in our playing days in Hong Kong. The annual Stragglers game against the Hong Kong CC was a well-contested highlight of the season and continues to this day. As our wicket-keeper, Willy's encouraging calls of 'Come on Stragglers!' from behind the stumps kept us all going in the hot afternoon sun.

This is a book all lovers of cricket will enjoy, and it speaks to a little-known chapter of the game's wonderful history, as well as recognizing those who have contributed to this famous club in its first century.

Sir Rod Eddington
Melbourne, Australia
December 2024

INTRODUCTION

IN 1925, India was very much the 'jewel in the crown' of British colonial possessions, as the old cliché has it, but it was also a country that was simmering with discontent. The power of the regime under the viceroy was ebbing away, unevenly and intermittently, attacked by nationalist agitators within India and by forward-thinking parliamentary liberals and others in the home country. It was a slim few years since the viceroy in 1912, Lord Hardinge, had almost been assassinated in Chandni Chowk, Delhi, while the massacre at Jallianwala Bagh, a garden near the Sikh Golden Temple in Amritsar, in 1919 – when Gurkha and Indian troops under Brigadier General Reginald Dyer cold-bloodedly killed 379 civilians – was fresh in the memory. Meanwhile, in 1924 E.M. Forster had published *A Passage to India*, a more nuanced look at the imperial experience than the Kipling that had sufficed thus far.

Into this febrile environment, a group of white British expatriates living in colonial India brought to life a new cricket club, the Stragglers of Asia – a club whose story over the next 100 years was inextricably linked with the story of Indian (and Pakistani) independence, the 'end of empire' and the cultural integration that these events drove. The tale of the Stragglers is intimately related to questions of decolonization and race, issues that were inconsistently addressed by individuals wrestling with their consciences, as the club made faltering progress towards inclusivity and diversity.

ONE ARM BOWLS A LITTLE

From foundation, the Stragglers were closely involved in the events of British India – they lost one of their number, B.E.J. Burge, to a murder committed by Bengali freedom fighters; the club then suffered grievous losses during the Second World War, many in heartrendingly tragic circumstances, including Lt. Col. L.V.S. Sherwood, who survived the six years of war only to be deliberately shot by one of his own soldiers; and in the decades following Indian independence in 1947, the committee displayed a stubborn reluctance to allow Indian members, an apparently equivocal position being taken by leaders like Tom Longfield, who became father-in-law to future England captain Ted Dexter. More positively, three members, including Stuart Barnes, a senior figure at Jardine Matheson, the iconic British trading house, made a huge contribution to the survival of the Hong Kong Cricket Club as it was ejected from its city location in the early seventies. This was just a couple of years after the Stragglers in the UK had finally admitted their first Indian member and begun to attract, through their very moniker, increasing numbers of non-white players.

By the 1990s the club had over sixty fixtures a year at its apogee, culminating in a 75th Anniversary Tour to India and the Festival of Wandering Cricket at Oxford in 2000. This festival celebrated wandering clubs, which are basically teams of like-minded individuals who have no fixed abode or ground of their own, but play using the grounds of their opponents or, where neither club has its own pitch, renting. Some wandering clubs have a close association with a particular venue, such as the Sussex Martlets with Arundel Castle Cricket Ground or the Bluemantle's with the Nevill at Tunbridge Wells, but very few have the luxury of owning a ground. For the Stragglers of Asia, the closest association historically was with Calcutta or, now, Hong Kong.

Today, the Straggler fixture card is around twenty-five to thirty games encompassing teams in England such as I Zingari (the oldest of the wandering clubs), the Somerset Stragglers and the South Oxfordshire Amateurs; meanwhile, the Hong Kong section keeps the Asian connection very much alive with an annual game or two. Tours have always been part of the Straggler tradition from its earliest days, when a 'Western Tour' was a key part of the 1930s fixtures. Forays to Hong Kong, South Africa, Sri Lanka (twice), Malta, Morocco, the Algarve and other exotic lands have been enjoyed and, in the Centenary year of 2025, the club embarks on a third visit to India, its original place of conception.

INTRODUCTION

Some of the themes covered in this account, especially concerning the racial aspect, are uncomfortable: my attitude is simply to use the primary sources we have to relate the story and resist judgement. I am critical of certain individuals, only in the context of everyone having their strengths and weaknesses - indeed, one of the joys of cricket is the way that different characters contribute to a team - and here the Stragglers, like any club, encompass a merry bunch of eccentrics, 'wrong 'uns', saints and straightforward retired army officers!

At a time when the game of cricket has come under attack for its historic racism in the Independent Commission for Equity in Cricket (ICEC) report of 2022, this Straggler story offers support for the view that the vast majority of cricketers of any ethnicity are definitely not racist and communicate across cultures much better than most people, learning those skills through the eternally absorbing game that is cricket.

Chapter One
BEGINNINGS
FOUR FOUNDERS AND THE MAHARAJAH
1925–1939

'In the early 1920s, when stationed in Ambala in the Gunners, I was invited by the late Maharajah of Patiala to take a cricket team to Chail every summer. Chail was in the Simla Hills, 7,000 feet up. The Maharajah had cut off the top of one of the peaks and made a cricket ground. It was the most tremendous fun, and we played them at everything. Cricket, hockey, tennis, billiards, and we even did our best in the whisky stakes. The Patiala peg was two fingers, measured with the first and little fingers. After we had done this for a few years, we discussed the possibility of forming a club.'

ONE ARM BOWLS A LITTLE

ON A VERY HOT SUMMER EVENING in early July 1925, after dinner at Simpson's in the Strand, four young men sat around the fountains and the statues in the shadow of Nelson's Column, Trafalgar Square, discussing the finer details of the club they were shortly to inaugurate. As described in the letter quoted above, written in 1956 by one of the founding members, Lt. Col. P.B. Sanger, they had been discussing it for some time.

Trafalgar Square, with all its historic statuary, was an ironic venue for the formation of a club that, over the next 100 years, was to embody imperial decline. The Stragglers - created shortly after the height of the British Empire (generally accepted by many historians as 1911, the occasion of the Delhi Durbar held to mark the succession of King George V as emperor) - reflect on a small scale, sometimes precisely, changes in the social history of the country over the century. The reason for the club was, in simple terms, to provide cricket for white colonial servants going home on leave every three or four years, when they generally took a 'long leave' of six months as allowed for in their agreements or terms of service.

'Tony' Sanger was a career soldier, educated at Cheltenham and Sandhurst, who had caught the end of the First World War as a young officer in the Royal Artillery. He spent the early 1920s in India and then went off to the Royal West African Frontier Force, before returning to India and entering the Indian Army in Prince Albert Victor's Own Cavalry - since he was a champion polo player, one imagines this transfer was one he lobbied hard for! It was also quite unusual to transfer mid-career from the British to the Indian Army and demonstrates that Sanger was a singular man.

How exactly Sanger found himself invited to bring a team to Chail is not obvious from the documents available, although we can say that he was clearly in the first rank of cricketers in India, as he was to play for the Army against the Navy at Lord's in 1925, an era when these matches were accorded 'first-class' status. He was certainly a member at the Lahore Gymkhana, which was the centre of cricket in western India. As a Straggler, Sanger played only fourteen games, but over a long period - 1925 to 1958. He was a committee member for many years and set up the first Straggler fixtures in Germany in 1954: as a player, he was a very good wicket-keeper/batsman, ending with nearly 300 runs for the club at an average of 20.

BEGINNINGS: FOUR FOUNDERS AND THE MAHARAJAH, 1925-1939

We have a grainy photograph of 'Sanger's XI' (actually nine, including one Indian player) against 'His Highness Patiala's Team' - of whom more later - in 1923. One of the Patiala team is the great Ranjitsinhji of Navanagar, who had been a close friend of the Patiala family for thirty years, depending on them for income after going bankrupt at one point. Ranji was the first Indian cricketer to achieve fame, captaining Sussex and playing fifteen Tests for England in the 1890s, scoring 154 not out on debut. His wristy batting style introduced a new shot to the game, the 'leg glance', as revolutionary at the time as the 'scoop' or 'reverse sweep' has been in the past decade or so.

Sanger was one of the four in London that evening, but modestly credits two of the others, Vernon Maynard and Alleyne Coldwell, as 'entirely responsible for working (the club) up to what it has become'. It seems that while Sanger had collected the teams to go up to Chail, it was Maynard who had the idea to organize elevens in England specifically for men home on leave - and the first of those teams had the Straggler name attached to it. In due course, it was Maynard who became known as the 'Founder'.

Among Stragglers today, there is a cadre who would love for Chail to be recognized as the birthplace of the club, and indeed a visit to Chail was undertaken on the 2000 Tour to India - and one is planned for the Centenary Tour in 2025. Reportedly the 'highest cricket ground in the world' at 7,500 feet (Sanger undersold it), cricket could be played in the summer months when the plains of northern India would have been at 40°C+ - even prior to global warming! The whole government of India annually moved from Delhi to Simla in the summers and the Maharajah's teams had plenty of potential opposition. Chail is an evocative place for the club - however, as the records assembled by the founders themselves record, the first game was played in England rather than in India, and this account prefers Chail as the site of conception, Eastbourne as very definitely the place of birth!

Vernon Maynard was born in 1893 and sent to Eastbourne College, where his name can be found today on a board in the pavilion, as a member of the First XI for five years and captain in 1911. Later, at Cambridge, he narrowly failed to get a rugby Blue and appeared for Harlequins Rugby Club as a scrum half. A soldier in the First World War, he left the Army because of wounds and took up a career in the burgeoning oil industry, at the time working for the Attock Oil Company, engaged in exploration work in what is now Pakistan. It is likely the wounds he suffered in 1917 were to blame for his lack of playing success for the Stragglers (he normally batted well down the order and bowled sparingly), but as many clubs know, the less keen players are often the greatest enthusiasts and best organizers.

It was Maynard who had the idea of playing against his old school in the fixture, which continues a century later. The team he raised in July 1925 is described in the school magazine as 'H.A.V. Maynard's XI', with, in brackets, 'The Stragglers of Asia'. According to the *Eastbournian*, it was the 'most enjoyable' fixture of the year for the school XI. We do not know the origin of the name, although it was not the first use of 'Stragglers' in the cricketing world – the 'Somerset Stragglers', who were to become sometime opponents over the 100 years, were founded in 1900, so possibly inspiration came from there. Certainly, the sobriquet of 'Straggler' fitted well when the participants came, to a man, from the far-off climes of India and Asia, and the name certainly stood out among the more prosaically named 'Gentlemen of Leicestershire' or – hard to imagine today – 'Gentlemen of Croydon'.

Alleyne Coldwell was a captain in the Northamptonshire Regiment who had served in France during the First World War and was posted around 1922 to the 2nd Battalion, which was resident at the time in Karachi, then part of British India. By 1925, reassigned to the Regimental Depot at Northampton, it was he who became the 'Honorary Home Secretary' of the club, effectively running its affairs and maintaining the membership records. He purloined a thick, almost-300-page hardbacked War Office exercise book that had briefly been used in the canteen of the regiment and reused it to become the register of members.

Over the next sixty or so years, Coldwell and his successors as honorary secretary listed those joining the club, split into alphabetically headed sections – providing a brief pen portrait of their cricketing attributes. Coldwell's in particular makes interesting reading: short, trenchant, often with dry humour. It is his description of A.J. Trollope, a member of the original XI at Eastbourne, 'One arm bowls a little', that inspired the title of this history. Reggie Senior, one of his regular team-mates, is described as 'Poor in all respects'; Lt. Col. E.C. Chesney is 'A useful bat, a very good fellow, good company on tour'; while Major Somers-Cox of the 4th Battalion, Baluch Regiment, is a 'better bowler than bat, not great at either'. Another character is described as 'Played

BEGINNINGS: FOUR FOUNDERS AND THE MAHARAJAH, 1925–1939

with me in 1930 and was utterly hopeless', despite being a member of MCC and the Free Foresters. Clearly a straight-talking character, Alleyne Coldwell (known to his friends as 'Willie') was an avid cricketer who, following his retirement from the Army, went into cricket administration as secretary of Northamptonshire County Cricket Club.

The fourth man in the group seated around the fountains on that evening was another soldier, Frank Mason-MacFarlane, in his mid-thirties, who had been serving in India during the Third Afghan War in 1919: he was a much-decorated officer from the First World War, with the Military Cross (MC) and two bars. Before the Second World War, he would be a military attaché at the British Embassy in Berlin and contemplated assassinating Hitler - 'He seems to have decided that such an attempt would have been injudicious, if not un-British', according to one historian. Others blame cold feet in the Foreign Office - according to another account, Mason-Mac was himself keen, pointing out that his flat in Berlin had a clear line of fire to where Hitler would speak celebrating his fiftieth birthday on 20 April 1939. Later, at Dunkirk, he led the hastily organized 'Mac Force', which defended the eastern sector - for which he received the next-highest award up from the MC, a Distinguished Service Order (DSO).

He was described by his Staff College instructors as 'an intense individualist' with ability 'above that of every one of his fellow students'. In early 1942, after briefly commanding a division as a Major General, he was appointed as Governor of Gibraltar, where he served with distinction in that crucial base, which controlled the Western Mediterranean, from early 1942 to 1944.

He was then appointed Chief Commissioner of the Allied Control Commission for Italy (an appointment that was effectively the temporary head of state) and it was while in this job that he violently disagreed with Churchill over the nomination for Italian prime minister. It was his dislike of Churchill that motivated him to stand as the Labour Party candidate for North Paddington in the 'khaki election' of 1945 (so called because millions of demobbed servicemen took part) - when he beat the playwright (and friend of Churchill) Brendan Bracken. A rare example, at that time, of socialist political leanings in a General Officer.

According to Sir Frederick Whyte in a tribute after his early death in 1953, 'Mason-MacFarlane could choose and direct a team and make them work overtime without noticing it'. He was described in *Time* magazine as 'one of Britain's ablest soldier-administrators'.

Sanger relates that the morning after the meeting in Trafalgar Square, the foursome plus his wife went to Fosters in St James's, the pre-eminent tailor of cricketing attire, to choose the club's colours. Vernon Maynard insisted that, whatever else it contained, the tie must have 'apple green' in it. The other two colours to some extent chose themselves – the four had agreed to have the keen cricketing Maharajah of Patiala as an Honorary Life Member, given his hospitality over many years at Chail, so royal purple was a natural selection, and, acknowledging the Indian origins of the club, black was the third. Uncomfortable as it may read to modern eyes, 'black' was often the shorthand used for India – for example, post-independence, British officers who transferred from the Indian Army to the Royal Artillery in the British Army were known informally as 'Black Gunners'.

'After much argument', according to Sanger, 'Eira, my wife, chose the tie'.

Settled on colours that allow members to sport blazers, ties and caps that still today stand out, albeit with rather more discretion than some other wandering or 'jazz-hat' clubs, the founders repaired to the Savoy, where they had a lunch appointment with their old friend the Maharajah.

His Highness Maharajah Bhupinder Singh was, even by the standards of Indian princes (there were over 500 princely states), a character.

His father, Maharajah Rajinder Singh, was a flamboyant figure who had been the originator of the Chail cricket ground in the 1890s, levelling the top of a mountain. He recruited English professionals and the best players from India to ensure that Patiala was the strongest cricketing state. He married an Irishwoman, having already sired a son, and the relations with the British government were 'tetchy' according to one account. Unfortunately, he died in November 1900 at the age of twenty-eight, leaving his nine-year-old heir, Bhupinder, who was carefully nurtured by the British establishment until he was of age to assume the title formally.

Bhupinder Singh became, as *The Times* said in its obituary, a 'striking and forceful Ruler', a 'tall and handsome figure' with 'fine expressive features and luminous eyes'.

According to one account, he would each year go on a royal progress through the streets of his capital, Patiala, naked on a carriage concealed only

BEGINNINGS: FOUR FOUNDERS AND THE MAHARAJAH, 1925-1939

by a flimsy curtain, accompanied by a few of his favourite wives, displaying his genitalia in full bloom, as it were, to reassure his subjects that he was a virile and capable ruler – since he apparently fathered more than eighty children, this display was perhaps unnecessary. He was certainly a *bon viveur*, known for his 'overflowing hospitality', and modern historians of India, such as William Dalrymple, who has written definitive accounts of the colonial era, describe him as a 'party animal' – hence the 'Patiala peg'. According to one biographer, quoted by Stephen King in *The Spectator* magazine in 2006, 'he was a sexual athlete who in his prime enjoyed a virgin a day, but in old age cut down to one a week'.

The Maharajah seems to have accepted British rule in India, to the extent that he recruited actively for the Indian Army in the First World War from his Punjab territories – historically and today a relatively wealthy part of India, thanks to the irrigation of the 'five rivers' (a translation of Punjab) and the resultant plentiful crop production. In 1917, there were already two *lakh* Punjabis serving the king in the Indian Army (a *lakh* is 100,000), and the Maharajah asked for two *lakhs* more, personally raising 15,000.

He was also a very keen cricketer, although of modest ability, ending with a first-class batting average of 17.4, well below the 35+ one would expect of a reasonable batsman. In 1911, at the age of nineteen, he was nominated captain of the first truly Indian team to tour England, and by 1934, he had become president of the Cricket Club of India (CCI), well experienced in the Byzantine politics of Indian cricket, which continue to this day – where riches even beyond the means of a Maharajah are in play (although not with the Stragglers, a strictly amateur club!). In that capacity, he pressured the Bombay government to grant the land on which he built the Brabourne Stadium, today's home of the CCI, and named after the departing governor, Lord Brabourne. For many years, CCI hosted Test matches in Bombay, or Mumbai as it became, and it was only with Wankhede Stadium's construction in 1974/75 that its role as the pre-eminent cricket venue in western India was usurped.

Politically, the Maharajah was also important, attending, as the 'Princely Member', the sixth session of the League of Nations in Geneva in 1925, with a large retinue. He was detested by Lord Willingdon, the viceroy from 1931 to 1936, allegedly because he made a pass at one of the viceregal daughters yet continued as the leader of the princes. In short, although 'many controversies gathered round his complex personality' (*The Times*), a more prominent sponsor of the Stragglers of Asia Cricket Club could hardly be wished for, and the association of the club with his family has continued to the present.

It might be considered ironic or strange that while the founding members of the club were happy to exult in its origins in India, and to have the Maharajah among their ranks, it was to be over forty years before another Indian member was admitted as a Straggler. Probably in 1925 it did not seem so odd – as mentioned, the brilliant batsman Ranjitsinhji had already blazed a trail in the cricketing world in the 1890s and links between the royal houses of India and the British establishment were tight. The princely states were an important component of colonial administration, where the rulers acted as the local government overseen by British 'political agents'. They governed millions of people and could easily cause problems for the colonial government in Delhi, with its limited forces. Naturally, the princes were the last people harbouring nationalist agendas and were happy to live with the colonial status quo.

An Indian prince as a patron was very acceptable, especially one who, as Sanger related, provided such significant hospitality at Chail. On the other hand, admitting ordinary Indians was never considered. The royals were seen as completely different people – far richer than most British aristocrats and people to be treated with respect and care. The 'luxurious world of Indian royalty was astounding, exotic and spectacular beyond reasonable belief', as one lady spectator wrote. Even an entirely English club, the Sussex Martlets, had Ranjitsinhji (by then His Highness the Maharajah of Navanagar) as one of three patrons in 1925.

Nevertheless, to the modern eye, the exclusion of Indians within Straggler ranks from the outset demonstrates the insular or even ignorant outlook of men not directly involved in matters of state. The movement for greater equality between the colonials and local populace had been gathering pace. In 1919, the Government of India Act, which was an initial recognition by the British of the inevitability of independence (although there was still a long and winding road ahead), opened the officer corps of both the elite Indian Civil Service and the Indian Army to men of Indian, rather than exclusively British, origin. As a result, by the 1940s, Indian Army infantry battalions were being commanded in battle by Indian officers, of equal status to whites as 'King's Commissioned Officers', as opposed to the more

BEGINNINGS: FOUR FOUNDERS AND THE MAHARAJAH, 1925-1939

junior 'Viceroy Commissioned Officers' previously, and in the civil administration the ICS had a cadre of perfectly competent Indian senior civil servants. It is unfortunate, if not surprising, that six years after the 1919 Act, the Stragglers were formed along the traditional colonial lines, 'locals' not admitted – and this is not the last time that actual practice on the ground lagged behind legislation.

Another example of the slow pace of social change can be seen in the first Indian cricket tournament organized in Bombay from the 1900s up to 1945; successively known as the Triangular Tournament, the Quadrangular and eventually the Pentangular, it consisted of teams divided along entirely religious and racial lines: the Muslims, the Parsees, the Hindus, the Europeans and the Rest – a category comprising smaller minority groups such as Indian Christians, Jews and Buddhists. Eventually, by the 1930s, people realized that communal cricket was doing nothing to help a very diverse nation become independent in a peaceful manner and gradually integration began; instances occur of teams being selected across racial divides for inter-zonal games in what became, at the instigation of the Maharajah of Patiala, the Ranji Trophy competition. By 1941, according to *The Times of India*, intercommunal cricket had become 'unsuited to conditions obtaining in the country' and it was 'beyond comprehension as to how sports could have anything to do with caste, creed and colour'.

In short, there is no doubt the Stragglers were born into a time of hesitant, confused and uncertain change, even in the confined world of Indian cricket.

As we have seen, the whole *raison d'être* for Vernon Maynard's club was to provide a team in England for white colonial servants to play for when returning to the mother country on leave. Before commercial aviation began, home leaves from India were taken by ship, necessitating a long absence of six months. Whether a man joined the Indian Army (or was posted with a British Army regiment in India like Mason-Mac, Coldwell and Sanger), the Indian Civil Service or one of the tea or trading companies, it was routine that he went east for around an initial three-year period. As such, for men departing England after university or, more often, on appointment aged eighteen or nineteen, there was little opportunity to join a club such as MCC or the Free Foresters, nor one of the geographically based gentlemen's cricket clubs, such as the Hampshire Hogs, the Band of Brothers in

Kent or the Somerset Stragglers. Faced with a long leave of six months, one can imagine there was an appetite among the young gentlemen for something other than low-standard games with their local village or estate team: many of them had played good cricket at university or elsewhere, close to 'first-class' standard – as MCC designated international, county and most professional cricket.

The first Straggler game was played in July 1925 at the end of the Eastbourne College term: the match was 'a great success in every way', according to the school. Interestingly, in a portent of customary practice in wandering cricket, when fielding eleven fit players is a constant worry, Maynard had to borrow one member from the school! The Straggler XI in batting order was:

Capt. A.F. Garnons-Williams – Royal Fusiliers, due to go to Staff College in Quetta
Capt. P.B. Sanger – Royal Artillery, stationed in Ambala
A.O.D. Taylor – Mackenzie Lyall and Co, Calcutta
Capt. Alleyne Coldwell – Northamptonshire Regiment, Northampton, recently returned from Karachi
Capt. A.W.B. Beecher – King's Own Yorkshire Light Infantry, stationed at Ferozepore
A.F. Senior – Indian Police Service in Kanpur
Lt. B.C.H. Kimmins – Royal Artillery, stationed in Meerut
G.S. Johnston – Shaw Wallace and Co, Calcutta
A.J. Trollope – details unknown
G.F. Branch – Eastbourne schoolboy
H.A.V. Maynard – the founder of the club, working with the Attock Oil Company in Lahore

The game itself was a close one, although no bowling analysis survives. The College batted first and reached 250 for 9 wickets at 4.10 p.m., with most of the runs coming from the tailenders, J.C. Corrie at No. 10 scoring 52 not out. One wonders if Maynard put on his weaker bowlers, perhaps even one-armed Trollope, after Beecher had removed most of the top order in taking 5 wickets – rather than grind an opposition into the dust. Such a gentlemanly gesture

BEGINNINGS: FOUR FOUNDERS AND THE MAHARAJAH, 1925-1939

is still typical of a wandering club, where short games are never the best games. The 'Eastbournian' takes up the story:

> The Stragglers included more than one first-class bat in their ranks and set about going for the runs at once in most determined fashion, scoring 110 in 35 minutes with only one wicket down.
>
> The rate of scoring, however, slowed down a bit, and with Morse keeping an excellent length, things looked better for us. It was at this point our fielding became quite first-class; catches were held and three of the opposition run out. AOD Taylor played a magnificent innings, but in spite of this we were able to get the Stragglers out on the stroke of time.
>
> Morres bowled some good balls and captained the side well, and Heath held a very fine catch (to dismiss Coldwell for a duck).

Alec Taylor, described by Coldwell's register as a 'very good left hand bat', was run out for 114 as the Stragglers ended up 16 runs short. One imagines Vernon Maynard, last in and last out (also run out), was disappointed not to win but delighted with the game.

Maynard's vision certainly found an appreciative market among the India expatriates, and an 'Honorary Foreign Secretary' was appointed at Calcutta, to spread the word; soon after, representatives were appointed all over the Far East and even in China, sending details of candidates to the foreign secretary for forwarding to Coldwell in Northampton, who helped candidates play two 'qualifying' matches when on leave. On the basis of performance (both cricketing and social) in these games, a player could be put up for membership at the next committee meeting.

A key qualification for membership was 'to have been in residence for at least one year East of Suez', as it was described in the first printed 'Rules' of the club, produced in 1928 - at the time, and for many decades afterwards, the term 'east of Suez' was in the national lexicon designating where the Asian part of the Empire began. It became a vital part of the Straggler brand too, the distinguishing feature of the club among its counterparts in the world of wandering cricket. By 1932, the requirement was increased to two years, rather than one, and then in 1934, this became 'two years in Asia east of Suez'. Over time, as we shall see, Rule 5 was tinkered with and diluted, as British commitments overseas gradually reduced, becoming by the 1970s 'East of Dover' (informally). Indeed, it was in the mid-1970s that the general British withdrawal from 'east of Suez' was accomplished. In the early 1980s, even before for certain individuals, the geographical qualification completely disappeared.

After the initial game in 1925, two were played in 1926 – at Eastbourne again and one against Lancing College.

The team was different and, given the three-year gap between typical leaves, the Stragglers XI varied from season to season and game to game, as today. One or two members of course, like Coldwell, had returned to England semi-permanently and were more prominent in the early years.

The Rules of 1928 noted that:

> Members abroad wishing to put up candidates for election may obtain membership forms from AL Hosie Esq., 9, London Street, Calcutta, or Capt E Cameron, 2nd/6th Gurkha Rifles, Shillong, Assam.

A.L. (Alec) Hosie is another important figure in early Straggler history: thirty-five in 1925, he was already captain of Calcutta Cricket Club and had played first-class cricket for Oxford University in 1913 (although without getting a Blue), Hampshire (for whom he was to appear eighty times over a twenty-two-year span), Bengal and the 'Europeans' team in India. He was in England during the summer of 1925, and he must have met up with Maynard in between the ten County Championship and two MCC games he played in; with his position in Calcutta as the pre-eminent cricketer, he was the ideal recruiting officer for the nascent club. In the event, the 'foreign secretary' quite quickly became Murray Robertson, probably because Hosie was too prominent and senior for such a role – he would go on to be chairman of the Indian selectors (to the understandable annoyance of the nationalists) when the MCC team toured in 1933-34. Hosie first played for the Stragglers in the summer of 1928, appointed before the season to manage the Oxford Tour: for him, no requirement for qualifying matches!

As a Straggler he was an effective batsman, making 1,179 runs at an average of 38 in 33 innings.

BEGINNINGS: FOUR FOUNDERS AND THE MAHARAJAH, 1925–1939

There are seventy-three members listed in 1928, forty-six of them army officers: twelve or so of the military men were Indian Army as opposed to British, from the exotically named Cookes Rifles, Deccan Horse, Punjab Regiment, Dogra Regiment, Baluch Regiment and Frontier Force Regiment – as well as the more familiar, to modern ears, Gurkha Rifles.

Fixtures for 1928 consisted of a four-day Cambridge Tour, with games against Gonville and Caius College; a two-day game against the Cambridge Crusaders (the Cambridge University Second XI) and Pembroke College; and a corresponding tour of Oxford, against Magdalen and Brasenose Colleges, and a two-day game against the Oxford University Second XI, the Authentics. There was also the match against Eastbourne College, as well as fixtures against the Northamptonshire Regiment (two days), United Services Portsmouth, Old Edwardians (two days) and Royal Artillery (two days). Altogether, sixteen days' cricket, 'match managed' by Maynard, Coldwell and Hosie.

In 1929, a significant figure in the wider Indian cricket story appeared in Straggler colours: Conrad Powell Johnstone (known as C.P. or 'Con') was a Cambridge Blue and Kent cricketer who worked for the Burmah Shell Company in South India. He had played for Kent in 1919 and played in the annual first-class game between the Europeans and the Indians at Madras (now Chennai) between 1926 and 1946, on one occasion in the same team as E.A. Cowdrey, father of the late Lord (Colin) Cowdrey, Kent and England captain. He captained Madras in the inaugural Ranji Trophy in 1934 and became president of the Madras Cricket Club in 1947. He represented Kent again when on home leaves in 1925 and 1929, and, after retiring to England in 1948, served on their committee, becoming president in 1967. Johnstone was awarded the CBE in 1948 for his contribution to the development of cricket in Madras.

His playing record for the club extends from 1929 to 1958 and he was certainly a Straggler of modern outlook. Johnstone sponsored the development of young Indian cricketers – for instance, M.J. Gopalan was given a job in the oil company, a stable income while he trained, and he subsequently played both cricket and hockey for India. Johnstone is remembered very fondly locally, to the extent that a new pavilion built at the Chepauk ground in Chennai was named the 'CP Johnstone' pavilion as recently as 1997, even though Johnstone had died in 1974. Importantly for the club, there is also evidence that he introduced the first Indian to play for the Stragglers in the early 1950s, although that did not lead to membership.

In the summer of 1929, a remarkable two-day game was played on the Cambridge tour against Pembroke College, who batted first, scoring an enormous 378 for 7. The Stragglers in reply were bowled out for 138 and the students asked them to 'follow on' under the laws of cricket for two-innings-a-side games, where the side batting second can be forced to bat again immediately if their first-innings score is more than 200 runs adrift. Captain Harold Webster, after a duck in the first innings, steadily accumulated 224 not out (still the highest individual score by a Straggler), with a declaration coming at 437 for 7, setting the College 201 to win. A student named W.H. Webster (no relation), having scored 95 in the first innings, scored 103 not out and took them to victory. Truly a Websters' match!

In May 1999, some seventy years later, Harold Webster's niece contacted the club and supplied some details of his life: he was in the Indian Army Service Corps and stationed in Peshawar in the twenties, where he became a Straggler. Unusually, he oversaw the mule transport, a vital part of the screw-gun mountain artillery, substantial guns being dismantled and carried by mules into the Khyber Pass – manoeuvres made famous by Rudyard Kipling's verse and song.

In cricketing circles, Webster was feted at the Peshawar Club for 'scoring a century before breakfast'. Owing to the heat of India, the practice was to start games early in the morning and take a long break mid-day.

Webster left India in 1935 on retirement at fifty-four and went to Mombasa in Kenya, where he opened a hotel. In 1939, on the outbreak of the Second World War, he immediately volunteered and became a Major in the King's African Rifles, 'responsible for malarial control'.

By 1930, the Straggler fixture list had increased to twenty-six days, with the addition of Bradfield Waifs, the Somerset Stragglers and Mr M.B.U. Dewar's XI, all two days. A game against Colchester Garrison was also added but this lasted only a year, while Coldwell was posted there. Two years later, the western foray to play Somerset Stragglers at Taunton expanded to Sidmouth at their picturesque ground and the Devon Dumplings at Exeter. In 1933, Coldwell was posted abroad, this time to the Caribbean, and George Blake took over as the secretary.

BEGINNINGS: FOUR FOUNDERS AND THE MAHARAJAH, 1925-1939

In his own way, Blake was as significant a character as any of the founding four. A cricketer of modest ability, described in the register as 'moderate bat, not good for more important matches', in 70 innings for the club he averaged 9 runs and bowled sparingly, taking 18 wickets. But it was he who organized the expansion of the fixtures through the thirties and then took the major responsibility, with Maynard and Coldwell, of reviving the club after the Second World War. In team pictures, Blake sits there, in Straggler blazer, in the front row, stern-faced and secure, moustache bristling. He spawned a club dynasty – both his son and nephew were to become Stragglers in the post-war period, and his grandson was in touch with the author in 2023.

Thanks to Blake's efforts, by 1937, the fixture list had grown to thirty-eight days of cricket; the Western Tour was eight days, taking in Devonport and Instow, and the fixture against the Hampshire Hogs first appears with a two-day game at Winchester. Meanwhile, the Cambridge Tour had taken in an additional college (Jesus), and two matches were added to the Oxford Tour (Christ Church and Balliol). To cope with this extended programme, a new rule was approved and published in the 1936 'List of Members' booklet:

> It is expected that all members home on leave or stationed at home play at least two matches for the Club during the season.

The finances of the club were simple. Funding was through the entrance fee of a guinea and no annual subscription was payable – collecting it from members spread far and wide across India would have been a challenge. Occasionally, men were elected who then failed to pay the fee, in which case, after due warnings, they were removed.

In 1935, the first recorded annual dinner was convened at the Metropole Hotel, London, presided over by Colonel the Honourable Sir Francis Stanley Jackson (an 'Honorary Associate Member' appointed by Maynard), who proposed the toast to 'The King'; George Blake then proposed 'The Founder of the Club and Stragglers east of Suez'. Two greeting messages were sent, the first to Buckingham Palace and the second to the viceroy, Lord Willingdon: Lord Wigham replied on behalf of the king, while Willingdon replied personally, thanking Stragglers and 'my old friend Sir Stanley Jackson' from the Viceregal Lodge, Simla.

ONE ARM BOWLS A LITTLE

A prominent politician and figure in pre-war London, as well as an England Test cricketer between 1893 and 1905, Stanley Jackson had been governor of Bengal from 1927 to 1932 and had narrowly escaped assassination while speaking at Calcutta University in February 1932: his assailant, Bina Das, was a young female Bengali anti-imperialist revolutionary. She missed with five shots and was tackled by the vice-chancellor, Hassan Suhrawardy, who was rewarded with a knighthood. An account records that 'even before the smoke had blown away, the Governor resumed his speech among cheers', which was typical of the *sangfroid* expected from senior leaders at the time. As we shall see, he was not the only Straggler to be shot at in that part of India.

On the other side of the coin, the brave Bina Das was imprisoned for attempted murder and given a sentence of nine years – subsequently, she joined the Indian National Congress in the struggle and later became a social worker. Some indication of the strong motivation of the freedom fighters can be seen in her statement:

> My object was to die, and if to die, to die nobly fighting against this despotic system of Government which has kept my country in perpetual subjection to its endless shame and endless suffering.

She was to live on in independent India and passed away in relative obscurity some decades later.

By 1937, the Straggler dinner had moved to the Hotel Victoria and the evening's president was Major Alleyne Coldwell, returned from the Caribbean; a senior civilian from Calcutta, Reginald Lagden, whom we will mention again below, gave a speech replying to the toast 'The Club and Stragglers east of Suez'.

As noted, the fixture card throughout the 1930s basically consisted of a week in both Oxford and Cambridge and then the 'Western Tour'. The university visits saw the Stragglers play a mix of the colleges and, in each case, the second team for the university, the Authentics or the Crusaders – although it should be noted that these XIs would not be a strict university Second XI, more a group of players on the fringes of the full Blues team who were vying for selection or simply available on the day.

BEGINNINGS: FOUR FOUNDERS AND THE MAHARAJAH, 1925–1939

Nevertheless, the Crusaders for sure, and no less the Authentics in Oxford, were formidable opposition. In eleven two-day games in Cambridge running up to the war from 1928 on, Stragglers managed to draw six and lose five - and in the three games after the war, the club recorded a single victory in 1950. The Crusaders won in 1952 by 128 runs and thenceforth the fixture lapsed. Against the Authentics, the record was no better - the Stragglers won the first game in 1928, then the Authentics won four of the remaining ten until the war: afterwards, the Authentics won three out of the six played until 1952, when again the fixture was discontinued.

By 1939, the fixture list encompassed forty-one days' cricket, with fourteen two-day games, including several military sides (the Ironsides at Bovingdon, RASC, the Northamptonshire's, United Services Portsmouth) and a mix of civilian teams (the Bradfield Waifs, St Edward's Martyrs, the Old Biltonians, the Somerset Stragglers); through the contacts of Reggie Senior, the club also played the Police College at Hendon, the day after the annual dinner - perhaps a challenging fixture. . .

The 1930s were a golden era: an account written twenty years later stated:

> The club was formed in 1925 primarily with the object of giving cricket to those coming home on six months' leave. There was a rapid build-up and in a very few years there was a large number of young and good cricketers falling over each other to play in the various fixtures. The quality naturally varied from year to year, but the standard was high and on many occasions the Straggler sides were little short of Minor County strength. These conditions led up to the outbreak of war. The club largely ran itself. The task of match managers was simple enough. It merely devolved in sorting out the best balanced side from the large number of applications from members and candidates wanting to play.

Around 1930, Maynard and Coldwell nominated fifteen Stragglers as 'Original Members' or 'OMs', although the reason for doing this, and what privileges or distinctions attached to these fifteen, is lost in the mists of time. In addition to the ten who played at Eastbourne in 1925, the others were Coldwell's elder brother, Capt. W.G.A. Coldwell (a much-decorated officer with OBE and DSO, who would command the 1st Battalion of the Northamptonshire's),

Frank Mason-MacFarlane, Capt. H.P. Mallinson of the Dogra Regiment, Lt. A.D. Middleton of the Northamptonshire's, and S.E. West of Indian Railways. The last survivor of the sixteen, and also of that first Eastbourne team, was Lt. Gen. Sir Brian Kimmins, who died in 1979.

OMs or not, the first Stragglers were a varied cross-section of men, from the military, civil service, police and commerce – by the time war intervened in 1939, the list of members was 285-strong, of whom 167 were military. Among the soldiers, a minority were from the Indian Army, between forty-five and fifty (it is sometimes hard to tell when regimental membership is not shown in the list), with more than 100 from British battalions based in India. The distinction between the armies was significant – in the Indian Army, an officer could live off his pay, while in the humblest British infantry regiment officers were still expected to have some private means to top up their salary: the Coldwells and their ilk came from well-to-do families in the shires. As a result, the Indian Army could afford to be selective, requiring applicants to pass out in the top third of the year at Sandhurst. Famously, Field Marshal Montgomery failed to, which, according to some accounts, prejudiced him against the Indian Army forever. Nevertheless, he was posted to India with the Royal Warwickshire Regiment and concluded that 'the average young officer went to India to drink gin, play polo and have a good time'. As a teetotal officer, uncertain mount and serious student of his profession, Monty never took to life east of Suez.

Although India was vast, by the 1930s, communications through the Raj were formidably powerful. The post office and telegraph systems were efficient and underpinned by the enormous railway network. While crossing the country could take days, assembling a team from nearby provinces to play a two-day game against the Punjab Wanderers at Lahore, as the Stragglers did over Christmas in 1934, was relatively straightforward. The Wanderers, incidentally, were made up of six white and five Indian players, a contrast to the all-white Stragglers.

With people like Hosie and Robertson in Calcutta, plugged into the civilian business community, and soldiers such as Captain Sanger and Captain Cameron scattered through the fifty-plus cantonments or military barracks of India, not to mention its members in the hallowed ranks of the Indian Civil Service, it is no surprise that word of the club spread quickly and successfully. Maynard's vision had filled a niche.

BEGINNINGS: FOUR FOUNDERS AND THE MAHARAJAH, 1925–1939

The club register generally shows a UK and an Indian address for each member, and the drill pre-war was for individuals to let the 'Foreign Secretary' know if they were progressing on leave to England in the coming summer, who would then inform the 'Home Secretary' (Coldwell and then Blake) in the UK – all by post. The names of potential players would be passed to the relevant match manager, who would confirm by a card in the post to the member's UK address: telephone was rarely used and only in the case of last-minute cry-off – and even that could be communicated by telegram. In an era where each household in London received three or more deliveries of post in a day, and in much of the country morning and afternoon deliveries were commonplace, running a wandering cricket club exclusively through the mail was achievable.

Of the civilians, many were based in Calcutta, still the commercial hub of India even if New Delhi was the administrative capital, working for the trading companies and 'managing agents' there, most of whose names have passed into history. Within India, Calcutta became the hub for the Stragglers, inasmuch as there was one, an annual game being played against 'the Rest' and then Calcutta Cricket Club.

In terms of social class, the members were distinctly 'officer' material, if not actual officers. The ICS and the vast majority of the firms recruited from public schools and/or university, and there was no shortage of people willing to try their luck in India, given the economic ills of the UK post-1918. However, class as much as race was important in India, perhaps even more so than in the home country.

Ten years after foundation, some early Stragglers were finishing their service in India and the Rules were amended in 1935 to allow for this:

The following members go on a Veterans List:

1. Members permanently residing at home.
2. Members who have not played for five years.

> They shall be subject to a donation of two guineas on application from the Hon. Secretary. The object of the Veterans' donation is to build up a reserve fund. It is hoped that Veterans will play for the Club.

ONE ARM BOWLS A LITTLE

The initial impetus was a statement in committee from Capt. Coldwell that with fewer candidates coming up for election each year he foresaw that 'at no far-distant date the expenditure of the club would exceed the income from entrance fees'. As ever, Coldwell was an efficient and canny administrator of great support to Maynard.

However, the take-up of the Veterans List was below-par, according to the committee minutes of 1937, with only twenty subscribers, and it was dropped as an idea after the war in 1946.

Chapter Two
MIDNAPORE AND ASSASSINATION

ON 2 SEPTEMBER 1933, the local District Officer (DO) and representative of the British Raj stepped on to a football field to play for the Midnapore Town Club, of which he was the ex-officio president, against the Mohammedan Sporting Club of Calcutta. He was a Straggler, but also played football as it brought him closer to the people he was responsible for. It was the end of half-time. Three Bengali teenage assassins who had been waiting among the spectators - the leader Brajo Kishore Chakraborty, Ram Krishna Roy and Nirmal Jeevan Ghosh - ran up to him and fired eight rounds from pistols into his body. Two white Indian Police Service officers, Philip Norton and Charles Smith, themselves opened fire and rushed to arrest the assailants, but there was no chance of saving the DO, who died at the scene.

It was an astonishing event, not the first assassination of a DO in that district, and further binds the Straggler story to the social history of the times and the hesitant and uneven progress towards independence for India.

ONE ARM BOWLS A LITTLE

As we have seen, the Stragglers were formed in an India that, to many in government and positions of power, was ineluctably approaching independence, with constant clamouring for self-government and loosening of control from London – but for many Indians, of course, it was far too slow. Queen Victoria had been granted the title of empress in 1877, and the Delhi Durbar of 1911 was celebrated with all the might of Empire on display, accompanied by tens of thousands of troops from the princely states such as Patiala, as well as the regular contingents from the British and Indian Armies. The Indian National Congress was inaugurated in 1885, with the express aim of promoting self-government, and there was a growing acceptance among many of its necessity.

Gandhi returned to India in 1915, following his studies in London and his legal practice in South Africa, where he first promoted his policy of non-violent resistance. It was then that the agitation for independence began in earnest. Institutional change was already underway by the time of the Straggler foundation – the first Indian barristers were enrobed in 1865-66, the first Indian graduates of Oxford and Cambridge had also emerged in the 1860s and the first full 'King's Commissioned Officers' for the Indian Army had passed out of Sandhurst in 1921.

Even prior to the turn of the century, the more enlightened members of the administration knew that the bell was tolling, even as the economic benefits to the home country of an Indian Empire were at their highest. As is proved time and time again, with Vietnam, Iraq, Afghanistan and Ukraine to name a few examples, invading a foreign territory peopled by a motivated nation eventually ends in failure, and the momentum for an independent India was already well developed by 1925.

The Jallianwala Bagh Massacre of 1919 in Amritsar raised many spectres of the 1857 Mutiny in British minds: after two Indian leaders of the local populace had been spirited away by the authorities in the night three days previously, crowds of agitators had gathered and, spurred on by some inept policing, committed crimes against white residents who found themselves isolated literally 'on the wrong side of the tracks'. A banker and railway supervisor were murdered, a white woman too, and another violently assaulted. Reinforcements arrived, under the command of the notorious Brigadier General Reginald Dyer: intent on teaching 'the natives' a lesson, he cold-bloodedly ordered his troops to open fire on a relatively peaceful gathering, killing, it is thought, 379 people.

This massacre, and the reaction to it, was to remain firmly in the minds of both sides through the succeeding years: on the British side, there was some considerable remorse, even as friends of Dyer created a campaign to raise monies for him as the person who had 'saved India and us from a repetition of the miseries and cruelties of 1857'. A debate in the House of Commons in July 1920 confirmed the general censure of Dyer for over-reaction and what one missionary had called 'an unspeakable disgrace, indefensible, unpardonable, inexcusable'. For the Indian freedom fighters, Jallianwala Bagh became the greatest example of how the brutal British were suppressing dissent all over India and undoubtedly encouraged a number of smaller, but deadly, agitations, at the same time as Gandhi was promoting non-violence.

One of these agitations was to have a devastating effect on a prominent Straggler. Bernard Edward John Burge was from the top echelon of the club; born in 1896 and raised in south-east London, he came from a Catholic family and was sent to school at Ampleforth, the monastic institution in Yorkshire, before going up to Merton College, Oxford. He was commissioned into the Royal Fusiliers in December 1914 and served in the London Regiment of the Rifle Brigade during the First World War, fighting at Gallipoli, in the trenches of France and latterly on the North-West Frontier of India, in the Third Afghan War.

In 1921, after the customary intense examination, he joined the Indian Civil Service (ICS), which was the bureaucratic elite of the British colonial administration – after the viceroy, ICS members ranked the highest in the order of precedence, above military officers, other civil servants, missionaries and, of course, people 'in trade' or *boxwallahs* as they were known in India. (It is worth saying that although the initial exploitation and conquest of India was perpetrated through the traders of the East India Company, by the early twentieth century they were towards the bottom of the British pile!)

As a member of this elite (there is the famous statement that an Indian Empire approaching 800 million people was governed by an ICS cadre of around 2,000), Burge was guaranteed a starting salary of £600 a year (approximately £50,000 in 2024) with, more significantly, a pension of £1,000 per year after twenty-five years' service.

ONE ARM BOWLS A LITTLE

Some flavour of the ICS is given by John Christie, who joined in 1928 and was in a very senior position by the time of independence, influencing events at the core of the colonial regime. Christie observed that whereas Plato's trained rulers were a philosopher's dream, the ICS was a reality. The Indian members took as much pride in it as the British, and among their compatriots the British members were known as the 'white Brahmins', intelligent, cultured and completely incorruptible. Some also considered them unapproachable, but they were taught what Christie termed 'the virtue of accessibility', whether touring their domains on horseback, handing down magisterial justice in court or carrying on their daily work, which often meant dealing with a long line of petitioners. This accessibility had fatal implications for some.

On reaching India, 'Bobby' Burge quickly resumed his cricketing career and joined the Ballygunge Cricket Club in Calcutta, becoming captain in due course. As such, and without the formality of a qualifying match, in 1927, he was elected a Straggler and is described by Coldwell in the register as a 'Good bat and bowler', seemingly faint praise but fulsome by the standards of Captain Coldwell. His home address was listed as Hope Fountain, Camberley, Surrey - and in India, c/o Imperial Bank, Park Street, Calcutta. This is typical: given the frequent movement of ICS and military officers across India and elsewhere, a bank address was normally more constant and reliable than a street one.

Home on leave in 1931, Burge played in no fewer than thirteen of the Stragglers' fourteen fixtures in England that summer, missing only the Eastbourne match. His highlight was against Old St Edward's, Oxford, where he took 5 wickets in the second innings as the Stragglers ran through the opposition to bowl them out for 103 and win by 133 runs. Then, after playing in the game against the Northamptonshire Regiment, where he scored 26 and 28 not out, batting at No. 8 (taking 4 wickets too), he went on the Western Tour and scored 115 opening against the Devon Dumplings at Exeter. Bradfield brought more success with scores of 69 and 24, as well as another 4 wickets. It was, one imagines, a very memorable season for Burge, the kind that every cricketer remembers if lucky enough to experience something like it. Usually opening the batting, Burge scored 570 Straggler runs at an average of 28.5 and ended with 34 wickets. In the ninety-plus years since, there is simply no example of a Straggler showing similar commitment over a single season. Aged thirty-five, he likely felt his opportunities of playing good cricket in England were running out and he made the most of his 1931 leave.

While he was enjoying this successful season amid the bucolic backdrops of Oxford and the West Country, back in India the 'Indian Freedom Movement' was gathering pace and especially in western Bengal, an area of the country that had long been at the forefront of violent movements. Specifically, the Midnapore or Medinipur region had seen the anti-Raj agitations of the Santal Revolt in 1776-77, the Chuar rebellion of 1799 and the uprising of 1857 – it was a hotbed of dissent with, by the 1930s, no shortage of recruits into the 'Bengal Volunteer Corps' and similar organizations. An area the size of Wales, it was one of the main indigo-growing centres in Bengal, very rural and quite behind the times. According to one writer, the local Indian version of greeting a European in the street went much further than a *salaam* – 'They would squat down at the roadside and put handfuls of earth on top of their bare heads in deference . . .'

In such an environment, it is hardly surprising that revolutionaries found a ready audience and strong support. Even after independence, West Bengal marched to a different drum, and indeed still does. It was the Communist and Naxalite agitations of the 1960s in Calcutta that led to the end of regular Straggler games in India.

Nor was the national picture a happy one when Burge returned from his leave: by 1931, there were over 100,000 Congress supporters in jail, a full-blown campaign of civil disobedience and the viceroy, Lord Irwin, was under considerable pressure to grant concessions – while fighting against the right wing in England, who objected to any concessions being made. Eventually, Irwin signed a pact with Gandhi just before the end of his five-year term. (As Lord Halifax, Irwin would go on to become one of the main supporters of 'appeasement' of Nazi Germany, before he was approached to take over from Neville Chamberlain as prime minister – being in the House of Lords, he demurred, allowing Winston Churchill his opportunity.)

The pact with Gandhi had little effect in Bengal. On 7 April 1931, the DO for Midnapore District, James Peddie, was assassinated by young freedom fighters while attending a school exhibition. The DO was the local face of British imperial rule, effectively the local tax collector and magistrate, and such murders were comparatively unusual in India, even in the febrile atmosphere of the 1920s and 1930s, when Indian leaders such as Nehru and Gandhi were being locked up regularly. Almost exactly a year later, on 30 April 1932, Peddie's replacement, Robert Douglas, was shot dead as he chaired a meeting of the District Board on a Saturday evening. The murders of two DOs in two years in the same district in the course of their public duties was remarkable, even in the context of the recent periods of unrest.

In response, Burge was sent from his post in Calcutta to replace Douglas in Midnapore – someone had to do it, the 'show must go on' was the typical attitude of the colonial government, even though the risks were obvious. His wife, Barbara Mary Isobel Burge (the daughter of an army colonel whom Burge had met in Calcutta), was certainly very afraid and, according to accounts we have, made a point of meeting any visitors that Burge had, before they went into his office to see him – with the thought that no freedom fighter or terrorist would stoop so low as to kill a woman first. She also accompanied him when he went 'on tour' around the district, often away for weeks at a time attending to the remoter towns and villages – this was exceptional, wives normally stayed in the DO's house or bungalow, sheltering from the uncomfortable climate and health risks of the Indian *mofussil* (rural expanses).

One observer noted that 'whilst at Midnapore, he was constantly under the threat of assassination', but apparently – and, one might say, in the finest traditions of Ampleforth, Oxford, the Army and the ICS – Burge and his loyal wife stuck to the task: 'They were both ill, but took no leave, and were doing their best to improve conditions in the Midnapore district.'

It is easy to see that Burge was unlike the normal caricature of the arrogant and typically 'colonialist' DO, portrayed in numerous British and Indian works of fiction and indeed memoirs: rather, similar to not a few of his colleagues, he displayed an empathy with the people under his rule. We are told that 'although beyond football age [he was thirty-seven], he himself resumed playing', as this brought him closer to the man on the street. A contemporary noted 'he was quick to realise the possibilities of personal contact on the field of sport'. Or, as Christie had termed it, 'the virtue of accessibility'.

On 2 September 1933, empathetic or not, he was gunned down in his football kit without remorse.

MIDNAPORE AND ASSASSINATION

Understandably, questions were raised in Calcutta and London. To the modern eye, the loss of one DO in a district could be unfortunate, the loss of a second deeply distressing, but to have a third, Burge, killed in the same town smacks of incompetence, arrogance and negligence. He was clearly one of the rising stars in the ICS and a grievous loss to them, his family of wife and daughter, and his cricket clubs. Curiously, a report in *The Times* from their correspondent in Calcutta took a very different line –

> The efficiency of the system which has been built up for combating terrorism in Bengal is not to be judged by the murder of Mr. Burge at Midnapore. Shocking as the crime was, it was an isolated episode; and in general, it may be said that, in spite of Midnapore, Government and police officers are confident of success in the war with terrorists . . . Not only has the Intelligence Branch been much strengthened, but the whole machinery has been improved, and reports show that the system is now working well. The accuracy of the information received about terrorists' activities is shown by the periodical successful raids on wanted persons and the seizures of arms and explosives, although to the general public the size of some of the recent seizures must seem disquieting.

One could say that on such obfuscation and complacency was an empire sustained – how their correspondent could write 'isolated episode' beggars belief. No doubt similar incidents were happening across other British possessions and to British interests elsewhere, in Ireland, Egypt, Turkey and China, to mention some of those reported in the same London newspapers; and the death of a youngish colonial administrator caused less comment than an equivalent incident would today, but Burge, with his impeccable background and attitude, was a sad loss indeed. In Calcutta itself, his murder was felt keenly:

> A requiem mass for the repose of the soul of Mr. Burge was celebrated at St. Thomas's, Calcutta, this morning. Sir John Anderson, the Governor, attended, accompanied by his Private and Military Secretaries. There was a crowded congregation of Indians and Europeans representative of many sections of Calcutta society. It is understood that Mrs. Burge, who was received by the Governor on

Monday, is returning to England almost immediately. The Corporation passed a resolution of sympathy with Mrs. Burge after some controversial discussion about the failure of the Government to suppress terrorism by their present methods.

An F. Rooney of the Calcutta Corporation (city government) wrote of Burge:

To a keen sense of humour and a frank and happy disposition was added an instinctive sympathy, a broadness of outlook and understanding, combined with a constant urge to know and to understand the people with whom he came in contact, in order that he might better assist them in their trials and difficulties.

He was laid to rest alongside his two predecessors in the environs of St John's Church, Midnapore, a full crucifix carved on his memorial, as a Catholic. At the base is carved a simple and true phrase, presumably at the request of his loyal and conscientious wife – 'The Price of Empire'.

The governor dispatched an Indian Army battalion to Midnapore in response to the murder, which was more symbolic than effective; the freedom fighters could celebrate another scalp, even at considerable loss to themselves. Reportedly, the soldiers (Indian sepoys except for seven or eight British officers) were only restrained with the 'utmost difficulty' from wrecking the town. After due legal process, where one imagines patience was low and the guilt was obvious, Kishore and Ram Krishna were hanged in Midnapore jail on 25 October 1934, followed by Nirmal Jeevan on 26 October. Nirmal Jeevan was eighteen years old. Several other individuals were imprisoned as accomplices, or transported to the Andaman Islands, where British India maintained a prisoner colony.

Around the same time, a road in Midnapore was renamed 'Burge Road'. Barbara Burge was awarded the Kaisar-i-Hind medal in the New Year's Honours of January 1934 – scant compensation, one imagines, for the loss of her talented husband. The two Indian Police Service officers involved were given the King's Police Medal – surprisingly.

Thus, eight years after their foundation, the Stragglers suffered the loss of a fine player in a high-profile incident that was, if not typical of the times, a

MIDNAPORE AND ASSASSINATION

symptom of the growing unrest in India and the underlying agitation towards independence. During the 1930s, various initiatives to speed Indian self-government were proposed by elements within and without Parliament, the home administration and Delhi – with very mixed reception and results. Constitutional change was necessary, and this attracted strong views on both sides of the argument. A further liberalizing Government of India Act was passed by Parliament in 1935, and elections held in 1937 – however, the arguments, demonstrations, violence and imprisonments went on through the Second World War until the famous 'Freedom at Midnight' moment in August 1947. All along, while the freedom and independence movements within India were not necessarily aligned, which in the long run led to the partition of India and Pakistan, and there were still to be plenty of stops and starts, the kettle was on the hob and the temperature of the water was rising. The Midnapore assassinations were but one aspect of the conflict, which was particularly violent in Bengal – and a counterpoint to the 'non-violent' doctrine that Gandhi promoted in vain.

Within the Stragglers themselves, Burge's death must have been received with a good deal of disquiet among the individual members, but the committee minutes do not reveal any comment. Indeed, looking at his entry in the secretary's register, there is a line to cross it out, with the scrawled note 'Died 1937', clearly incorrect and presumably added some years later. As an Oxford man and ICS member, there is no doubt that Burge was highly rated within the Stragglers, even before his cricketing prowess and ability was counted, where a record of playing thirteen out of fourteen possible fixtures in a season is unequalled. It is perhaps unfortunate that no memorial to him exists within the club, unlike another prominent young man taken in his prime some decades later.

After the rather dispassionate report of Burge's death, *The Times* was to publish a more emotive notice in June 1934, noting the passing away, less than a year later, of Burge's father, John Edward, at the age of eighty-three – 'he never really recovered from the assassination of his son'.

Chapter Three
WAR
THE STRAGGLER SACRIFICE

THE ASSASSINATION OF BURGE was the first time that a Straggler was lost in the service of the country, but it was not to be the last. This is unsurprising for a club whose membership was largely drawn from the military and civil service and it was of course the outbreak of the Second World War in 1939 that produced the most severe loss. Along with every other similar club, the Stragglers of Asia fell into a dormant period, sustained in the UK by J.R. Coulthard, who acted as secretary and treasurer from 1940 to 1945; he was appointed *pro tem*, in succession to George Blake, who had been in the post of secretary from 1934, alongside A.F. 'Reggie' Senior, the treasurer. Both Blake and Senior served overseas, Blake earning an MC with the Army in Mesopotamia, and each returned to his post in 1946.

The final game before war was declared took place in Southampton against the Hampshire Hogs on 21 and 22 August: Stragglers, having lost to the Hogs in 1937 and 1938, made it three in a row - in their second innings they were bowled out for 115. It was a poor omen. There was scheduled to be a game on the following two days against the United Services Portsmouth, but this was cancelled as the country slipped into war.

Nothing survives in the club archive from the war years, no correspondence nor minutes of meetings, simply because there were none as most of the individuals were either already serving in India or dispersed to far-off lands, even the civilians.

Like all British institutions, large and small, the Stragglers suffered losses and had their own 'Roll of Honour', as the lists were named. Researching seventy-plus years later, the enormity of the nation's losses in the war is hard to comprehend - on many days, the list of the dead in the national press had several hundred names on it. Having said that, it was of course a lighter loss than that suffered in the First World War. In total, with 15 known fatalities out of a list of 285, the Straggler losses were roughly in proportion with that of the country, around 4 per cent.

For the club, fourteen were listed in the post-war Members List of 1947: eleven army officers, a naval lieutenant and two civilians, including a member of the ICS. A further Army death was noted in committee - the individual had been elected but never paid the entrance fee. Two of the officers were Brigadiers and six were Lieutenant Colonels: thus, eight of the fifteen were commanding either brigades (3,000+ men) or regiments/battalion-level units (600+ men). Six of them had played first-class cricket.

They all merit a brief description, if only to emphasize the randomness of the conflict, the way in which Stragglers were dispersed to all corners of the fighting effort and, not least, the quality of the members. In the list below, several interesting vignettes appear - the distinguished father of a later Straggler president, two civilians killed in aircraft crashes not related to enemy action, another pair of soldiers who lie by chance in the same North African cemetery, a Commanding Officer shot by one of his own soldiers, a victim of suicide and a sailor whose last resting place was only identified in October 2023.

WAR: THE STRAGGLER SACRIFICE

Brigadier Bernard Howlett DSO (Aged Forty-Four)
Buried in Italy

Howlett merits the first mention, as the most senior Straggler officer to be killed in the conflict, and probably the best cricketer among the fifteen.

Bernard Howlett was the only son of the vicar of Snaresbrook, a small village in Essex. His nickname was 'Swifty' and by all accounts he was, as an opening bowler for Kent in the twenties. He made his debut in 1922 and played six times that season, then in the following year was restricted to four Second XI appearances: he went to India with the Queen's Own Royal West Kent Regiment over 1926/27, returning in 1928 to play almost the full season with Kent, as a regular with the First XI.

In a side that contained Tich Freeman, Les Ames and Frank Woolley, all England Test-playing legends, Howlett was not one of the stars, but still took 108 wickets over 42 first-class games, at an average of 29. He was also in demand in India, playing against the touring MCC side in 1926/27 on four occasions and representing the Europeans in the Bombay Quadrangular tournament.

He was elected to the Stragglers in 1928 and is described simply as 'Very good fast bowler. Played for Kent most of 1928.' In his first match against the Northamptonshire Regiment, he took 7 wickets in the Northants first innings, but poor batting meant he ended on the losing side.

By 1942, he was commanding the 6th Battalion of his regiment: he won not just one DSO but two, the first in North Africa and then again during the invasion of Sicily. Selected for rapid promotion to Brigadier, he commanded first 36 Brigade, and then 139 Brigade. It was during the advance up Italy, around the town of Abruzzo, that Howlett was instantly killed by enemy shellfire and is buried in the Sangro River War Cemetery. He left his wife and son, Geoffrey.

That thirteen-year-old boy was to follow his father into the Army, becoming General Sir Geoffrey Howlett and a very prominent Straggler in the 1980s/90s, serving as club president between 1989 and 1993.

General Sir Geoffrey was to speak movingly of his father's death when in 2019 he was asked to appear before one of the seemingly interminable Northern Ireland hearings, as a retired soldier of eighty-nine, about the shootings on 9 August 1971: he could have avoided it, yet not only attended but asked the coroner if he could address the relatives of the victims:

I have enormous sympathy with you all as relatives of those who were killed in this case on the ninth of August 1971. I know something about bereavement because my father was killed in Italy in the war when I was thirteen and I wanted to know everything about how it happened as well.

Captain R.F.H. Philpot-Brookes (Aged Twenty-Seven)
Buried in Belgium

A member of the 'Straggler Regiment', the Northamptonshire's, Philpot-Brookes was the youngest and most junior of the Straggler casualties. Joining in 1936, having been based with the 1st Battalion in Jullundur (now Jalandhar), his first game had been against the Punjab Wanderers at Lahore during Christmas 1935 (one of the two fixtures the Stragglers played in India each year), when he scored 108. He went on the Cambridge Tour in 1936 and played two games in 1938, before a final game at Hendon in 1939, top-scoring with 35.

A talented cricketer, he played two first-class games for the 'Europeans' in India, during the 1938/39 season, scoring a century in one and taking 11 wickets across the two fixtures.

He was killed serving with the 2nd Battalion, early in the war, on 28 May 1940 during the hectic retreat to Dunkirk. Mentioned in Dispatches (the award just short of a gallantry medal, signified by a leaf insignia on the relevant campaign medal), he is buried in the Bus House Cemetery, Belgium.

Lt. Col. (Acting Brigadier) F.R. Mackintosh-Walker DSO (Aged Forty-Six)
Buried in France

A Straggler from Scotland, unusually, Mackintosh-Walker was commissioned into the Seaforth Highlanders: he had an outstanding record in the First World War, winning an MC and two bars.

He became a Straggler in 1930, described as 'No. 6 bat and change bowler', qualified by his posting on the North-West Frontier. After some useful contributions in his first season, he did not play again until 1936, where he made 30 and 63 at Northampton. This was his last game.

WAR: THE STRAGGLER SACRIFICE

His war record is quite remarkable. In the dark days of the retreat to Dunkirk and the French coast, between June and August 1940, he was commanding the 4th Battalion of the Cameron Highlanders, as part of the 51st Highland Division, expected to extract through the Cherbourg Peninsula. Much of the division was 'put in the bag' (captured), but Mackintosh-Walker, with another officer, Major Thomas Rennie, escaped and proceeded to evade recapture over six weeks as they walked and bicycled south through German-occupied France, eventually reaching Spain and then neutral Portugal, where their first act on reaching safety was to play a round of golf before returning to the UK!

Back in the army, he was given command of a brigade, the 227th Infantry Brigade, part of the 15th Scottish Division. Gallantly, he led them to capture a couple of important bridges over the Odon River in Normandy, before being unfortunately killed in action on 17 July 1944, aged forty-six. He was awarded a posthumous DSO. He is buried in the Hottot-les-Bagues War Cemetery, France.

A contemporary noted: 'Although his golf and cricket styles were unorthodox, he always seemed to win and to work himself into a side.'

Sadly, Tom Rennie, his companion in the long escape and evasion, was also killed later, in March 1945, by then a Major General.

Reginald Lagden MC (Aged Fifty-One)
Killed in Aircraft Accident, India

If Howlett was the senior soldier killed, Lagden was the senior Straggler, although a less talented cricketer. Born in 1893 in Basutoland, educated at Marlborough and Pembroke College, Cambridge, Lagden won his Blue and played at Lord's in each of his three years at the university (1912-14), as a batsman. He scored 222 runs, averaging 37 across 6 innings: cricket was not even his best sport - he played hockey for England in 1913-14 after winning a Blue for that too.

More impressive than his varsity match record are his six first-class centuries for Cambridge against the counties and being selected for the Gentlemen against the Players in 1913 - the traditional games where the best amateurs took on the best professionals.

Serving in the First World War with the Rifle Brigade, he was awarded an MC, but lost his older brother, an Oxford man and England rugby player, who was killed in action. Lagden then decided to make his career in Bengal in business and was invited to join the Stragglers as early as 1926, by which time he was ascending the ranks of commerce and the cricketing fraternity in Calcutta. In due course, he became president of the Calcutta Cricket Club, then president of the Cricket Association of Bengal. He was among those who invited Lord Harris to send an MCC team to India in 1926, leading to their first tour.

He took part in the only Straggler victory over the Authentics in 1928, scoring 32 and taking four catches. In December 1929, he played against Calcutta CC and again in January 1931, scoring 100, then 1 in the following year. It seems he then decided to stop playing but continued a keen involvement.

In 1934, home in the UK on leave, we find Lagden chairing the Straggler committee meeting held at London's Grosvenor Hotel on 1 December – at the time there was no designated 'chairman' of the club and the committee members took turns at electing a chairman of the meeting – who then signed the previous meeting's minutes (at which he may not have been present!).

In May 1937, when he was awarded the Order of the British Empire (OBE), he was serving as the chairman of McLeod, one of the large tea firms in Calcutta.

Too old to rejoin the army in the Second World War, at forty-six when it started, Lagden's obvious leadership abilities were used commanding the Special Constabulary of Calcutta. He became vice president of the Bengal Chamber of Commerce and would have been president the following year if fate had not intervened.

Returning on 20 October 1944 from another trip to the UK, he was aboard an RAF Liberator, which overshot the runway at Karachi; the accident was survived by the five crew but, tragically, not the four passengers, who, towards the rear, died in an explosion, Lagden among them. The accident report suggested pilot fatigue as a contributory factor and the unserviceable state of 'George', the autopilot function – primitive in those days, but still an effective aid for airmen. While Lagden was, at fifty-one years old, a man of some means and considerable stature, he left a widow and six children with no breadwinner, in an age where senior businessmen's salaries were more modest than they subsequently became. After a six-year legal battle, his widow was awarded £17,400 in compensation (equivalent to around £750,000 in 2024).

The Calcutta Cricket Club, of which Lagden was president, erected a stone memorial arch, known as the Lagden Gate, at the club's Eden Gardens ground. Lagden's successor as president, Alec Hosie, wrote:

> Reggie was held in such affectionate esteem in Calcutta that there was not an office in Clive Street or any club or public building in Calcutta that did not fly a flag at half-mast when the news of his death came through.

Major C.M. Warren (Aged Thirty-Three)
Buried in Libya

Warren has one of the more acerbic comments on cricketing abilities in the secretary's register. Joining in 1934, he is described as 'An incredibly bad wicketkeeper and bat. Very keen, will go miles to play.' His record is indeed modest, a total of 245 runs across 31 innings at an average of 8: almost half of these runs were scored playing against the Ironsides, his Tank Corps colleagues at Bovington. His best score of 64 was also his last, in 1939.

He was killed as a Major at thirty-three, during the war in the North African desert. He is buried in the Knightsbridge War Cemetery in Libya.

Lt. Col. J.H.C. Wooldridge (Aged Forty-Three)
Buried in Singapore

Hugh Wooldridge was part of the Gresham's School First XI, photographed in 1914. While he was to survive the First World War, poignantly, six of his team-mates in the photograph did not. He was elected to the Stragglers of Asia in the early thirties.

He was Indian Army through and through, father a brigadier, and brother of another Straggler, J.W. Wooldridge, who proposed him. He played on the Western Tour in 1934, taking a good number of wickets, 15 across three two-day games; his next and last fixtures were in Oxford in 1939, albeit without the same success.

By 1942, he was commanding the 5th Battalion of his regiment, the Royal Garhwal Rifles, part of the forces stuffed into Malaya and Singapore in a desperate attempt to stave off defeat. As is well chronicled, in the event a superior British force and powerful garrison was surrendered to the Japanese after a campaign lasting no more than nine weeks – a stunning reversal for the Empire and one that destroyed the reputation of the British Army in Asia. The Royal Garhwal Rifles were part of the problem – described as 'raw and under-equipped', the 5th Battalion had only recently been raised and, like many of the war-raised battalions, lacked enough experienced officers and NCOs. According to one historian, Brian Farrell, the brigade it belonged to, 45th Indian Infantry Brigade, was 'at best "semi-trained" for desert warfare' – hardly preparation for action in Malaya, where it arrived on 2 January.

Wooldridge was killed a bare ten days later on 12 January 1942, at the age of forty-three, and lies in Kranji War Cemetery, Singapore, alongside many of his men, with the heart-rending inscription on his grave of 'Sleep Well, My Darling', as requested by his widow, Lesley.

Reportedly, many captured men of the 5th Battalion fought on the other side for the Japanese as part of the 'turncoat' Indian National Army, which was raised from the Indian prisoners of war – an action that earned complete opprobrium from those Indian soldiers who stayed loyal to the Crown, to the extent that INA men were often killed if captured later in the war. As the Army Commander in Burma commented: 'Our Indian and Gurkha troops were at times not too ready to let them surrender and orders had to be issued to give them a kinder welcome.'

At any rate, the 5th Battalion Royal Garhwal Rifles was not raised again.

Lt. Col. G.C. Thorne DSO (Aged Forty-Four)
Lost at Sea in the Bay of Bengal

Thorne played cricket at a high level, for the Army XI against Oxford University (which counted as first-class in 1927), and was put up for membership just prior to the war. He was, again, a highly decorated soldier – DSO and two bars. Originally from the Royal Norfolk Regiment, he was commanding the 2nd Battalion of the Cambridgeshire Regiment in the battle for Singapore. As the fall of Singapore to General Yamashita's troops became inevitable, several highly valued officers were selected to try to escape and fight again another day: Thorne was one, presumably because of his outstanding leadership and gallantry, proved on three occasions at least. He was evacuated on the SS *Rooseboom*, a Dutch vessel that took around 500 mainly military personnel from Padang, bound for Colombo.

Unluckily, the *Rooseboom* was torpedoed by a Japanese submarine on 1 March 1942 and while there were some survivors, a few of whom spent several weeks drifting in a boat, Thorne was not one of them. He is commemorated at the Kranji War Memorial in Singapore.

His loss was noted with regret in the Straggler record at the committee meeting of October 1945, when it emerged that his entrance fee was outstanding: he had played against Brasenose and Balliol in 1939 as qualifying games.

He is also recorded on the Free Foresters CC 'Roll of Honour' in the Lord's Pavilion, along with forty-three others – reflecting the larger size of the Foresters.

Lt. Col. S.D.G. Robertson (Aged Thirty-Five)
Buried in Tunisia

Elected in 1934, the secretary's note was – 'Good bat, can bowl a googly.' He seems to have played just two games to qualify and made only 4 runs in each. He played one more game in 1936 and none further.

Originally from the Suffolk Regiment, Robertson was killed in North Africa while attached to the Royal Armoured Corps, as a young Lieutenant Colonel of thirty-five. He is buried at the Medjez-El-Bab War Cemetery in Tunisia. His widow ordered a gravestone inscription with the message: 'He died not for the peace of England but for the peace of the world.'

Lt. Col. W.B.S. Wilberforce DSO (Aged Thirty-Eight)
Buried in Tunisia

Resting in the same cemetery at Medjez-El-Bab as Robertson, Bill Wilberforce was another talented young officer, who was originally commissioned into the King's Own Yorkshire Light Infantry but was commanding the East Surrey

Regiment in North Africa. On 6 May 1943, he had just heard that he had been awarded the DSO by his Brigade Commander and was sitting in his jeep at Regimental HQ when a shell landed close by. A large chunk of shrapnel killed him and crippled his Intelligence Officer, who was sitting next to him.

Aged thirty-eight, he came from the famous Wilberforces of Markington Hall in Yorkshire – one of his direct antecedents being the leading campaigner against slavery, William Wilberforce. His grandson, who of course never knew him, recalls the family stories of his tall figure racing in to bowl at pace.

As a Straggler, he had been elected in 1935, was a 'good bowler, fair bat' and represented the club on seven occasions. A tribute noted: 'One can picture him playing cricket always with a smile on his face and enjoying every turn of the game.'

Lt. Col. L.V.S. Sherwood DSO (Aged Forty-Four)
Buried in Greece

Sherwood has a memorial in the chapel of his old school, Bedford, which does not do full justice to his tragic story. Having survived the war as an Indian Army officer in the 10th Baluch Regiment and won a DSO and bar in Abyssinia and then the Western Desert, he was commanding a battalion in Greece during the Greek Civil War against communism: on 2 September 1945, some months after VE Day (Victory in Europe), Sherwood was shot dead by a 'psychologically disturbed soldier' from his own unit. At the same time, the soldier killed the Subedar Major of the battalion – the senior non-commissioned rank, equivalent to the British Regimental Sergeant Major (RSM).

C.K. Rhodes ICS (Aged Fifty-One)
Killed in Delhi Airport

From Charterhouse, Rhodes won an Exhibition to Brasenose College, Oxford; not a regular First XI cricketer at school (although he did take 5 wickets for 5 runs on his first outing!), he won a Blue for golf, but not cricket. In 1913, he passed the examinations for the ICS and was posted initially to Shillong in the far north-east of the country, where soon after arrival he commissioned a nine-hole golf course, later expanded to eighteen holes in 1926.

He joined the Stragglers in the early thirties, proposed by Maynard himself, and was described as 'a really good all-round cricketer, bowls fast medium, keeps a beautiful length will bowl all day. Very keen.'

In 1916, he married Margaret Herbert, daughter of the Inspector General of Police in Shillong. She was something of a social campaigner, principally against the Hindu tradition of *sati*, where a widowed woman would throw herself on the funeral pyre of her husband. After twenty years' service, Rhodes was awarded the Companion of the Indian Empire (CIE) decoration.

Unfortunately, he was killed on board an Indian National Airways aircraft that crashed shortly after takeoff from Delhi on 6 January 1941. Had he survived, one imagines that he would have been one of the Stragglers pushing to diversify the club, given his seniority, intellect and close knowledge of the country.

Lt. K.J. Harper, Royal Navy (Aged Twenty-Eight)
Lost at Sea Off Norway

The only sailor among the fallen Stragglers, Harper was elected in 1937, as a fast bowler – he went on to take 5 wickets in an innings against the Ironsides in the summer before the war, 8 in the match. His father was a retired colonel living on Harpers Farm in the picturesque village of Litton Cheney, nine miles west of Dorchester in Dorset, and one imagines he may well have been watching just down the road at Bovington for those two days.

Harper was a Lieutenant, serving as the Second-in-Command of HM Submarine *Thistle*, which was ordered on operations off Stavanger, Norway, during the German invasion in early 1940 (one of the first substantive clashes of the war). *Thistle* encountered a German U-boat, *U-4*, on 9 April and at 1604h fired four torpedoes at her from periscope depth. Unaccountably, all missed as *U-4* crash-dived. Later that same night, at 0213h on 10 April, *U-4* found *Thistle* herself on the surface, recharging batteries. *U-4* fired two torpedoes and the second of these decisively sunk the Royal Navy submarine with all hands, a total of fifty-nine men. On this occasion, German discipline and training, at a relatively higher level early in the war, had won the duel.

In a strange coincidence, as this book was being researched, the wreck of HMS *Thistle* was discovered in spring 2023 and formally identified as such in October. She has been left as is and the remains of her crew, including our twenty-eight-year-old Straggler, lie undisturbed nearly 500 feet below the waves.

Major H. Gardner RA (Aged Forty-Seven)
Buried in Libya

Gardner was commanding the 34th Light Anti-Aircraft Regiment in the Desert War when he was killed at the age of forty-seven. Unusually, he held an Air Force Cross (AFC) and Territorial Decoration (TD), awarded for long service in the Territorial Army. As a cricketer, he was a member of the MCC, Free Foresters and I Zingari, elected to Stragglers in 1928 as a 'very useful bat'. While not a very regular player, he scored 70+ twice in 1929 and captained the Straggler team on several occasions.

Lt. Col. C.B. Rubie ED CBE (Aged Forty-One)
Died at Hove

Born in 1898, Rubie was a prominent amateur first-class cricketer who represented the Europeans regularly in the Bombay Quadrangular Tournament from 1921 to 1926. He was very involved in the development of cricket in Karachi and captained three teams against the MCC tourists of 1926/27, who included Arthur Gilligan and Maurice Tate. In 1930, through these connections, he played four times for Sussex. He was employed by Phipson and Co, wine merchants in Bombay, Karachi and Rawalpindi.

As a Straggler, he first played in the second and third matches, in 1926 against Eastbourne and Lancing colleges, and then a couple of games in 1930.

His military career was rather unconventional in that he is first listed in the Ceylon Planters Rifle Corps as a Corporal and then climbed the ranks to Lt. Col. in the Indian Reserve of Officers, gaining an Efficiency Decoration (ED), which was awarded to members of colonial reserve/volunteer forces. He was also made a Commander of the British Empire (CBE).

In 1939, he was appointed to manage the upcoming tour of an England team to India over winter 1939/40, which was to play twenty-six fixtures, including three Tests. The tour was cancelled after the outbreak of war in early September and Rubie unfortunately died of a heart attack after an operation on 3 November the same year.

Capt. A.A. Shaw (Aged Thirty-Seven)
Buried in New Delhi

Alexander Shaw was the sixth Straggler first-class cricketer to die during the war, in Delhi on 19 July 1945. He played two first-class games, one for Sussex against Cambridge University in 1927, when he caught 3 and stumped 3 in 1 innings, and the second six years later for the Europeans against Bengal in the 1935/36 season.

Coincidentally, as a schoolboy he had opened the batting for Eastbourne College against the Stragglers of Asia in their first game in 1925, run out for 27. As a Straggler, he played twenty-seven matches for the club through the 1930s, including five of the annual games in Calcutta, where he worked as a tea broker. Coming home on leave in 1930 (when he played his qualifiers), 1933 and 1936, he scored three centuries and compiled 973 runs at an average of 32, just failing to appear in the 'Career Records' table, which requires 1,000 runs: of course, add the 27 he made against the club, and he would have got there!

As an 'Emergency Commissioned Officer', recruited in the rush to meet the Japanese threat in 1941, he served with the 11th Sikhs and died just as the war was ending, by suicide. The story goes that his wife had left him for another officer.

Apart from the casualties, there were a number of Stragglers who won awards for bravery and survived – one example being Colonel Roger Welchman, who commanded the 5th Sherwood Foresters as they crossed the River Cosina in northern Italy in November 1944; according to a later obituary, after an earlier attempt had been driven back, 'he went forward under heavy fire and organised a bold plan. The operation was entirely successful and was considered a brilliant example of infiltration tactics.' Welchman had been posted in Rawalpindi with the Welch Regiment (appropriately!).

ONE ARM BOWLS A LITTLE

There is also the curious case of acting Major General Jackie Smyth VC – not a casualty, more an interesting story that almost all military Stragglers after 1945 would be familiar with.

Smyth was the only Straggler to hold the highest award for gallantry, the Victoria Cross (VC), which he had won with the 15th Ludhiana Sikhs during the First World War. Smyth's entry in the Secretarial register is curiously brief: he was 'elected a member by Capt. Bicher' in a year unknown and his cricketing ability is simply recorded as 'good bat'. Moreover, he only seems to have played in one game and this writer suspects that he was recruited into the Stragglers as a matter of prestige, since even then the number of cricketers with a VC was very few and Smyth might have been expected to burnish and help spread the name of the club. As a matter of fact, he had played two first-class matches for the British Army in India and he remains the only cricketer of that level to have held a VC.

The Second World War found him itching again for action, although he was comparatively older at forty-seven; thanks largely to his incessant lobbying, after first commanding a brigade in the debacle of Dunkirk, he was able to inveigle himself into command of the 17th Indian Division, which was part of the force defending Burma in 1942, another campaign of disastrous retreat, and another ignominious defeat for the British. Having been recently operated on for an anal fistula, he was passed medically fit by a board headed by the senior doctor in his own division – a slight conflict of interest, one might imagine, and probably a premature decision.

A key incident in the retreat through Burma, with the Japanese in hot pursuit, was the destruction of the Sittang Bridge, an important crossing point on the road to Rangoon. Smyth, a 'brave, talented and much-admired officer' according to one account, was in this case generally adjudged as supremely foolish in ordering the premature blowing of the bridge while approximately two-thirds of his division (around 10,000 men) were the wrong side of it. This left thousands of Gurkhas, never famous for their water skills, and other Indian and British troops to swim a very broad river, with countless unnecessary casualties – not to mention the loss of valuable weapons such as artillery and personnel carriers. In fact, the Sittang Bridge debacle was a case study in how not to defend river crossings, still being taught by the Directing Staff (DS) at Sandhurst some fifty years later, where most Stragglers would have heard Smyth's name.

WAR: THE STRAGGLER SACRIFICE

Smyth was sacked at once by General Wavell, not an unsympathetic commander normally, and sent home to the UK. He subsequently resurrected his reputation somewhat by entering politics after the war. Smyth served as an MP for over fifteen years and became Sir John in 1956. However, his brief Straggler career had ended, perhaps fortunately for the reputation of the club, even before the infamous Sittang incident. The register is clear: 'Resigned, 1939'.

An interesting postscript to the war years came from Straggler George Brown, quoted in the newsletter of 2002:

> I was delighted to read of the Eastbourne College celebrations and of the intention to present a bench for the cricket ground. As an Old Eastbournian and a Straggler, and having played on the ground in both capacities, I am pleased to enclose a contribution towards the bench. It is the only ground on which I have played cricket to the sound of gunfire! I was in the College XI in '42 and '43 when we had evacuated to Radley, but we used to return to our home ground to play an annual fixture against the Royal Navy, who occupied the school premises during the war. They had an AA [anti-aircraft] gun on top of the College tower to shoot down low flying German aircraft and periodically during play, the gun would open fire; the Navy said it was to make sure it was in working order; but there was no way of telling if in fact it was for the real thing. I also began to suspect that they used it to put us off at critical moments!

Chapter Four

RECOVERY IN THE FIFTIES AND THE QUESTION OF NON-EUROPEAN MEMBERS

ON 6 OCTOBER 1945, a small notice appeared in *The Times*:

> Stragglers of Asia CC – An Extraordinary General Meeting will be held in London on October 24th, 1945. Will any member that can attend please advise the Hon. Secretary, 16 Chelsea Park Gardens, SW 3, when time and place will be notified.

Encouraged by Maynard, Coulthard and Senior, who were in the UK, George Blake, resuming his secretarial duties interrupted by war, had put it there. After six long years, the war had finally come to a close in September 1945, although this was not to be the end of operations for Straggler servicemen and many have continued to see action over the following eighty years in various theatres, from Korea and Suez in the fifties, right up to the more recent conflicts in Bosnia, Iraq and Afghanistan. On the cricketing front, there had been a revival of the first-class game in 1945 and, in anticipation of better cricketing opportunities ahead, the Stragglers lost no time in trying to revive the club.

The attendance in Chelsea proved to be rather fewer than anticipated at only six: Maynard, Blake, A.F. Senior, J.R. Coulthard, G.N.R. Morgan and M. Robertson. Murray Robertson, who had retired from being 'foreign secretary' in Calcutta, was elected to chair the meeting. The minutes reveal that a modest restart of three or four fixtures for 1946 was proposed and Blake was deputed to arrange the fixtures, which were published in due course on a small card the size of a cigarette packet. The balance at hand in the bank was £42, roughly £2,000 in 2024 value. At the close of the meeting, Robertson proposed, and Morgan seconded, 'that it should be recorded in the Minutes a deep sense of sorrow at the death of Mr R.B. Lagden who was one of the original members of the Committee'.

In raw numbers, the Stragglers re-established during the late forties and fifties, and the membership list grew quickly as so many officers in the forces had served two years east of Suez, either fighting the Japanese directly or aiding the war effort from India and elsewhere. The *raison d'être* for the club, to provide cricket for those coming home on leave, was unchanged, even if the leave patterns were gradually to shift – long leaves every three or four years were to become more regular and even annual trips became the norm for some as air links improved. From 285 in 1939, the membership list grew to 471 members in 1949.

Although only six games were played in 1946, the secretary, Blake, stated at the committee in October that he planned to stage a much more ambitious programme. Most of the pre-war fixtures were revived, with the exception of the Western Tour, where difficulty arranging accommodation was cited as the reason. The annual committee meetings were now held at Maynard's home in London and the report in October 1947 was definitive:

RECOVERY IN THE FIFTIES AND THE QUESTION OF NON-EUROPEAN MEMBERS

This year we have endeavoured to get back to our pre-war fixture list and had arranged 18 matches. We had been more successful than we could have expected, winning 6, losing 4 and drawing 8 matches.

At the same time, there were concerns about watering down the Straggler ethos - 'we must be careful not to propose any candidates for qualifying matches if they do not conform to the social standards aimed at by the club'. The leadership wanted to remain a club for the 'officer class', which had been somewhat diluted by the exigencies of war - some 'Emergency Commissioned Officers' were from the lower fringes of middle-class respectability and, as the new Labour government imposed itself, there was a general drift towards more egalitarianism within the country.

Twenty-five candidates were elected (compared to fifteen in 1946), and a further twenty-nine in the following year.

With India independent and fully self-governing since August 1947, the withdrawal of the British Army from India and Pakistan, and British officers from the Indian Army (although some British officers stayed on short-term three-year contracts), the Stragglers of Asia's status as an all-white club must have been beginning to look rather exceptional, at least to the more intelligent members. At this distance, it seems odd but, again, history, and the motivations of individuals, do not move in straight lines. For instance, in the wider world, around the same time in 1949, Nehru, the prime minister of India and one of the principal architects of Indian independence, was denied membership of the MCC.

For the Straggler hinterland of imperial India, while the temptation is to think the date of independence marked the start of a clear, smooth and ordered transition, it was far from that - Mountbatten was installed as viceroy in February 1947 with a clear mandate to achieve independence as quickly as possible. The deep communal divisions in India, which had been smothered by colonial rule, came to the surface. The horrendous partition of the country into India and Pakistan, along lines on a map hurriedly drawn by a British-based academic, and the consequent relocations of communal populations (very broadly, Hindus/Sikhs from Pakistan to India and Muslims from India to Pakistan), dragged on for many weeks, with concomitant massacres and senseless slaughters, and the results continue to reverberate through the subcontinent today.

ONE ARM BOWLS A LITTLE

Many Straggler members, especially those in the Indian Army, were intimately involved – there was a hastily constructed Punjab Frontier Force constituted under Major General 'Pete' Rees, and evidence suggests that the multi-communal, disciplined Indian Army stayed neutral before being split apart. Auchinleck, the revered Commander-in-Chief, did his best to ensure the exit of the British officers was handled properly – the mess collections of silver, pictures and mementoes, accumulated over nearly 200 years in some cases, were handed over to their new custodians, and remain in the messes of Indian and Pakistani regiments today.

As a princely state, Kashmir was left in the balance too long by a vacillating Hindu ruler, who eventually declared for India, even though his state was (again broadly) Muslim – an incursion of Pakistani irregulars and some troops was met by a rapid deployment of the Sikh Regiment to Srinagar and a brief conflict, which has left the 'Kashmir' issue to be resolved by the UN (it never has been, to the ongoing regret of governments and cartographers everywhere). At the time, the commanders of both the Indian and Pakistan forces were British (on contract), a situation one cannot imagine occurring in a similar transition today.

What does this have to do with the Stragglers? Well, the point is that the environment was still relatively confused for some years after independence and while it is hard to defend the foot-dragging and slow movement towards opening the club to non-Europeans, that was largely reflective of the atmosphere and the *Zeitgeist* at the time. Reading the extant committee minutes from those years, one senses much discussion and argument behind the written words, with members taking firm stances and probably entering into some passionate debates.

The 'non-European' issue was first raised in the committee meeting of 17 October 1947, soon after independence for India and Pakistan in mid-August. The minute reads:

> The question of Indians being eligible for membership was also discussed and it was decided that the present time was not opportune.

Alleyne Coldwell, George Hirst, Reggie Senior, Vernon Maynard, Jim Hechle and George Blake were in attendance, all of them Stragglers of some

RECOVERY IN THE FIFTIES AND THE QUESTION OF NON-EUROPEAN MEMBERS

experience, and on the surface this minute seems dismissive, although the committee focus was clearly on re-establishing the fixture list and ensuring the financial viability of the club. We do not know whether the issue was raised in the immediate aftermath of independence because it was seen as the 'right thing to do' or whether some specific members, perhaps based in India, proposed the change: likely the impetus was not coming from the UK-based committee. Of the six, Hirst and Hechle were in Calcutta, the others in the UK.

As a civilian based in Bengal, Hechle was to become a significant member of the club leadership in the 1950s. He played against the club first in December 1929, then qualified as a Straggler while on leave in 1930: he went on to play almost fifty games, scoring 1,344 runs at an average of 30.

Kit Cowgill, a member of the Indian Police Service who had joined the Stragglers in 1937, volunteered to become honorary secretary after George Blake stood down in 1952. Blake had done a fantastic job building and then rebuilding the fixture list and membership. Cowgill was to remain in post for almost thirty years; according to Stuart Barnes, the first Hong Kong secretary from 1969, he was 'fanatical about the Stragglers' and it was doubtless the key enthusiasm in his life. Living back in England after the war, he became involved in all aspects of the club's administration and, not least, continuing the secretary's role of writing cricketing pen pictures as new members joined. As a partner in a printing firm, he also helped with producing the club's annual fixture cards and lists of members and results - Straggler literature has always been second to none in the wandering club world.

In 1948, shocked by the increased cost of cricket balls and the tripling of the printing bill, Coldwell and Maynard sponsored the introduction of an annual subscription of 10 shillings (50 pence), which came on top of an increase in the entrance fee from 2 to 3 guineas the previous year. This would help the club pay for umpires and 'tips to groundsmen' out of central funds rather than the team of the day.

More significantly, almost as soon as he was appointed in October 1953, Kit Cowgill organized an 'Extraordinary Committee Meeting' for 30 April 1954, where the committee considered again the admission of Indian members. At the meeting, Cowgill tabled a proposal from the foreign secretary in Calcutta (E.B. 'Ted' Leigh since 1950) 'to admit non-Europeans as members to the club, either as associate or full members'. Cowgill was someone who had mixed closely with the Indian population in his professional life as a policeman, and one imagines he was positive about the proposal and happy to arrange the meeting.

At this distance and with only the committee minutes to depend on, it is dangerous to assume positions or to try to reconstruct what the arguments were. From the UK view, given that the club existed to cater for white colonials returning to the home country on leave, there was no urgency to admit Indians as members, but the picture in Calcutta was much different – the war had broken down racial barriers, the Indian population was now empowered by independence, and the status of a 'whites only' policy in any club was looking increasingly anachronistic.

No doubt there was a great deal of discussion around the proposal – we learn that it was 'gone into at length' by the chairman of the meeting, Coldwell. The Founder, Vernon Maynard, and Reggie Senior apparently proposed that 'Indians be invited to play for the club at no expense to themselves' – which one can interpret as an acceptance of Indian players appearing for the Stragglers, but not becoming members per se. However, for the proposal itself, the minutes record that it was 'unanimously negatived', a curious and apparently rather ungrammatical form of words – although the word 'negatived' has its uses in parliamentary procedure and would not be as unusual as it is today. The five present aside from Maynard, Coldwell and Senior were Blake, Tom Longfield, Hechle, H.R. Power and E.E. Goward. Since Cowgill was not actually present for the meeting, he could not dissent – he was, however, granted a minuted vote of thanks for making the proposal.

Later that summer, it appears that the 'unanimously negatived' decision did not preclude Maynard's suggested experiment of 'asking Indians to play as guests'. S.K. Khanna played three matches for the club, and, according to the minutes of the committee in October 1954, 'proved an unqualified success'. Khanna had been introduced by Straggler C.P. Johnstone in Madras, one of the more enlightened members who was always pressing the case of Indian cricketers.

Specifically on Mr Khanna, the minutes recorded that 'The Royal Marines and St. Edward's Martyrs, with both of whom he stayed [they were two-day matches], were most impressed with him socially and as a cricketer. Mr Khanna

RECOVERY IN THE FIFTIES AND THE QUESTION OF NON-EUROPEAN MEMBERS

had written to the Hon. Sec. expressing the pleasure he had derived from playing with the club and sent his thanks to the committee and members concerned, for the courtesy extended to him.'

It is worth looking at the experiment in some detail: at Deal against the Marines, on 19 and 20 July, in a very low-scoring game where the Stragglers were bowled out for 84 and 90, versus 77 and 223 from the Corps, Khanna scored 8 and then was bowled for a duck. The following day, against Sir Roger Manwood's School, he scored 37 batting at No. 3. Last, at Oxford on 30 and 31 July, he kept wicket and stumped no fewer than five batsmen, catching another, in the St Edward's first innings of 185. He then scored 17 batting at No. 3 in the Straggler reply of 260 for 9 declared, before helping the team, with another stumping, to bowl out the Martyrs for 143, leaving a target of 69 to win. Again, batting at No. 3, he sealed the 9-wicket victory with 37 not out.

Given these performances, especially the tally of five stumpings in an innings, which has yet to be matched, allied to the sterling references from the opponents in two-day fixtures, one must question why S.K. Khanna was not to be proposed as a member of the Stragglers.

The answer possibly lies somewhere in the minutes of the same committee, which continue: 'GNR Morgan's letter on this subject [non-Europeans] was discussed but it was agreed that all he said had been dealt with at the Extraordinary Meeting, at which Mr. Longfield was present. As there was no fresh evidence to warrant any change it was decided to take no action, save asking the Hon. Sec. to obtain the views of the members in India.'

Unfortunately, we don't have Morgan's letter. He had joined the Stragglers in 1928 and was a *boxwallah* in Karachi; he played a good amount in the 1929/30 period as a fast bowler, but little else is known of him. The mention of Longfield is also intriguing – Morgan and Longfield had played together in the two-day Cambridge Crusaders fixture in 1931: Longfield had taken 10 wickets in the match, Morgan 5. Twenty years on, both retired from playing, was there some disagreement between them, with Morgan pressing for Indian members and Longfield resisting? This is one interpretation from the outline of Morgan's letter above.

Tom Longfield is an important character in Straggler history. Educated at Aldenham and Cambridge, he earned Blues in 1927 and 1928. He scored two centuries against the counties and took 40+ wickets in each university season. Playing in his first university match at Lord's in 1927, he earned the description from Sir Pelham ('Plum') Warner of 'a capital all-rounder'. Warner had been captain of England, founded *The Cricketer* and was the foremost cricket administrator of his day. After making his Kent debut in 1928, Longfield went to work in India with Andrew Yule and Company in Calcutta, the city where his father had also been employed, by Royal Insurance: this restricted his Kent career, but he still played forty matches for them as an amateur over the period 1928-39 when home on leave. Andrew Yule was the largest and most established of the twelve or so British-owned 'managing agents' that largely controlled business in Bengal and Assam, in tea, indigo, jute and general trade.

Longfield became captain of Calcutta Cricket Club (CCC) and then the Bengal Cricket Association, leading the Bengal team to Ranji Trophy success in 1938/39 and playing a total of eighty-two first-class matches in his career for three teams, Cambridge University, Kent and Bengal. It is not immediately obvious what he did during the war. Afterwards, he negotiated with the Bengal Cricket Association the move of the CCC from Eden Gardens to Ballygunge - which included the relocation of the 'Lagden Gate'. The association paid the CCC a total of five *lakhs* (500,000) rupees in compensation for moving them - a large amount of money, £37,500 at the time - incredibly, equivalent to over £1 million in 2024!

Longfield first encountered the Stragglers in December 1929, making a century against the club for CCC, and then played his qualifiers at Cambridge in 1931. He was introduced by the CCC captain ('snobbish to the core', according to one chronicler), Alec Hosie, mentioned above. For the Stragglers, Longfield, as a first-class cricketer, was a star. He was an effective batsman, scoring 1,346 runs at an average of 34.5, with three centuries: he was arguably even more valuable as a bowler, taking 116 wickets across forty-two games between 1931 and 1951. One commentator wrote of him: 'he was the complete cricketer and, in addition, a captain of vast insight.'

By 1951, Longfield was appointed to the Straggler committee and started attending the meetings in person by 1956, when he had retired from India. Between 1960 and 1972, he acted as chairman for most of the Straggler committee meetings held, and it was only when Johnny King-Martin appeared on the scene in 1972 that he was moved on. As someone whose name is attached to each occurrence of the 'non-European' issue, and remembering Morgan's letter referred to above, it is tempting to blame Longfield for slow adoption of non-Europeans into the Stragglers of Asia - however, conclusive evidence to that end is, to be fair, lacking. The old managing agency firms of Calcutta have been described as 'notoriously racist' by at least one historian - but again, it would be an unreasonable stretch to apply this general description to Longfield. He had played on several mixed-race teams in India through the thirties and it seems incredible that he could have adopted a stubbornly prejudicial position.

When the final decision was taken by the Straggler committee in favour of Indian members in 1969, which we will cover below, it was passed unanimously and Longfield was at the meeting. Even if he had dragged his feet, he was intelligent enough to realize that the 'wind of change', in Harold Macmillan's famous phrase of ten years before heralding decolonization, had well and truly come.

On a lighter note, probably Tom Longfield's greatest contribution to English cricket was his daughter Susan, who married Ted Dexter - the dashing and innovative Sussex and England captain of the early 1960s. Dexter had a long association with English cricket, serving as an England selector among other appointments, and his wife was a huge support to him throughout.

After the EGM of 1954 and the missed opportunity of Khanna's appearances, some eight years passed before the non-European question came up in committee again (at least in a minute): at this point, October 1962, L.J. Goddard, who was the foreign secretary in India, raised the issue again. Possibly he was influenced by two events: first, in November 1961, a D.K. Mukherjee had appeared for the club against Calcutta CC, which was surely one catalyst behind Goddard's approach to the committee. Second, more broadly, in January 1962, India had won two Test matches in Calcutta and then Madras, to defeat England in a series 'for the only time in history', as *Wisden* put it (of course there were to be plenty more of these historical events in years to come!). Even if a few top players had stayed at home, like Cowdrey, Trueman and Statham, this loss, under Dexter's captaincy, must have had an effect on the remaining British population in India. The Nawab of Pataudi 'gave a dashing display' in the fifth Test and scored 103 in two and a half hours.

ONE ARM BOWLS A LITTLE

A further angle to this proposal is Goddard's own background. Elected in 1957, he is specifically listed as 'non-playing' and was proposed by senior Straggler Ted Leigh, who presumably had an idea that Goddard could run the Calcutta administration. While Leigh himself was from a blue-chip background, educated at Winchester College and employed by Shaw Wallace, one of the more prominent firms in India, Goddard came from a humbler background, albeit with a Cambridge degree. He was a schoolmaster, head of St Paul's School in Darjeeling, and it is not unthinkable that his views were more liberal than many in the Stragglers.

The committee discussion from 1962 is not recorded. The resolution, however, is: 'LJ Goddard's proposal to admit non-Europeans could not be accepted.'

Reference was made to the '1954 resolution' (although it was minuted as something less than a resolution) that permitted non-Europeans to play as guests, and a further rider was added: 'Such guests may be allowed to pay for their meals if they wish.' Again, it is hard to understand the point that is being made here, but possibly the one or two Indian guests who played felt uncomfortable being treated as guests and dependent on their team-mates funding meals for them. There is anyway no evidence that Indian guests did play again after S.K. Khanna in 1954 and before Mukherjee.

The participants in the 1962 meeting included Longfield, of course, and again it is tempting to ascribe to him the unyielding position on this point. If he really was anti-Indian, then he was unfortunately far from alone in this attitude - a decade earlier, in what was to become a famous exchange, the then secretary of the MCC, Colonel Rait Kerr, said to Geoffrey Howard as he left St Pancras to take the 1951/52 MCC Tour to India: 'Well, good luck, old boy, rather you than me, I can't stand educated Indians.'

This has been quoted often, by Stephen Chalke and others, to illustrate the prevailing attitudes among some of the cricketing elite of the 1950s, and it was to take decades before the old prejudices and racial bias were completely eliminated within the establishment. Curiously, Rait Kerr had spent six years or so in India as a soldier and played for the Europeans in the Quadrangular tournament - but obviously was still prejudiced. He was not Indian Army, rather, a Royal Engineer.

Therefore, on three occasions, in 1947, 1954 and 1962, the Straggler committee of the day had considered the issue of allowing Indians to become members

RECOVERY IN THE FIFTIES AND THE QUESTION OF NON-EUROPEAN MEMBERS

and no substantive progress had been made – the consensus on the committee was still negative, it seems, despite the efforts of Cowgill, Leigh, Goddard and probably many others. As we have seen, compared to institutions such as the Indian Army and the ICS, the Stragglers were positively backward in reaching out across the racial divide. It might be easy to blame Longfield, Maynard and Coldwell collectively for dragging their feet, but Maynard died in 1956 and Coldwell in April 1962, before the October meeting. Tom Longfield was effectively chairman from 1960 until 1972, a period that eventually included (in 1969) the election of 'non-Europeans'. Kit Cowgill remained as secretary of the Stragglers until 1980, a run of twenty-six years, and, again, was in place when the move was finally made.

It can only be conjecture, but it is fascinating that none of the committee were from the Indian Army or ICS and thus there was comparatively little experience of working with or playing sport with Indian team-mates, except as opponents. Coldwell was a British Army officer who would have no mess mates of another ethnicity. Maynard had a more progressive view but stopped short, it seems, of recommending Indian members – because he, more than anyone, understood the original *raison d'être* of the club as being for British colonial servants to have a club in England to play for while on leave. Reggie Senior was an Indian Police Service officer from 1922 to 1938, possibly scarred by the endless internal conflicts, where the IPS, as we have seen, was having to protect colonial servants on the ground against the considerable forces of change. Nevertheless, his attitude was as progressive as Maynard's, even if they were both part of the unanimous vote against Cowgill's proposal in 1954.

Tony Sanger, one of the 'founding four', had a more positive attitude: in a letter to Cowgill after Maynard's death in 1956, sent from Germany where he was serving as a colonel, he asks whether the second Maharaja had passed on the 'Honorary Life Membership' to his son.

> If not, may be better not or we should have to reconsider taking Indian members, though I'm not sure the time hasn't come when we should?

One can sense, unstitching the double negatives, that Sanger was also moving with the times and had at least understood the travesty of having a Maharajah as an Honorary Life Member but allowing no Indian rank-and-file members:

his remark also gives the impression that he well knew there were committee members not in favour of the idea.

Difficult as it is to interpret these references and the conversations recorded in brief minutes at a distance of decades, when all of the participants are dead, we can see the indecision and how it would take the more enlightened members a long time to rectify the missed opportunity of that EGM in 1954. Fortunately, that EGM, the experiment of S.K. Khanna and the rejected proposal from Calcutta in 1962 were not the end of the matter.

Turning to other aspects of these years, a contributing factor to the debate around Indian members was that the club had more than enough membership applications in the years after the war, especially during the fifties, and there was no need to widen the traditional recruiting ground of white army officers and other individuals living in the East. As we have seen, the principal financing of the club was through the entrance fee of 2 guineas, which was raised to 3 - by 1952, the bank balance was £107.19.2 (pounds, shillings and pence); by 1963, it was £416.17.7, equivalent to around £8,500 in 2024, a healthy number for a wandering cricket club.

In 1954, there were area representatives installed in Baghdad, Ceylon, Central Malaya and Singapore, as well as the beaten track of Karachi and Calcutta. Recruiting was good. There was no intent to recruit anyone other than white colonial servants in those places (all were colonies or, in the case of Iraq, administered by the UK), along the same lines as India.

Thanks to the satisfactory finances, apart from lowering the entrance fee from 3 guineas to 2 in 1955, the club was able to donate to various entities through the fifties - in 1954, 15 guineas to the Northamptonshire Regiment; in 1958, 10 guineas to the Eastbourne College Building Scheme; in 1963, in memory of H.K. Christian, the club's current all-time highest wicket-taker, 10 guineas to the Cancer Research Fund.

Lt. Col. Henry Christian was, in some ways, the most successful cricketer in the club. When he joined in 1946, he was described as a 'very good left hand opening bowler, No bat'. Already thirty-eight, he was to assiduously gather wickets for the Stragglers over the next fifteen years in a manner never before seen, appearing in over one third of the games. He also played eighteen matches for Surrey Second XI over the period 1947-57.

RECOVERY IN THE FIFTIES AND THE QUESTION OF NON-EUROPEAN MEMBERS

From 1946 to 1960, he took 388 wickets for the Stragglers, appearing on 102 occasions, twelve of which were two-day games. Unfortunately, for the early period (until 1951) bowling analyses are not available, but we know his last 138 wickets were taken at an average of 19.1 runs conceded. In his best performance, he took 12 wickets in 2 innings against the Royal Engineers in July 1952.

A close contemporary of his was Graham Skinner, a very talented cricketer who had made his debut in minor county cricket for Buckinghamshire at the age of seventeen. He played first-class cricket, representing the minor counties against Oxford University and the West Indies in 1933, then playing for Bengal – and scoring a century in the final when they won the Ranji Trophy in 1938/39. He joined the Stragglers in 1938 and by 1963 had accumulated 1,839 runs at an average of 41 and taken 110 wickets in fifty-six games: the 61 wickets he took after bowling analysis was recorded were at a very respectable 16.9. In the 1990s, the newsletter noted: 'AG [Alfred Graham] still appears at Stragglers matches, particularly at the Cross Arrows fixture at Lord's where he proudly continues to sport the club colours in the form of a tie on which the colours are almost totally homogenized and which has a patina which would be greatly admired by the experts on the BBC's Antiques Road Show.'

A *boxwallah*, Skinner was with Balmer Lawrie in Calcutta and played in the Straggler fixtures there in 1947 and 1948, before returning to the UK. He was a true Straggler – apart from Lord's, he used to watch the club at Eastbourne, and the author recalls meeting this eighty-two-year-old gentleman with the faded tie in 1992, having no idea what a distinguished Straggler and high-class cricketer he was, proud to come out and watch his old club play.

In 1955, funds were spent to acquire a large silver cup, which was presented to the Northamptonshire Regiment and engraved 'to mark our association with the Regiment of 30 years which began in 1925'. This was to be played for annually in the long-standing fixture, which had started in 1928 and been contested on twenty occasions, with the Stragglers winning six and losing five, the rest of the matches being drawn. The photograph of the two teams in 1955 has the cup as its centrepiece – ironically, the game was only to be played once more, in 1956, also a draw.

The cup now lies in the collection of the Northamptonshire Regiment Museum in Abington Park, Northampton. Very curiously, the lid of the cup has a faint, unrelated inscription around it:

> Presented to the Officers of the 3rd Battalion Northamptonshire Regiment by Major H.W.K.M. on his retirement 1900.

Was this perhaps a random piece of silver found in the mess, which was deliberately used as part of the new trophy? Had the main body of the major's original cup been lost across one of the regimental moves to and from India or the Caribbean? The answer is unknown, but artfully the design of the cup reflects the design of the lid, making one think Coldwell had thought it through carefully.

It is a mystery why the game was dropped in the 1957 season, as noted in the minutes that October. Coldwell had been the great sponsor of the regimental fixture. He had retired from the Army in 1946 to move just down the road to Northamptonshire County Cricket Club as secretary. Clearly, over the years he had managed to convince previous Honorary Colonels of the Northamptonshire's (the ceremonial heads of regiments, frequently with royal connections) to be supportive, among them General Sir Henry Knox and Brigadier W.J. Jervois, both of whom were given Associate Member status in the Stragglers (more significant than it sounds!). But it is not surprising that by 1957, a two-day cricket match against a wandering side might be deemed extravagant, given the costs to the regiment of putting it on. Potentially, the focus of the officers had changed to the upcoming amalgamation with the Lincolnshire Regiment, as the Army entered one of its many downsizings.

At any rate, the splendid cup is retained in the museum of the Northamptonshire Regiment, which, after initial merger with the Lincolnshire's, itself ceased to exist in 1961, its remnants being absorbed into the Royal Anglian Regiment.

In the mid-fifties, the tours to Cambridge and Oxford were also dropped, owing to the expense of accommodation – they were replaced by fixtures with fellow wandering clubs like the Dragonflies, the Bluemantle's and the Free Foresters, who requested a game that was played at Hurlingham for some years. Notwithstanding the loss in Northampton, increasing numbers of

RECOVERY IN THE FIFTIES AND THE QUESTION OF NON-EUROPEAN MEMBERS

military sides were taken on – including Woolwich Garrison, Aldershot Services, the Royal Army Service Corps. In 1955, in an interesting echo of empire, the Stragglers played 'A Nigerian XI' at Sanderstead – a team that was entirely composed of expatriates working in Nigeria. By the next year, when the fixture was against the 'Nigeria Cricket Association', at least three Nigerians were playing.

In a major development for the club, the large number of members serving in the British Forces Germany (BFG) led to the creation of a fixture list there. As ever, one individual was the driving force, none other than Colonel Tony Sanger: as one of the original four in Trafalgar Square, founding a team for the British in India, it is entirely appropriate that he introduced the club to the British Army of the Rhine (BAOR). In many ways, for the young officer of the 1960s-90s, a posting to BAOR was what a posting to India was half a century before. In 1954, two matches were played, against Headquarters Lübbecke District and then the full BAOR side, in a two-day game.

Capt. Martin Maynard – son of the Founder – played against the BAOR side the following year, keeping wicket and then scoring 119 not out in the second innings to take the Stragglers to victory by 9 wickets.

It was in Germany that the club most obviously joined in the move of wandering cricket away from being an exclusively middle- and upper-class recreation: whereas before the war the roster of players would never have included non-officers, in the fifties and sixties the club began to mirror the social developments of the age, with 'other ranks' appearing in its teams. Cricket, one could argue, became a catalyst in this new spirit of egalitarianism – the BAOR side that the Stragglers played in 1967 had just one officer, a fifty-year-old colonel, presumably to keep the young troops in line (to be fair, he did also score a half-century!). As everyone who has ever crossed a boundary rope on a bright, sunny morning knows, cricketing success or failure that day has no correlation to rank, race, religion or even reputation!

Meanwhile, in England, the later fifties saw a patch of poor seasons, in terms of results. While the club had done well to re-establish the fixture list and by 1951 was playing twenty-nine games, including two in India, the number of games fell to only fifteen by 1959.

ONE ARM BOWLS A LITTLE

The minutes are not exhaustive, but occasional comments give us the drift of the conversations. In 1955, the committee notes 'grave doubts about the Club raising a side on a Monday', perhaps not surprisingly, even in those more leisured days. In 1956, 'the Suez crisis caused difficulty', as games against the Royal Army Service Corps and the Airborne Forces were cancelled: at least one Straggler, the youthful Captain Geoffrey Howlett, son of Bernard, was a member of these Airborne Forces and parachuted into Suez to capture the El Gamil airfield under fire. Others also saw action, including Johnny King-Martin, who was awarded a DSO as CO of his Artillery regiment. In Germany, the Stragglers were due to visit Berlin, but Tony Sanger wrote that 'Nasser [the Egyptian president] rather ruined the tour as General Hughie Stockwell [the general in Berlin] was whipped home just before his game...'

Back home, 'There had been considerable difficulty raising sides and on a number of occasions guests had made up the side. Four non-members played against RAC, four at Northampton, four against Royal Marines, five against Sir Roger Manwood's School and three against the Nigerian XI.'

It seems that while recruiting was generally successful, persuading members to play was a challenge – and this was an era before family life became as prominent a reason to forgo cricket as it is now!

The death of Vernon Maynard in June 1956 undoubtedly cast a further pall. Maynard was only sixty-four and his obituary in *The Times* conveyed a sense of his devotion to the Stragglers. Committee meetings had been held at his home throughout the late 1940s and early 1950s, and special mention was made in the minutes of his wife Jane's hospitality; in recognition, the club donated a pair of silver sauce boats, which were to re-emerge in the 1980s. Meanwhile, Jane Maynard wrote to Kit Cowgill:

> So few people have realized it was Vernon's idea originally which explains why he has always been so very very keen on the club. In fact, a life's hobby.

Something about his wife's words can only reinforce the humble manner that Maynard exuded, even as he founded and promoted the club: apart from his insistence on 'apple green' in the colours, it is hard to find an ounce of self-promotion in his leadership. Happy to delegate chairmanship of committee

RECOVERY IN THE FIFTIES AND THE QUESTION OF NON-EUROPEAN MEMBERS

meetings to others, even when he was present, he would be captain on the field, yet hardly bowled and batted himself at No. 9 or lower. A true servant leader before his time.

Results in 1957 and 1958 were woeful and further losses among the OMs cannot have helped morale. Colonel Reggie Senior, who as we have seen played a significant part in the administration of the club, died unexpectedly on 8 April 1957 in post as Chief Constable of East Suffolk - he was also the current treasurer of the Stragglers and had to be replaced rapidly by R.H. McLeod. Only sixty, Senior had led an eventful life in the forefront of policing, not just in India, as a tribute written by Colonel G.H.R. Halland recounted: the close interaction between British and Indian policemen was emphasized - and dilutes the negative picture of the white English police officer in India conveyed by the novelist Paul Scott in his *Raj Quartet*, among others.

> His fine personal qualities and charm of manner at once endeared him to the Punjabis of all ranks, who were quick to appreciate him as a real leader and trusted friend... In 1930 when I went to Delhi, I found Reggie there as Superintendent in charge of the provincial CID. The local situation was then difficult for the police as the safety of the Viceroy and general security were menaced by a determined and well organized gang of revolutionaries. Largely through his initiative and the loyal support of his Indian subordinates the secret headquarters of this gang in the heart of Delhi City was discovered and raided and the gang broken up.

'Later, from 1948 to 1953', Halland continues, 'I had the privilege of making the regular annual inspection of the East Suffolk Constabulary and saw how much their high standard of efficiency was due to his leadership as chief constable, his knowledge of all ranks, and consistent personal concern for their welfare.'

Towards the end of 1957, Cowgill sent a circular letter to all members, inviting them to volunteer for matches. The early optimism after the war had dissipated:

ONE ARM BOWLS A LITTLE

> The number of Europeans playing cricket in the East has been considerably reduced and some of the clubs out there have had to amalgamate. Also, there is now no Indian Army such as previously existed, and which was a fertile recruiting ground . . . Moreover it is now unusual for those working out East to have a long leisurely six months summer leave. Either leave is confined to shorter periods of three months or if six months is taken this is likely to be January–June or July–December, in either case embracing a relatively short period of the cricket season.
>
> During the 1957 season only one match was won out of fifteen fixtures (in England) . . . What is more inexplicable is that from statistics compiled for seven recent years, out of 132 members elected as many as 43 have never played for the Club since election and a further 29 have played during one season only.

The club was foundering, it seemed to many, and the committee was faced with a crisis.

It did not help that the committee meeting of October 1959, held at the Public Schools Club, had contradictory information. On the one hand a communication had come from India that 'there has been an extraordinary influx of promising young players into Calcutta, and a strong potential in the Assam Tea Gardens'. This development was somewhat against the flow, it would seem, but again it is a myth to think that British civilians were somehow at once unwanted in or ejected from India after independence. The fifties were a time of relatively benign socialist economics and the hard-left nationalization and indigenization of business in Bengal started in earnest only in the early sixties.

At the same time, however, the committee was asked to address obvious symptoms of decline. Results for some years had been poor, although the object of wandering cricket has never been to win at all costs – and the success of a fixture is rarely judged solely based on results. However, few want to play in a side that loses much more often than it wins, and the record of Stragglers was dire. Most sides in wandering cricket reckon on a roughly balanced win/lose percentage, with many games being drawn too, but the three seasons

RECOVERY IN THE FIFTIES AND THE QUESTION OF NON-EUROPEAN MEMBERS

1956-59 saw only 20 per cent wins and a loss almost every second game - a dispiriting picture.

The merchant of doom in this case was Jim Hechle, who worked for a managing agent in Calcutta, Thomas Walker & Co., and had been the club's foreign secretary in 1936 before returning to England and becoming a committee member. He acted as chairman for the meetings between 1958 and 1961: in 1959, he sent a report on the season to the members before the October meeting. A grave agenda item titled 'The Future of the Club' was debated. The club had won five games but lost eight, scoring only 75 against West Kent and 68 in the first innings against St Edward's Martyrs; one of the sole bright spots was twenty-two-year-old John Edrich, the future England Test opener, guesting against Beckenham and scoring 90 not out as Stragglers chased down 122. Regrettably, the Hechle report does not survive, and we have to imagine the talk around the table - in the end, 'after a lengthy discussion', a resolution was passed:

> That the club be carried on for the next two years, but with the rider that there must be a marked revival of enthusiasm amongst Members abroad, and recruitment of new Members from overseas. If, after that period there is further deterioration, **then steps should be taken to phase the club out.**

Fortunately, the discussion did prompt a revival of enthusiasm, it seems, and, by the meeting of October 1960, the committee had seen 'considerable improvement in the last few years'. The cumulative effect of Cowgill's missives, renewed efforts at recruiting in Calcutta and Hechle's serious approach to the danger paid off. When Hechle sadly died not much later, in 1963,

> The chairman [Longfield] recalled the real debt of gratitude the club owed to Jim Hechle for all he had done for the club as chairman elect and particularly during one very difficult period when, but for his efforts, the club could well have folded up altogether.

Chapter Five
SIXTIES AND SEVENTIES
RESOLUTION OF THE 'NON-EUROPEAN' ISSUE

OUT IN THE EAST, the club kept the Indian connection very much alive through the fifties and early sixties, playing an annual fixture, sometimes two, against the CCC at Eden Gardens initially and then, from 1949, when the CCC moved, Ballygunge. The British community in Calcutta, while smaller, was still significant and the teams were relatively strong. One participant, Chris Strachan, who had moved east in 1959, having done national service in Cyprus, remembered these games:

> I well recall the Stragglers games in Calcutta . . . Played at the Calcutta Cricket Club in Ballygunge they were almost entirely an intraclub event with about half of the Straggler teams made up of members and the

remainder being qualifiers. The games were keenly contested, and the cricket was of a fair standard.

Because of the heat, it was generally felt unreasonable to bat on after the lunch interval. Lunch itself was a flexible event, timed to coincide with the declaration. If insufficient runs had been scored the lunch hour was extended by mutual agreement so that the target for the team batting in the afternoon was a stretching one. Beer, pink gin and curry was the typical menu.

Chris was a formidable middle-order batsman with strong arms and a good eye, who, in an era of lighter bats, more defensive attitudes and longer boundaries, hit sixes with aplomb. He was also a useful bowler and lightning-fast fielder. He is the only Straggler to have played for the club both in Calcutta and in Hong Kong (as well as England), moving companies from W.S. Cresswell, tea brokers in Calcutta (where he was from 1959 to 1965), to John Swire & Sons in Hong Kong.

John Quin is another Straggler with memories of those games. He was with a trading firm called C.C. Wakefield before joining Castrol and then BP - living in Calcutta during the late fifties and then in Malaysia during the sixties. Asked about the relations between the Indian and British community, he mentioned that some clubs were still expatriate only in the fifties - the Calcutta Swimming Club and the Tollygunge - but the CCC (which later became the Calcutta Cricket and Football Club) was fully integrated even before independence.

> Our Indian visitors were hosted within and without, fully invested with ale (or nimbu pan [sweetened lemon water with black salt and spices]) plus the inevitable array of pakoras, samosas and like Indian fare which a galaxy of street vendors were traditionally allowed to offer from the parking lot as the evening wore on.

The impression one has is of games played in a possibly less competitive atmosphere than in England, the idea being to enjoy exercise during a hot, steamy day off, among a genial group of friends - and integrated racially.

SIXTIES AND SEVENTIES: RESOLUTION OF THE 'NON-EUROPEAN' ISSUE

As noted, D.K. Mukherjee appears in the 1961 Straggler score sheet in Calcutta, indicating that the 'eastern' part of the club was moving quicker toward integration and diversity than those at home.

Beyond the boundaries, the end of the colonial era was fast approaching: the seismic event of Indian independence in 1947 was followed through the fifties and sixties by the cessation of British colonial rule in a plethora of Asian and African countries. For the Stragglers in India, after the optimistic tenor of the late fifties (as reported to the committee in 1959) the political and economic circumstances of West Bengal were deteriorating.

In 1962, there was a severe incursion by the Chinese army on the border, which caused most of the European tea planters to evacuate, on the orders of the Indian government: to aid the rescue, RAF transport aircraft from Singapore were deployed into Guwahati and other aerodromes. The evacuation was only temporary as the Chinese troops quickly withdrew, having embarrassed the Indian Army severely, but the tea estates were never the same afterwards. The sight of the privileged Europeans and their families being evacuated, leaving their local employees to face potential invasion, understandably left a sour taste for many.

The trend, described by one commentator as 'European planters being eased out in place of the local Indian trained staff', was set to continue through the 1960s and 1970s. Many planters and other civilians left with meagre pensions, 'barely enough to cover the cost of his whisky', as the son of one wrote. They retired in some cases after generations of service in both colonial and independent India, bound for the seaside towns of Eastbourne or Torquay, often to name their houses along Indian themes. Others, younger, went to jobs in provincial English towns with a more humdrum existence ahead of them, probably deeply missing the light, colours and exotic routines of India; some very fortunate might have friends in the City of London, perhaps comrades from the war, who would arrange relatively well-paid jobs administering personnel departments, which helped to recover their pensions.

Meanwhile, in Calcutta itself the government was gradually falling into the hands of trade unionists and the left wing - the most extreme were the so-called Naxalites, who espoused a form of communist ideology that held no place for private business, especially foreign-owned. Quite quickly and encouraged by the policy of the socialist Central Government, the foreign institutions were closed or sold; the trading companies and managing agents largely disappeared or were taken over by Indian owners. Even Andrew Yule, the largest and most prestigious of Calcutta firms, eventually went bankrupt before being revived under public ownership in the 1970s. The Indo-Pakistan War of 1965 did nothing to boost confidence and the devaluation of the rupee in 1966 (by 57 per cent, from 4.76/$1 to 7.5/$1!) was for many the last straw. The Stragglers of Asia fixture in Calcutta therefore became inevitable 'collateral damage' amid the wider social and economic changes – the last game was played on 26 December 1965.

In 1968, the club's foreign secretary reported that he was still making an effort but could only find three Stragglers left in Calcutta to play – and while he reserved a date for the following year with the Calcutta CC, there was to be no recovery. Indeed, there was extensive civil unrest in that year and Calcutta (which became Kolkata in 2001) was set for decades of decline and deterioration.

In 1969, John Quin was to get a Straggler fixture going in Kuala Lumpur, where the Stragglers played at the Selangor Club, otherwise known as 'The Dog'. The Selangor Club scored 210 and the Straggler chase was curtailed by the all-too-common afternoon downpour at 20 for 1. The following year, two Straggler games were played at Singapore Cricket Club (SCC) on the Padang, one against a touring Hong Kong Combined Services side, and the next against SCC itself – both, as it happens, lost by the club.

The results in the sixties were slightly better than in the fifties, with a static list of fixtures, a lesser number than the modern-day Straggler card. In the committee, there was often talk about how difficult it was to find players and the number of late cry-offs. There was also concern about the possible recruiting pool, with the shrinkage of the Army east of Suez. The committee began to debate the dilution of Rule 5, initially agreeing to drop the words 'for at least two years' from the residence qualification. Then, after consulting with the two Original Members (Coldwell and Sanger) on the committee, Hechle oversaw an Extraordinary General Meeting on 1 December 1961, which altered the rule to read:

> To be eligible for Membership it is necessary for a candidate to have been in residence East of Suez, or in Africa, **or to have served in H.M. Forces overseas.**

SIXTIES AND SEVENTIES: RESOLUTION OF THE 'NON-EUROPEAN' ISSUE

For army officers, east of Suez had become 'east of Dover', as clearly the centre of gravity for the Army outside the UK had decisively moved away from Asia to Germany, where at the peak over 100,000 British servicemen were stationed.

One or two people were especially diligent in recruiting, particularly Brigadier Johnny King-Martin, who we will come back to, in Malaya; he was given special authority to recruit members:

> Brig. King-Martin has been empowered to elect to membership suitable officers now serving in the east and the formality of a qualifying match has been waived.

The last clause is very unusual across wandering cricket clubs - basically, total faith was placed in King-Martin to vet both the playing and social qualities of potential members.

As a Brigadier, Commander Royal Artillery (CRA) for the 41st Gurkha Division in Kuala Lumpur and a pre-war Straggler, King-Martin clearly already held a lot of influence within the club. Although the division was fully engaged in the Malayan Emergency of 1948-60, that gradually wound down during the period of his command (April 1961 to March 1963), allowing him the time to propose no fewer than twenty-one members in 1963.

Meanwhile, in Germany, building on the initial games started by Tony Sanger in the mid-fifties, several good players came to the fore - notably Peter Salisbury, another Artillery officer. First appearing in 1966, Salisbury went on to play 199 innings for the Stragglers, up until 2000, scoring 4,494 runs with five centuries and eighteen fifties: a gritty opening batsman with a good eye and penchant for the leg glance (if not quite as elegant as Ranji's), he played for the club every year over thirty-four years, apart from 1976 and 1993.

Salisbury was prominent in Army cricket, running it in Germany, and well disposed to organize some more casual games as practice - however, he took the Straggler fixtures very seriously and did his utmost to win. His account of one match against bitter Army rivals the RAF is revealing:

ONE ARM BOWLS A LITTLE

It was the first time the Stragglers had played in the Rheindahlen Cricket Week, and it was the first time they had played against RAF Germany. Ken Hider was the Match Manager, and he rang me just beforehand to say that he had pulled a muscle, and would I take over running the side? When I asked what the team was, he read out 7 names of players whose average age was well over 40. I was 44 at the time. He said he would ensure that there would be 11 players there on the day. I said "No" and that I would run the side if I could recruit the remaining players myself and that they may not be Stragglers.

Salisbury at once recruited two young captains (one a wicket-keeper) and two even younger soldiers (non-officers), both of whom bowled nagging away-swing medium-pacers. Batting first, Stragglers made only 124 after reaching 73 for 2. Fortunately, the conditions were hot and humid - ideal for the young bowlers, who demolished the RAF upper order to 50 for 6 - despite having to rest these openers after 17 overs each (!). Forty-seven-year-old Steve Goldring took 3 for 19 to bowl out the RAF for 106.

Salisbury spent over sixteen years of his career in Germany and played for the full BAOR side a record number of times, captaining it in 1967 and 1976.

By all accounts, his successors, John Eden and Tony Skipper, were more relaxed but no less effective in shepherding and growing Straggler cricket during their postings in Germany.

BAOR was a generally cushy existence, whichever regiment or corps an officer or other rank was serving in. Tax-free alcohol meant that the booze was usually cheaper than the mixers, leading to heroic drinking sessions as the core of the British Army faced the Russian threat during the height of the Cold War. Equally, tax-free petrol or 'benzine' meant that driving to a match, even though it might involve a journey of several hours between the different British bases, was affordable. Moreover, on the basis that Germany was more expensive than the UK (if not for petrol and alcohol), a 'Local Overseas Allowance' was paid, leading most single officers and soldiers to enjoy a standard of living higher than they could expect in the UK.

It was a pleasant existence, only disturbed, for the 'teeth' arms (Infantry, Armoured, Artillery, Engineer and Signals units), by regular four-month tours in Northern Ireland, trying to deal with the 'Troubles' between 1969 and the

SIXTIES AND SEVENTIES: RESOLUTION OF THE 'NON-EUROPEAN' ISSUE

1990s. Of course, in later years other conflicts also interfered: the first Gulf War required huge support from the army and RAF in Germany, and the 'Former Yugoslavia' campaign later in the 1990s similarly.

The author served in an Artillery regiment in 1976 whose officers' mess, in the garrison of Hohne, overlooked a cricket pitch. The rhythm of BAOR life meant there was plenty of time for sport. The big military exercises were always scheduled in September, when the cricket season was over, and up until then regiments largely made their own programmes, allowing much time off for their sports teams. As a young Second Lieutenant, the author spent his days between May and August practising and playing cricket, while also training for and entering athletics, swimming and orienteering events - military skills were subordinated while the regiment (commanded by a Commando and Parachute-qualified Lieutenant Colonel) tried to win everything at any sport, in brigade, divisional and finally corps competitions. Outside these, the Free Foresters also had a BAOR section playing a two-day game against the Corps Commanders XI, and other cricket was arranged by keen players.

The Stragglers in Germany played a variety of military teams including a two-day game in the then-separate enclave of West Berlin, playing against the local General's side over a weekend, after a long drive up on the Friday evening through the closely supervised 'corridor' traversing communist East Germany. Berlin had a notably hedonistic side to it, even by German standards, accentuated by the barbed wire and minefields, Checkpoint Charlie and other accoutrements of the Cold War. The team would stay at the bland and basic 'Edinburgh House' accommodation run by the Army - however little time was spent there. Given the nightlife, it was not a place you wanted to be 'not out' overnight in a two-day game.

All the cricket, both in Berlin and elsewhere in BAOR, was played on coconut matting laid over shale, or occasionally concrete: on shale, the ball would often 'sit up' and the unwary batsman would be caught at cover or mid-off. At the Rheindahlen Headquarters, close to the Dutch border, the best possible wicket was prepared for the more important games, when the BAOR side would take on RAF Germany, or good teams from the UK, Denmark and the Netherlands. Many touring sides visited BAOR from the UK - including the Stragglers UK, who sent a team in 1976 and 1977.

ONE ARM BOWLS A LITTLE

Back in England, the club was playing an average of sixteen matches a year, still losing rather more than they won, still attracting some good players – none better than former England wicket-keeper Roy Swetman, who represented Surrey from 1954 to 1961 and appeared in eleven Test matches over 1959/60.

In 1962, Swetman turned out for the Stragglers with 73 runs against Aldershot Services and continued to play two or three games a year for the next five years, scoring 795 runs at the remarkable average of 61. He scored three centuries and five fifties, also bowling, with a best return of 5 for 67 against the Butterflies at Hurlingham in 1967, a season when he was keeping wicket for Nottinghamshire, having come out of retirement in 1966 for two years. The Hurlingham game was on the Sunday (no first-class cricket was played on Sundays) of the Middlesex vs. Nottinghamshire game at Lord's! For Stragglers, he avoided the wicket-keeping gloves.

Swetman was to blot his copybook severely with the club when he did not show up for the Beckenham fixture in 1968, and, despite being written to, failed to provide an explanation. As a result, the committee had almost resolved 'that his name be removed from the Club register', until Bertie Joel, his original proposer, intervened and he was given another chance. Some thirty years later, with his son Rupert playing great cricket, he was to reappear in Straggler colours.

In 1966, the pre-eminent cricket journalist (by his own account) E.W. Swanton published a massive 1,165-page tome titled *The World of Cricket*, declared as 'probably the most ambitious and extensive work ever produced on a game which has a history and literature second to none'. For a year or two before, the editors had been in touch with Straggler honorary secretary Kit Cowgill, who contributed a few paragraphs, including a neat summary of the club's issues:

> The changed pattern of home leave for overseas members, the scarcity of free time for those at home and increasing costs have all combined to put paid to the one-week tours at Oxford and Cambridge and the West Country, even though as a wandering club with no expensive ground to maintain the annual subscription is very small.

SIXTIES AND SEVENTIES: RESOLUTION OF THE 'NON-EUROPEAN' ISSUE

For the Straggler committee, the key event of the sixties was the resolution of the 'non-European' issue. The catalyst was a young Punjabi Indian, Shiv Datt, the son of an Indian Medical Service officer, Major General Dev Datt, OBE. Shiv was a product of the Doon School (the Eton of India) and moved to Oakham School in the UK when his distinguished family emigrated from India. He was an immediate star on the cricket pitch. *Wisden* 1966 comments for Oakham in its 'Schools Cricket' review: 'The [1965] season was remarkable only for the batting of S.D. Datt who headed the batting averages [379 runs at an average of 38] for the second season running and has two more years at the school.'

In the 1966 season, he scored 442 runs at an average of 34, including 146 not out against Kimbolton School, winning a free bat from sponsors Slazenger, who were just breaking into the cricket bat market. He followed this with 334 runs at an average of 30 in 1967 and went on to read Electrical Engineering at Southampton University, where he set about qualifying as a playing member of the MCC. At this point he met Major Bill Withall, at the time the best Straggler batsman. A worldly Royal Engineer officer who took up flying helicopters in the Army Air Corps, Withall at once saw that Datt would be an ideal recruit for the club. Datt tells the story:

> It was in 1969, my first MCC qualifying match, that I opened the batting with a young, dapper Sapper Major – immaculately turned out, his MCC cap at the merest hint of a tilt to support an easy grace, all as much to teach a young aspiring MCC candidate the style to which MCC was accustomed, as to project the man himself. We scored a 50 each, his more elegant than mine, before making way for 'others to have a bat!' As we strolled around the boundary, Bill invited me to join a wandering club which he was also a member of, the Stragglers of Asia CC, where, he assured me, I would enjoy excellent cricket on good pitches at top-class venues with likeminded and most interesting people. It was an invitation I could not refuse.

Datt played three qualifiers, United Services Portsmouth (bowled for 3), Beckenham (bowled for 13) and the Bluemantle's at Tunbridge Wells (bowled for 40 and 5 overs, 1 wicket for 18). Not a fantastic start, but his class would have been evident to all, and with Withall's sponsorship there was no likelihood of him not being put up for membership.

As remains the practice today, candidates for election are considered at an autumn committee meeting. So came the fateful day. Shiv Datt was on the list of candidates at the committee meeting on 17 October 1969 at the Oriental Club in Stratford Place, in London's West End. Kit Cowgill, despite being sympathetic to Indians joining the club for almost twenty years, was unable to record his name correctly and the prospective member is recorded in the minutes as 'C. Datt'. 'Shiv' evidently proved to be beyond the ability of some committee members to pronounce (despite their many years in India, in some cases), so he was given the name 'Charlie'.

It is relevant first to note the number of people and the seniority of the Stragglers present at that meeting: Paul van der Gucht, Tom Longfield, Bertie Joel, Brigadier Johnny King-Martin, Major General Terence McMeekin, Lt. Col. (by then) Bill Withall - all these key Stragglers were there, plus R.J.S. Franks, Commander G.E.M. Naylor, C.W. Langford, Kit Cowgill and the honorary treasurer, R.H. McLeod. Also attending was an influential and senior member recently returned from the East, J.W. Anson, 'by special invitation'.

Before the list of candidates was to be discussed, there was an agenda item from 'Matters Arising' of 'non-Europeans'. Clearly, the issue had come up in the previous committee of 1968, although no record of that exists.

That there was a long discussion on the subject is obvious and it seems natural that Tom Longfield, as chairman and with the added stature of being the most experienced first-class cricketer in the room, would have taken the lead. He was also the committee member who had been present at all the previous considerations of the non-European issue.

Even if he had seemingly dragged his feet over the previous years, Longfield was surely intelligent enough to realize that times were changing. Whatever his private thoughts, there were any number of reasons not to delay any further the entry into the club of Indian members, and no doubt the name of 'C. Datt' on the list of candidates was in Longfield's and everyone's mind. The unprecedentedly high number of attendees at the meeting (twelve) is maybe a signal that some intensive lobbying was going on.

It is worth quoting in full the relevant minute for this agenda item:

SIXTIES AND SEVENTIES: RESOLUTION OF THE 'NON-EUROPEAN' ISSUE

The Chairman said that the question of admitting non-Europeans to the Club had been raised and he asked members for their views. After considerable discussion it was agreed that proposals for non-Europeans would be accepted in the normal way but that the proposer must ensure that the candidate was in every way suitable and ensure particularly that the candidate had sufficient resources in the UK to pay his dues to the Club and that he would pay them. It was further agreed that the Committee must be discriminating in all such cases which come up for election. It was proposed by R.H. McLoed, seconded by T.D.H. McMeekin, that non-Europeans who are in every way suitable and with adequate resources in the UK should be admitted as members of the Stragglers of Asia C.C. This resolution was carried **unanimously**.

One imagines that Bill Withall made a strong case for his protégé Shiv Datt, who was making runs in his qualifiers for MCC even if not many for Stragglers: presumably Cowgill also spoke in favour - as he had been positive since joining the committee fifteen years before; and it seems the senior army officer present, Major General Terence McMeekin, was a keen supporter, since he seconded the motion. The treasurer, McLeod, was the proposer of record, a sign of silent endorsement, one may speculate, from the chairman.

Some might view the very careful wording of the resolution around the financial issues as being patronizing - however, in the committee's defence, there were very pernicious foreign currency controls in India at the time and some concern that the Indians would have difficulty paying their way was natural. Having said that, the additional clause 'and that he would pay them' at the end of the sentence certainly seems gratuitous!

The meeting progressed through the treasurer's report, followed by some discussion about cricket ('It was reported that there was an acute shortage of wicketkeepers now available'); then the cohort of fifteen candidates came up for approval, of which ten were duly elected, including 'C. Datt'.

Also elected that year were a future president of the club, Billy King-Harman, and the secretary of the Hong Kong Cricket Club, Stuart Barnes.

Thus, nearly twenty-two years after the 'non-European' issue had first been mooted, and some forty-four years after the formation of the Stragglers, and in the wake of several false starts, it was finally accepted that a 'non-European' could be elected to membership. It was a highly significant moment for the club to settle the race issue, albeit rather later than most institutions had resolved it.

Writing in 2024, with all the current focus and ambient noise around the negative history of colonialism, it is tempting to ascribe the delay in admitting Indian members to racist motives on the part of some, potentially Longfield in particular, who had been present at all the meetings since 1947, where the issue was discussed, but this would be unfair. Even apparently seminal moments in history such as the independence of India can take decades to trickle down in their effects on individual behaviour, and the intriguing aspect of the Stragglers story is the obviously different perspectives that white British colonials of varying experiences held. It would be easy to virulently criticize some of those on the committee as being 'racist', but there is simply no clear evidence of that – rather, it seems some simply saw the Stragglers as a 'British' club and saw no need to allow Indian members as the original purpose of the club did not encompass them.

To ascribe this to racism is too simplistic – rather, there was a continuum of views from the 'highly resistant to change' Longfield, it seems, to those behind the appearances of Mr Khanna as a guest, who were all too aware of the need to become multi-racial and inclusive.

General society had moved on rather faster than the Straggler committee, and there was also a pertinent cricketing event that must have moved some closed minds in the body, if that is what they were. A year earlier, the 'D'Oliveira' affair had rocked the cricketing establishment and, indeed, the government. Enormous controversy had been generated when the South African 'Cape Coloured' Basil D'Oliveira was left out of the MCC side to tour South Africa in August 1968, a story that others have recounted in minute detail, in particular Peter Oborne, with his magnificent biography of D'Oliveira, published in 2004. The affair brought into sharp relief the racist attitude of the South African government, still hell-bent on maintaining apartheid in all its horrible vestiges: D'Oliveira had left Cape Town some years before and qualified for England after several years, playing first in the Lancashire league, then for Worcestershire.

The South African government was so keen to avoid the image of a non-white coming back to tour with MCC that they resorted to subterfuge at a government level and even tried to bribe D'Oliveira himself. Sadly, some in

SIXTIES AND SEVENTIES: RESOLUTION OF THE 'NON-EUROPEAN' ISSUE

the English cricket establishment were less than straightforward, leaving him out of the initial tour party although he had scored 156 not out in a Test just before, and hence the affair acquired even more notoriety.

Rich Evans in *Wisden Cricket Monthly* later commented that with its inept handling of the D'Oliveira affair, 'MCC echoed the identity crisis of post-imperial Britain'. One has to make the same judgement on the Stragglers' handling of the 'non-European' question, particularly as it had stretched out over decades – but by 1969, no Straggler committee member could have been blind to the necessity of resolving the issue.

Most people are, to some extent, 'prisoners of their experience' and the varied lives of individuals surely affected their view of the 'non-European' issue. A man like Johnny King-Martin, brought up by a father in the Indian Forest Service and fighting the war in the North African desert and Eritrea alongside Indian troops of multiple faiths and, increasingly, as the war went on, Indian officers, was bound to have a different view from someone like Tom Longfield, raised and working in all the studied formality of a great managing agency establishment in Calcutta. It would take a PhD thesis to definitively prove that Indian Army officers adopted a much more open attitude than their civilian colleagues, but in this modest history of a cricket club, perhaps some evidence already exists. The important point, though, is that individuals have individual views and perspectives, and while the activist wants instant results, real deep societal change often happens incrementally.

Sadly, Datt's election to the club in 1969, while a watershed, did not see the complete cessation of the 'non-European' issue, as we shall see.

Shiv Datt has been a fantastically committed Straggler, although for much of his career he was overseas, tackling projects in Nigeria, Iran and Abu Dhabi, among others. Nevertheless, he is the second-highest run-scorer in the club's history, with 6,524 runs from 241 innings, including eleven centuries. He never bowled much, filling in as a wicket-keeper if necessary, and was capable of the highest standards of fielding. In the epic contest between the touring Stragglers from the UK and the Stragglers of Hong Kong in 1993, he swooped low and fast at first slip to catch the Hong Kong team's key man Martin Sabine for 55, when it seemed he might run away with the match. As it was, the home team was restricted to 206 for 9 declared. and the tourists overhauled it by two wickets – again largely thanks to Datt's 84 opening.

He has been a leading light in many ways, not least in developing tours to India in 2000 for the 75th Anniversary and in 2025 for the Centenary and maintaining the vital links between the club and India.

Another important event at the start of the seventies was the introduction of Johnny King-Martin into the club's administration, after his retirement from his distinguished career in the Army. King-Martin introduced a zest and bias for action that was sorely needed, especially in recruiting a higher level of player. He was also aware that the club's governance by means of an annual committee meeting every October, with a rotating chairman elected at each meeting, was inadequate; also, that fundamentally the members of that body were too old – two had died in office the year before.

King-Martin first joined the club just pre-war in 1939, having been commissioned into the Indian Army in 1935, serving in that evocatively named regiment, the 12th Frontier Force.

During the war, he saw action in Eritrea, the Western Desert and Italy, but it was after 1945 that he really made his mark. Transferring from the Indian Army to the British Royal Artillery (thus becoming a 'Black Gunner'), King-Martin won an MC in the Malaya campaign, followed by a DSO in the very brief Suez campaign, as Commanding Officer of 50th Medium Regiment, RA. As mentioned above, he served with the Gurkha Division in Malaya, and then in BAOR, retiring in 1970 with a CBE. While in general Indian Army officers after transfer to the British Army struggled to be promoted above Lt. Col. (they were joining regiments relatively late in their career and the army was contracting after the war), King-Martin did as well or better than anyone – and was an unusual soldier in winning two gallantry awards during the colonial campaigns.

General Sir Geoffrey Howlett, a successor as president, wrote of him:

> We were going through a pretty lean period in the 1960s and when Johnny retired from the Army in 1970, he, more than anyone else, put this right, first as Match Secretary and then as Chairman. His energy, his setting of standards, and above all his surface pomposity that was, so wonderfully, only skin deep, made him an ideal sporting leader.
>
> There was an occasion, on a German tour, before the plastic card was 'the norm', when he rashly admitted that he had an American

SIXTIES AND SEVENTIES: RESOLUTION OF THE 'NON-EUROPEAN' ISSUE

> Express card after a long, expensive Club evening in a Dusseldorf nightclub. I only hope that he eventually got all our shares back!
>
> On another tour, of Denmark, including a match in North Jutland, at the rather dangerously named town of Horring, he was again in charge. As the very senior tourist, manager and umpire, he asked me, then a Divisional Commander in Germany, whether he might possibly borrow a staff car for the evening. This was theoretically to save him having to stay up most of the night with the younger cricketers in Hamburg on their return journey to my house from Jutland. I believe that I have now retired long enough to admit that I did 'fix' it. The team eventually all got back to my house at 3.00 am, the staff car and Johnny at 4.00 am.

Another Straggler, Peter Salisbury, wrote of King-Martin:

> He was a crusty old Brigadier who didn't suffer fools gladly and had a terrible temper if anyone upset him. In the late 1960s he was Commander Rhine Area (a largely administrative role) and played regularly for the Stragglers ... Later, back in the UK, I served on the Stragglers committee when Johnny was chairman. Johnny was an excellent chairman. He insisted on the highest standards and served the Stragglers extremely well. He was very keen on accurate records being kept and insisted that on the score sheets submitted by match managers all players on both sides had full and correct initials. Ken Hider used to make up initials for opposing players when he did not know them. Goodness knows what Johnny would have said if he had known!

As a cricketer, King-Martin preferred to open the batting and take the bowling on - his average in fifteen post-war games was 14, with a top score of 45 at Eastbourne and quite a few ducks at No. 1. It was as an administrator that he really made his mark for the Stragglers - importing his enthusiasm and urgency. He had an attitude about him that could come across perhaps as brusque and overbearing at times - it obscured what was a very caring and interested spirit, who was able to extract the best performance from his teams. His newsletters, started in 1972, were legendary and give some feel of the club's poor state and his efforts to turn it around. Indeed, 1972 was something of a nadir for the Stragglers – out of eighteen games started, eleven were lost and, again, only one won – and that by the narrow margin of 3 runs against the Dragonflies.

The Brigadier was officially match secretary but instituted a 'management sub-committee' of himself, Cowgill and others co-opted as necessary, which ran the club day to day. Bob Bairamian continued as treasurer and by 1972, the fixture card noted an 'Hon. BAOR Secretary Maj. K.G. Hider RA'. More surprisingly, perhaps, it also noted an 'Hon. Foreign Secretary' again, M.R. Smith of James Warren & Co. in Chowringhee Road, Calcutta. However, as we have seen, the Stragglers had played their last game in that city seven years before.

After a couple of years, King-Martin instituted real change, as he reported in the newsletter:

> On 26 March 1973 both the Annual Committee meeting and the first ever Annual General Meeting took place at Lord's . . . the retiring Chairman of the club nominated his successor and the first ever President of the Club, P.I. van der Gucht, who was unanimously elected.

At the same time, Shiv Datt was also elected to the committee, along with an energetic Australian doctor, Darryl Cantor. Although perhaps 'crusty' in the office, Johnny King-Martin was not going to let any lingering colonial prejudices derail his club.

> A cocktail party took place (after the AGM) to which some 35 members came. Wives and attractive girlfriends provided a backcloth for hopes of better things to come and members are asked to keep this in mind and are encouraged to bring wives and girlfriends in the future.

The man King-Martin supplanted was of course Tom Longfield, who had been on the committee since the early fifties, as often as not chairing it since there was no official position in the club's Rules. He was graciously retired and later presented with a Parker Knoll armchair from the club, a present he had, one suspects, quite typically specified himself.

SIXTIES AND SEVENTIES: RESOLUTION OF THE 'NON-EUROPEAN' ISSUE

Paul van der Gucht assumed the new position of president, and still no full-time chairman was appointed until 1982, when King-Martin assumed the role.

Thus King-Martin, the much-decorated artilleryman, had not only shaken up the administration of the club but, in taking Shiv Datt on the committee, had made it crystal-clear that no questions of race would further intervene in club membership or administration. A frontline soldier with an Indian Army pedigree, King-Martin presents an interesting counterpoint to the much better cricketer Longfield, whose stewardship of the club's affairs over many years had seemingly shirked the key question.

Van der Gucht was also an impressive cricketer - a Radleian, he played with Wally Hammond in the Gloucestershire side of 1933, where he kept wicket for thirty games. His wicket-keeping was of a very high standard, and he recalled that Sutcliffe, the England opener, was his 'rabbit', dismissing him in both innings while playing for MCC against Gloucestershire. Once he left for India in 1935, working as an engineer with a firm called R.A. Lister, he became an important figure in Indian cricket too.

There he played for the Europeans in the Bombay Quadrangular tournament, and for Bengal in the years running up to the war, with Longfield leading them to the Ranji Trophy in 1938. He was known as 'the smartest wicketkeeper between Kanchenjunga and Cape Comorin', according to an Indian newspaper. Just before Christmas in 1935, we see him playing for the 'Viceroys XI' against the Indian University Occasionals, among whom were the Stragglers Alec Hosie and Tom Longfield again. What is important to note about this fixture is that both teams were mixed - three Europeans appeared on each side, providing further evidence that diversity was establishing itself, even if not among the Stragglers. Among van der Gucht's team-mates were Yuvraj of Patiala (the son of the Maharajah) and the Maharajah of Cooch Behar.

Joining the Indian Army for the duration of the war, van der Gucht was captured in the Western Desert and incarcerated in Italy for over two years.

Van der Gucht retired from India in 1949 (at only thirty-eight) and returned to the UK. In 1968/69, he played for the Radley Rangers in the Cricketer Cup (a competition for Old Boys' sides), aged fifty-eight, still wicket-keeping. Becoming the first Straggler president in 1973, he was, by all accounts, an avuncular but slightly distant figure. One contemporary, Graham Skinner, said of him: 'He was a patient, kindly man, immensely modest and with strong religious beliefs.'

Dennis Silk, the president of MCC, said in the memorial address at Radley College Chapel in 1994, 'He was a patrician who maintained the highest standards of true gentlemanly and sporting behaviour.'

As a Straggler, he had an important role to play in simply managing King-Martin's enthusiasm. Peter Marno, a later chairman, describes King-Martin's *modus operandi*:

> I played a very enjoyable season of qualifying matches and waited with bated breath to see if I would be elected to the Stragglers. Sometime after the end of the season I received a telephone call from Brigadier Johnny King-Martin who asked if I would run a couple of fixtures the following summer. I responded that I did not know if I was yet a Straggler whereupon, raising his voice, he asked again 'Will you run two fixtures next year?' I said 'Yes' – his response was 'You are now a Straggler.' The two matches were midweek and a few days apart – one against the Brentwood Martyrs and the second against Reed's Choughs. I seem to remember that we lost the first by a considerable margin and I don't think we were invited back.
>
> I think I complained too strongly about being given two midweek games close together for my first matches. The following season I found myself a member of the committee where I stayed for some time in one role or another.

Indeed, Peter – having been elected to the committee – was to serve terms as chairman twice!

By 1974, the results had improved, and the newsletter noted:

> . . . a young schoolboy, Gower, playing for the King's School, Canterbury, against the club, made 100 before lunch – a remarkable performance by any standards more particularly so at that age.

SIXTIES AND SEVENTIES: RESOLUTION OF THE 'NON-EUROPEAN' ISSUE

Of course, when King-Martin wrote this he could have had no clue that the young schoolboy was going to be one of the most elegant batsmen of any era, captain of England and an extremely popular figure in the cricketing scene.

David Gower himself always recalls this innings fondly – it was an important century for him.

> In what turned out to be my final season at King's we played a lovely touring side called the Stragglers of Asia, and I got a hundred. Someone saw my innings and reported back to Leicestershire and on the back of that I got an intro. The following season I left school in March and decided to take up the option of playing full-time. My heart was not really with the Law, my heart was with Leicester.

Subsequently, Gower would mention the Stragglers in his autobiography and on air several times during his broadcasting career.

Also in 1974, Major John Eden, on his long Gunnery course at Larkhill, took 6 wickets for 6 runs as the Stragglers bowled Worcester College out for 99 at Oxford. Regrettably, the score card is only a summary, so the number of overs is not recorded.

In the middle of the decade came the 50th Anniversary Jubilee in 1975: the seniors decided to ask the Army for help with a venue for festivities. Fortuitously, Brigadier (by then) Bill Withall was in charge of Aldershot Garrison and astutely he and Johnny King-Martin had Paul van der Gucht write to Lieutenant General Sir James Wilson, the Commander of South East District, also the president of the Army Cricket Association. It helped, no doubt, that Wilson had been a Straggler since 1947 and his immediate predecessor in the District, General Sir Terence McMeekin, was as well. Wilson, an officer of much experience in 'Unusual Undertakings', as his autobiography was titled, was only too delighted to assist. As an aside, he had been closely involved on the staff of the Pakistan Army during the Kashmir incident.

> The Army owes a great deal to the Stragglers since many young officers have been able to learn about the right kind of club cricket largely as a result of their membership of the Club. That the geographical location of those serving abroad has changed matters not a bit; the same

principles apply, and we have every reason to be grateful to the Stragglers for what they have done to help cricket in the Army.

With appropriate blessing and support, various festivities were organized, the centrepiece being two games at Aldershot on 3 August. One was a '55 over' contest between the Stragglers and the Army side, who were gearing up for the Inter-Services tournament in ten days' time (which they won). The Stragglers batted first and opened with a good, if slow, partnership between Withall (40) and Datt (41) of 80 off 40 overs; clearly, runs were needed and wickets were lost, the club ending their innings at 153 for 9 - below par, one might think. Unexpectedly, 'the Army were soon in trouble against some excellent quick bowling by Fursdon and Hamblin'- 39 for 5, all out for 107, largely 'done' by the pace of Fursdon, Bryan Hamblin (3 for 21) and Peter Cattrall's leg spin (4 for 24).

Cattrall deserves a paragraph of his own - at The King's School Canterbury in the 1965 season, he had taken the astonishing number of 66 wickets across seventeen games, a school record, and unsurprisingly the school won twelve of them. Perhaps too attacking a bowler to get a Blue, he joined the Stragglers in 1972 as a 'Useful hitter, v. good leg-spinner, superb cover' - proposed by Bob Bairamian and seconded by Johnny King-Martin. Definitely in the 'top ten' Straggler bowlers, he took 1,128 wickets at an average of fewer than 15 runs each - outstanding figures for a leg-spinner. His Straggler credentials were complete when he married the daughter of Major General Bill Withall!

The second game played on the 50th Anniversary celebrations saw a side captained by Geoff Downman take on one skippered by Richard Hawkey, two senior Stragglers: in the event, a close draw resulted, but the game was not officially recorded as a Straggler fixture, unlike the similar intra-club game on the Hong Kong Tour in 1993.

After the two matches, there was a party at the Royal Engineers officers' mess at Minley Manor, attended by no fewer than 160 members. King-Martin's comment was straightforward:

> One could not find a more perfect setting to celebrate such an occasion, for the terrace at Minley, on a fine warm summer evening overlooking the fields and woods, was truly beautiful.

SIXTIES AND SEVENTIES: RESOLUTION OF THE 'NON-EUROPEAN' ISSUE

A presentation was made to Kit Cowgill, honorary secretary for twenty-two years – Paul van der Gucht presenting a silver salver, which had been subscribed for by appreciative members.

A couple of weeks earlier, a wooden bench was presented to Eastbourne College and the headmaster, Simon Langdale, to mark the anniversary. Notably, two 'non-Europeans' were part of the side, the ubiquitous Shiv Datt and a fellow Punjabi, Saeed Hatteea, who had earlier appeared against the Band of Brothers at Sutton Valence. Shiv Datt tells the story:

> Hatteea arrived late at Sutton Valence, having had trouble finding the ground, and we were in the field. He was also in jeans and leather slippers [*chappals* as worn by the Punjabis in the height of summer], which did not make a good first impression. However, he came on to bowl at once and after the first ball, David Baxter, wicket-keeping, took six steps back: Hatteea removed their middle order, three of whom were top class Stragglers as well as Brothers – Hamblin, Heroys, and Streatfield – taking 4 for 40 off 20 overs. He was quick.

Later, at Eastbourne, Hatteea scored 31 not out, but only took 1 wicket off 10 overs. He was a very useful player who had played state cricket in India; unfortunately, not keen, it seems, to join the Stragglers.

That year – 1975 – was also a good season for results, with eleven wins and seven losses: unusually, only one game was lost to the weather. Additionally, some notable candidates were elected to the club, including Brigadier Geoffrey Howlett (aged forty-five) and Major Bill Kincaid. Probably the standout performance was David Baxter's six wicket-keeping victims against Reed's Choughs: four stumped and two caught.

The highlight of 1976 was a visit to Germany to take part in the Rhine Army cricket festival - against RAF Germany and BAOR XIs, and also another club side from UK, the Adastrians. There were two two-day games against BAOR (drawn) and RAF Germany (lost), then a limited-over one-day competition where Stragglers beat the RAF and then went on to beat the Adastrians, to win the festival – a great achievement. King-Martin reported to the president:

ONE ARM BOWLS A LITTLE

> Unbounding energy, unlimited good humour, politeness and charm to others were the key notes. Leg pulling, ribaldry and so on were unending and I personally came away dead tired and weak for laughing!

Elsewhere, 1976 was another good year, with ten wins and only five draws; several games in July and August were cancelled because of the prolonged drought.

In 1977, the Straggler BAOR section played at Rheindahlen against the BAOR side and lost by an innings and 13 runs, being bowled out for 69 and 81, a game that marked the debut of future chairman Jack Hyde Blake. Another lowlight in the season was controversy at Reed's on 14 July: after a bright start, the Stragglers were struggling - Richard Hawkey came in at No. 7 and was controversially given not out by a Straggler umpire filling in at square leg when, as one witness put it, he 'was run out by yards'. Going on to make 64 not out, he helped the club to 277 for 7 declared. Reed's Choughs started well but with Lloyd-Jones taking 6 for 24 to wrap up the tail, they lost by 127 runs. The Hawkey incident left such a sour taste with John Savage, the Reed's convenor and senior master, that the Choughs promptly dropped the fixture for a couple of years, and it was only revived in 1980.

The latter years of the seventies saw around thirty fixtures a season and, after the inevitable cancellations, a preponderance of wins over losses. The outstanding players of the era were Bill Withall, a General still accumulating runs at the top of the order, Bryan Hamblin, a three-year Oxford Blue and dangerous all-rounder, David Fursdon, also an Oxford Blue fast bowler, and Richard Heard - fast-scoring middle-order batsman and lively fast bowler. Heard's father, an Indian Army officer with the Frontier Force Regiment, had qualified for the Stragglers in 1939, appearing in the last game before the war. When not on Kent duty, Charles Rowe played occasionally too - son of George Rowe of Hong Kong fame.

Meanwhile, in Germany, Peter Salisbury, Dennis Williams and John Eden were the leading lights, the latter an off-spinner with an accuracy he seemed to import from his day job as an Instructor in Gunnery (IG). IGs earned a red band around their hat from a two-year course and were feared by ordinary mortal artillerymen for their withering criticism of poor procedures - although John was a kind man overall!

SIXTIES AND SEVENTIES: RESOLUTION OF THE 'NON-EUROPEAN' ISSUE

The newsletter of 1980 sounded a clear warning that things were getting tougher in terms of assuring a full eleven on the day: 'a spate of members crying-off at the last moment, in some cases as late as the evening before the game, leaving the wretched match manager in a hopeless position'. A theme that recurs time and again in the Straggler story, and no doubt that of every wandering cricket club!

On a happier subject, the tour to Jersey was a success, not least with General Withall personally flying four members of the Stragglers across the Channel in an Army helicopter – something that would certainly lead to questions in Parliament today. All three games were won, apparently – the record of one is missing, at least in the club. Perhaps it lies with a middle-aged lady somewhere, tucked into the pocket of a teenage dress kept for sentimental reasons, a thought stimulated by these final sentences in the tour report:

> The tour ended with the Stragglers being entertained royally by a very generous tax-exile at a Bistro. They found themselves sitting next to a party of attractive schoolgirls (always lucky our touring sides!) celebrating leaving school. One gathers that senior Army Officers and business executives alike were not slow in seizing upon the opportunity to whisper words of worldly advice whilst shuffling on the dance floor . . .

A report rather showing its age now, of course.

The Stragglers of Asia have always kept records well, beginning in the 1950s when the committee of the time collated all the documents/scorecards from the first three decades.

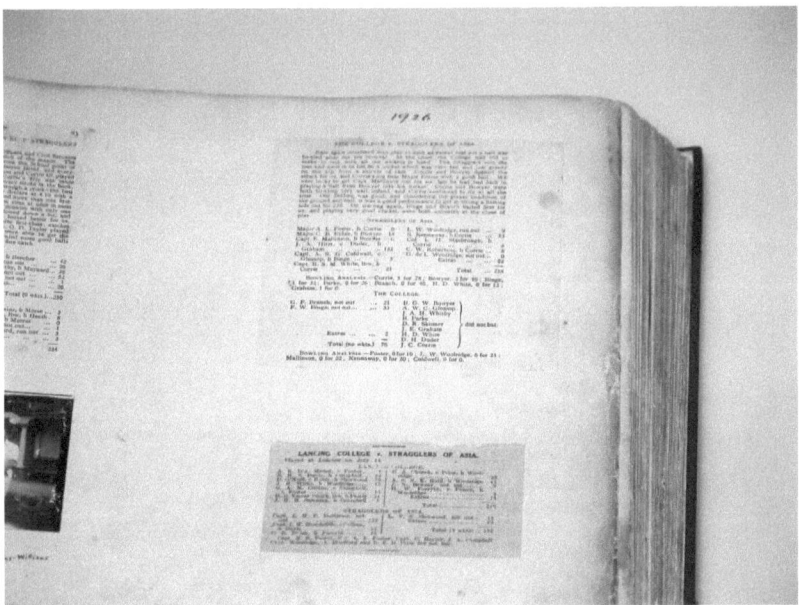

The first scorecards from 1925/26 at Eastbourne and Lancing.

P.B. Sanger's team in Chail in 1923. He is standing, third from the left, whilst Vernon Maynard is fifth from the left.
All six men standing became Stragglers.

Sanger with the Maharaja's XI in 1923; the famous cricketing prince, Ranjitsinghi (by then aged fifty-one), holds the ball up.

The Stragglers at Portsmouth in 1930, playing the United Services Club.
One of the four founders, Mason-McFarlane, is seated on the far left.
Next to him is Rubie, a prominent figure in Sussex and
Indian cricket between the wars.

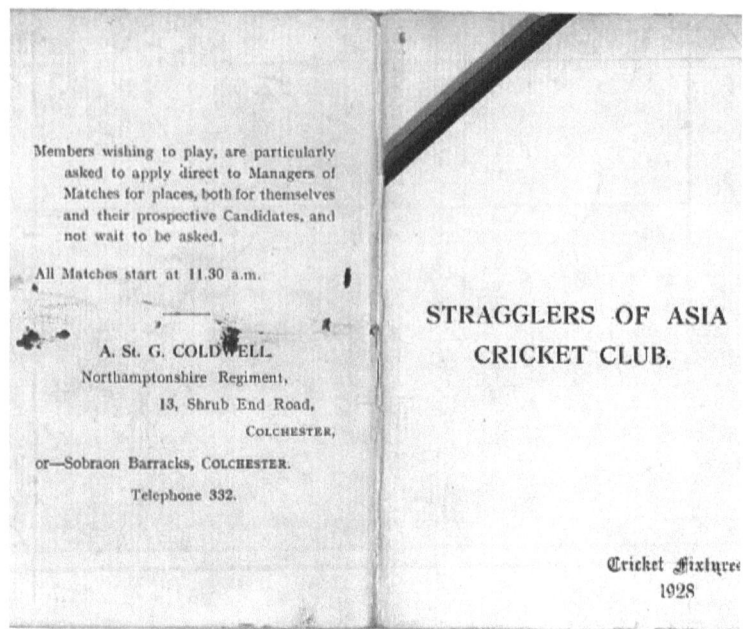

The first fixture card for 1928 was printed in late 1927 by the Hon. Sec. Alleyn Coldwell, posted at the time in Colchester.

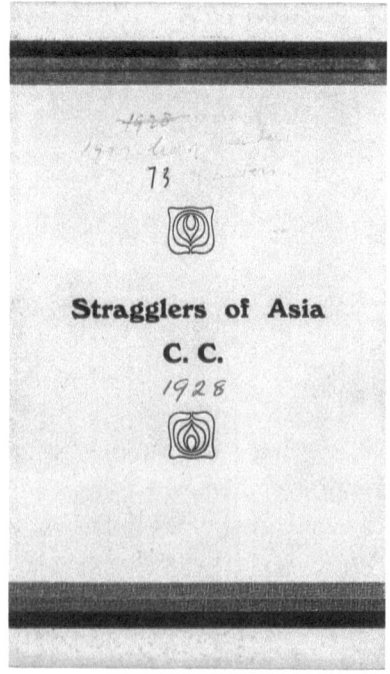

Around the same time, a booklet containing the club's simple Rules and a Membership List was produced.

R. GRESHAM, c/o Messrs. Heatly & Gresham, 40, Wood St., Westminster, S.W.
L. GUISE, c/o Messrs. Thomas & Co., Calcutta.
T. B. HARVEY, Fairley Rectory, Southampton.
pt. L. L. HASSELL, South Staffordshire Regt., Junior Naval and Military Club, 96, Piccadilly, W.
pt. R. L. W. HERRICK, Deccan Horse, 30, Regent St., Nottingham.
pt. J. W. HINCHCLIFFE, Northamptonshire Regt., The Barracks, Northampton.
A. E. HIRST, R.A., c/o Lloyds Bank, 6, Pall Mall, London, S W. 1.
HORLEY, Naval and Military Club.
L. HOSIE, 9, Louden St., Calcutta.
V. HUGHES-HALLETT, Seaforth Highlanders, Berkeley House, Hay Hill, W. 1.
ajor C. E. HUXFORD, 2nd/8th Gurkha Rifles, Shillong, Assam.
S. JOHNSON, c/o Messrs. Shaw, Wallace & Co., Calcutta.
KIMMINS, R.A., Meerut, U.P.
H. KINDERSLEY, 1, Southwicke Crescent, W. 1.
W. KENNAWAY, c/o Thomas Cook & Sons (Mail Dept.), Berkeley Street, London, W. 1.
B. LAGDEN, c/o Messrs. Macleod & Co., Calcutta.
E. LUCAS, Croftmoor, Dean Park Road, Bournemouth.
F. LUMSDEN, 21, Napier Road, Edinborough.
G. MACKENZIE, I.C.S., East India United Service Club, Pall Mall.
ajor F. N. MASON MACFARLANE, Turin House, Forfarshire.
pt. E. H. P. MALLINSON, 10/17 Dogra Regt., Jullundur, Punjab.
A. V. MAYNARD, Brandon, Pittville Crescent, Cheltenham.
ajor A. D. MIDDLETON, Moor Grange, Far Headingley, Leeds.
ajor B. H. MATHESON, United Service Club, S.W.
ajor T. S. MUIRHEAD, 2nd Northamptonshire Regt., Colchester.

STRAGGLERS OF ASIA C.C.

RULES.

1. The affairs of the "Stragglers of Asia" are regulated by a Committee.

2. The Committee is to consist of six members, which may be increased if necessary. It will include the Home Secretary (ex-officio).

3. The duties of the Committee are to assist the Secretary in arranging matches, to elect members, and generally to forward the interests of the Club in every possible way.

4. Each newly elected member shall pay an entrance fee of one guinea to the Hon. Secretary for printing, postage, etc. There is no annual subscription.

5. To be eligible for membership, it is necessary for a candidate to have been in residence for at least one year East of Suez.

6. All candidates must be proposed and seconded by two members, who should state the cricketing abilities of the candidate they are proposing.

7. An Election of Members will be held annually, at the end of the cricket season, and at least one qualifying match should have been played.

The first Rules included the requirement of one year's service 'East of Suez' - later increased to two. This defined the origin of Stragglers for the first half-century of the club's existence.

8. The number and election of candidates will be limited, and must necessarily vary according to how many members are at home on leave each year and the number of fixtures arranged.

9. Members abroad wishing to put up candidates for election may obtain membership forms from A. L. HOSIE, Esq., 9, Louden Street, Calcutta, or Capt. E. CAMERON, 2nd/8th Gurkha Rifles, Shillong, Assam, to whom they should be returned when completed.

10. Members are asked to notify any change of address (particularly when going on leave), if possible before the end of the year preceding that of going home.

11. The accounts will be passed by at least two members of the Committee.

NOTE.—Fixtures are now being arranged for 1928, and it is hoped that fixture cards giving dates of matches, with managers' addresses, will be sent to all members by December.

Owing to the difficulty of organization by reason of time and distance, it has been considered impracticable for the home Secretary to arrange sides for managers entirely, as previously. Managers of matches should endeavour to arrange the nucleus of their sides in India, and the Home Secretary, who will have records of all members and candidates on leave, will assist managers in every possible way to complete their sides on their arrival home.

LIST OF MEMBERS.

Capt. D. S. AIKENHEAD, R.A., Green Trees, Duffield, Derby
Capt. A. W. B. BECHER, K.O.Y.L.I., c/o Lloyds Bank 6, Pall Mall, S.W. 1.
Maj. A. C. BIRD, Hqrs. Western Command, Quetta.
J. H. BOYD, R.E., 1st A/A Brigade, Blackdown, Hants
N. L. BOR, I.F.S., Kilkoran House, Callan, Co. Kilkenny
B. J. BURGE, I.C.S., Hope Fountain, Portsmouth Road Camberley.
E. P. BURKE, I.S.E., Wellington Club, Grosvenor Square S.W.
M. F. F. BUSZARD, 2nd Northamptonshire Regt., Colchester.
Capt. E. L. CAMERON, 2nd/8th Royal Gurkha Rifles Shillong, Assam.
I. P. F. CAMPBELL, c/o Messrs. Turner, Morrison & Co. Calcutta.
Capt. A. ST. G. COLDWELL, 2nd Northamptonshire Regt. Sobraon Barracks, Colchester.
Capt. W. G. A. COLDWELL, 2nd Northamptonshire Regt. Hong Kong.
J COMPTON, 136, Kensington Park Road, Notting Hill London, W. 11.
J. H. CRACK, I.P., c/o Lloyds Bank, 6, Pall Mall London, S.W. 1.
Capt. C. M. CHRISTIE, R.A., R.M.A. Mess, Woolwich.
Capt. W. H. R. DUTTON, 1/13 Cookes Rifles, 3, Goldsmic Road, Brighton.
Maj. A. L. FOSTER, R.A.M.C., 48, Murray Road, Wimble don, London, S.W. 19.
P. M. FOWLIE, 23, Cannon Place, Hampstead, N.W. 23.
W. C. FURMINGER, 2nd Northamptonshire Regt. Sobraon Barracks, Colchester.
Capt. R. F. GARNONS WILLIAMS, Royal Fusiliers, Staff College, Quetta.
Capt. M. A. GREEN, Northamptonshire Regt., R.M.C. Camberley.

Less than three years after founding, the instructions for gathering teams and the geographical spread of members demonstrated the success of Maynard's vision. Leave in England might come only once in three or four years, but the keen cricketer had the Stragglers to play with when home.

Stragglers of Asia v. The Rest
Eden Gardens, Calcutta
Xmas 1936

G. Wilkinson A.C.T. Blease E.H. Page F.C. Kidd H.B. Trinder
W.G. Carter H.S. Connolly A.A. Shaw P.N. Miller L.H. Gilbert R.F. Scott G.F. Carter
S.R. Gresham S.W. Bohrend E.E. Gomard W.S. Scott A.L. Hosie K.F. Keag J.R. Hechle R.A. Gourlay

The fixtures in Calcutta were generally played around Christmas – the lush sub-tropical environment provides the backdrop. Alec Hosie, the captain and pre-eminent cricketer in Calcutta, leans forward into the camera. Jim Hechle is seated two places to the left. In the second row is the tall Alexander Ward, part of the Eastbourne College XI in 1925; he was to commit suicide in 1945.

By 1938, Tom Longfield and Paul van der Gucht (both in rear row) were in Calcutta and had joined the Stragglers.

Stragglers of Asia vs. Northamptonshire Regiment, 3/4 July 1936: H.A.V. Maynard is front centre, Reggie Senior is seated on far right. The Stragglers bowled the Regiment out for 42 in the first innings but were unable to take more than 8 wickets in the second, resulting in a draw.

Stragglers of Asia Cricket Club.

ANNUAL DINNER

Thursday, 11th July, 1935

HOTEL METROPOLE,
LONDON.   W.C.2.

Menu

Grape Fruit Cocktail Cerisette
Variétés Norvégienne

Consommé Double Yvette
Crème Shéridan

Timbale de Homard Newburg
Riz Pilaff

Médaillon de Ris de Veau Anthelme
Pommes Darphin
Petits Pois Frais

Blanc de Volaille en Gelée Yorkaise
Salade Favorite

Pêche Glacée Oriental
Mignardises

Canapé Ivanhoë

Café

In London, the first Annual Dinner was held at the Hotel Metropole and messages of loyal support were sent to the King and the Viceroy in India. The Stragglers ate well.

DATE	MATCH	Where Played	ADDRESS OF MANAGER
Wed., June 19	Eastern Command	Hounslow ...	G. S. Blake, 16 Chelsea Park Gardens, S.W.3 Tel. Flaxman 9352
Wed. June 26 & 27 Thurs.	United Services	Portsmouth ...	Lt.-Col. R. J. B. Snook, R.A. 4 R.A. Training Regt., Larkhill, Wilts.
Sat., July 6	Eastbourne College	Eastbourne ...	H. A. V. Maynard, 3 Courtfield Road, S.W.7. Tel. Frobisher 2073
Sun., July 7	Staff College	Camberley ...	Lt.-Col. H. M. Leapman, 74 Temple Chambers, E.C.4 Tel. Central 7987
Sat., July 27	R.A.S.C. Aldershot	Aldershot ...	J. R. Coulthard, Sundial, Forest Row, Sussex. Tel. Forest Row 201
~~Mon., Aug. 5~~ Wed., Aug. 7	Royal Marines Deal	Deal ...	G. N. R. Morgan, Canon Barn, Sandwich, Kent Tel. Sandwich 146

STRAGGLERS OF ASIA CRICKET CLUB.

Members wishing to play are particularly asked to apply direct to Managers of Matches for places both for themselves and their prospective Candidates and not wait to be asked.

All Matches start at 11.30 a.m.

G. S. BLAKE,
16, Chelsea Park Gardens,
S.W.3.
Tel. FLAXMAN 9352.

Cricket Fixtures
1946

With Maynard's support, Hon. Sec. George Blake successfully restarted the club after the war - the six fixtures for 1946 were printed on a card no bigger than a cigarette packet.

STRAGGLERS of ASIA v THE NORTHAMPTONSHIRE REGIMENT 8'-9' July 1955

By 1955, the teams were playing for a cup (on the ground in front of the seated dignitaries). Sadly, it was only to be contested once more, in 1956. Kit Cowgill, long-serving honorary secretary and under-rated player, is seated third from left, Alleyne Coldwell third from right.

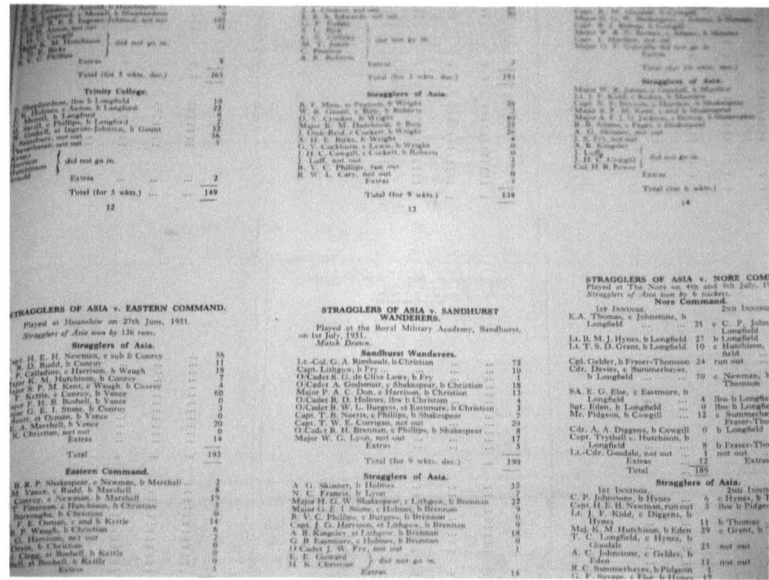

Scorecards from the early fifties show a mix of military and non-military players: H.K. Christian is prominent as a bowler, on his way to the record number of wickets (388) for a Straggler.

A boundary shot from the successful Cyprus tour of 1998 with Sye Razvi waiting to bat in the foreground, Stragglers of Asia's all-time record run-scorer (7,121).

The Stragglers vs. the Pilgrims (the cricket team of a certain regiment in Hereford) at Wormsley in 1998. John Stephenson is flanked by Peter Marno and Ramesh Sethi; Geoffrey Hartley stands on the right.

Two prominent Stragglers - Peter Marno, twice chairman, and Tony Hooper, talented all-rounder who continues to defy the years and is touring India in 2025.

General Sir Geoffrey Howlett, president of the Stragglers 1989-93, and Christopher Martin-Jenkins, prominent cricketing writer, share an amusing anecdote.

A group of military Stragglers: standing, Tim Lerwill (current Straggler president) and Nigel Russell; seated, Kerry McLean, Willie Bicket, Mike Reeve-Tucker and Malcolm Watson.

Thanks to John Stephenson, Alec Bedser came to speak at the dinner in 2002, with his twin brother Eric, the energetic Straggler Chairman Jack Hyde Blake in between.

The current Maharaja of Patiala, H.H. Captain Amarinder Singh, pointing out the various properties within his Baradari Gardens Estate in Patiala on the Seventy-Fifth Anniversary 2000 tour, to the first 'non-European' member and tour organizer Shiv Datt, alongside Hyde Blake.

A modern Straggler team: against Northchurch, 1 September 2024. Standing (left to right), Joe Reid, Faris Haider, James Allsop, Conor Brown, Matt Suckling, Pradeesh Surendran; kneeling, Harry Chapman, Charles Fidler, Danny Dawson, Rob Pollock-Hill, Tony Hooper.

The artist Jim Russell painted the Stragglers in the field at the Hurlingham Club in London, one of the oldest venues for the club; the original is in the Hurlingham's collection.

Chapter Six
THREE STRAGGLERS RESCUE THE HONG KONG CRICKET CLUB

THE LAST STRAGGLER GAME in Calcutta was on Boxing Day, December 1965. The decline of the city as a commercial centre, from what had been the 'economic core' of the British Empire in India, had been relentless since 1947 and hastened in the early sixties: the communist agitations had worsened, and the number of members left in the city was a handful only.

By the meeting of October 1967, clearly the committee in London was very disappointed at the loss of Straggler cricket 'east of Suez'; there were discussions about reviving it in Malaysia, Singapore or Hong Kong - with the result that John Quin was successful in arranging the game at the Selangor Club.

Committee member Brigadier Terence McMeekin was also helpful in arranging for details of the Army members in Singapore and other bases to be updated. While the forces were just about to undergo a withdrawal from the eastern bases, this was not immediate. In Hong Kong, the Gurkhas would stay right until 1997 in the event, and McMeekin was in touch with Major C.J. Pike of the 10th Princess Mary's Own Gurkha Rifles - a battalion that had a long tradition of non-conformity.

C.W. Langford chimed in that he knew 'a prominent member of Hong Kong Cricket Club and volunteered to try and get him to join the Stragglers. It was also agreed that any Straggler games which may be played in Hong Kong will count as qualifying games for candidates.'

Rather redundantly - typical, maybe, of the wishful thinking club committees can indulge in, especially sitting rather far away from West Bengal - 'It was agreed also that the annual match against Calcutta C.C. would in future count as a qualifying game for candidates' - of course, it was never played again.

The 'prominent member' of Hong Kong Cricket Club (HKCC) was George Rowe, a civil servant in the colony, who was president of HKCC. Having been approached by Langford, Rowe, who was at home on leave in September 1968, played against Beckenham on 1 September with his son Charles (who was to go on to a professional career with Kent and Glamorgan). Charlie, aged sixteen, scored 15 and took 3 for 56 off 19 overs: his father, aged fifty, was less successful, scoring 1 batting at No. 9, in one of the few Stragglers tied games. In due course, both were elected at the October 1968 committee meeting.

Together with the HKCC secretary, a Jardine Matheson accountant, Stuart Barnes, Rowe planned a Straggler game in Hong Kong, which was first played in late 1968 according to Barnes, featuring several Stragglers who were in Hong Kong, including Major Pike, who became Barnes's proposer. 'The Mad Major', originally educated at Hilton College in South Africa, had been a Straggler since 1963 - he was a useful all-rounder with a great liking for copious amounts of alcohol and the local ladies, allegedly: his DSO earned in Malaya fighting the communist terrorists certainly made up for any trivial character deficiencies.

The first firm record of a game in the Straggler annual booklet is for December 1969, meaning the score card for 1968 has been lost. Enquiries at HKCC have yielded nothing.

THREE STRAGGLERS RESCUE THE HONG KONG CRICKET CLUB

Barnes himself was elected at the committee's meeting of October 1969, having played three qualifiers in England that summer. ('A useful LH opening bat. Good slip field', Cowgill recorded.) The HKCC game at the end of the year saw Charles Rowe and Vaughan-Arbuckle (a guest) both score 103 not out trying to chase down HKCC's 234 for 6 declared. They ended 6 short for a draw. Barnes, after taking 2 for 14 off 3 overs, was out for a duck and the only other batsman to lose his wicket was Peter Davies, a very correct opener who was to become a Straggler and also a fixture in the Colony XI and the HKCC sides - he is known in local circles as 'The Great Man', a forerunner perhaps of the GOAT ('Greatest of All Time') sobriquet applied to a few cricketers today!

Hong Kong was facing its own decolonization, of course, although it was not until 1980-82, when the handover to China in 1997 was coming within fifteen years (the term for many business loans), that attention was really focused - and the famous Thatcher/Deng Xiaoping meetings resulted in the negotiations leading to the Basic Law agreement, which was intended to keep the Hong Kong Special Administrative Region as a separate enclave, to some extent, within the People's Republic of China for fifty years.

Of more pressing interest to the HKCC hierarchy was the end of the lease in 1971 on its pitch at Chater Road, where HKCC had been founded in 1851 on an old parade ground (which was still used for military musters at events such as the accession of new monarchs). By the 1960s, it had become a much-photographed patch of green beside the tall Hilton Hotel, flanked by the stolid Bank of China and Legislative Council buildings, and overlooked by the Hong Kong Club - similar in atmosphere to the Armoury House ground in the City of London, where Stragglers play the Honourable Artillery Company. 'It was like playing cricket in the middle of Piccadilly Circus', according to one observer.

Further, the Chater Road HKCC was not just a cricket club - its facilities became a lunchtime and evening haunt for many of the expat bankers, merchants and executives working nearby, especially if, as 'juniors', they had not yet qualified for the Hong Kong Club or were unable to enter that lofty establishment for other reasons. The Cricket Club was also an easy refuge during the autumn typhoons where offices closed if the Signal No. 9 went up, as one member recalled: '... so it was off to the Cricket Club for a bit of a "beat up". If the typhoon hit late, we would sleep or pass out on the Club floor once the siesta chairs were full, and it was a sorry and bedraggled group that came to in the morning.' The drinks were cheap and there was a 'Men only' bar upstairs, while ladies were permitted in the ground-floor restaurant.

The club's Centenary in 1951 was celebrated with a lavish dinner attended by the governor, Sir Alexander Grantham, who, according to HKCC's *History*, 'to the surprise and delight of those gathered announced the intention of the government to grant us a lease for a further 10 years'. The surprise and delight were due to the periodic calls for the club to move as it was sitting on very valuable land. Indeed, in 1947, after the Japanese occupation, the colonial secretary (the senior civil servant under the governor) was apparently making an argument that HKCC was occupying the land illegally, since no lease could be found - it had likely been destroyed during the fighting and occupation - and in 1948, 300 members had turned up 'to voice their views on the Government's injunction that they should give up their club and ground for the new Defence Force by the end of April 1950 and accept an alternative site at Happy Valley', the *China Mail*'s front-page account related. 'The President emphasized that unfortunately the club was only a tenant at will, and the Government had every right to resume the ground and premises on it.'

Somehow, the balance of public opinion at the time swayed in HKCC's direction, but the issue 'always bubbled just below the surface', as their history puts it.

In 1963, after another ten-year extension in 1961, the issue was raised again in the Legislative Council and the colonial secretary stated that the government would find a less central site for the club. Rumours of a move made the press in 1965, and by early 1966, the government had set up an 'Advisory Committee on Recreational Leases' to be able to give any recreational club sufficient notice of eviction. Come 1967, it was also on the agenda of the Urban Council and in 1968, their debate on open spaces specifically focused on HKCC - according to Peter Hall, councillor D.J.C. Blaker said conditions had changed entirely from the time when HKCC originally took the land: 'It is now in the midst of a thriving, bustling city. I hardly think that it is a symbol that the majority of our community would choose to have as its City Square.'

THREE STRAGGLERS RESCUE THE HONG KONG CRICKET CLUB

Another councillor said in March 1968: 'It is disappointing that we have had to have racial discrimination in the centre of town. The cricket club is symbolic of discrimination.'

At that, George Rowe was moved to write in the sternest tone to the *South China Morning Post*:

> There is no racial discrimination at the HKCC, and many members would resign if there was. I certainly would. Membership is not restricted by race, colour, creed or nationalities; indeed, we probably have more nationalities than any other club in Hong Kong.

Interestingly, Peter Hall (a Eurasian), writing in the mid-nineties, begged to differ: 'Well spoken, George, and I'm sure you believed it to be true. However, I'm afraid in reality the picture was different.' Hall's comment was backed up by no evidence, but clearly keenly felt. Others have commented that while HKCC was nominally multi-racial, in practice the only non-white members were those who had played for the colony and were automatically enrolled in the club as a result.

In any event, by 8 March 1969, the government had decided definitively not to renew the lease, which was running out in 1971, and advised the club officially.

At the first committee meeting following the communication, and after it had been established the government was offering an alternative site some distance away with a measly degree of compensation, the mood was very gloomy. Senior members had been living with the uncertainty of the leasehold ever since the war – the justification to have a fundamentally expat club occupying a prime piece of real estate was non-existent, really, and in the small world of Hong Kong then, where government and non-government mingled frequently, combined with pressure from some of the local Chinese community, many faint hearts inevitably wondered whether the time had come to simply shut the club. Blaker, quoted above, was just one of a group who believed a new reality had emerged.

Alan Bailey, one of the committee, was to write later:

> The Government's proposals carried very ungenerous surrender terms and some extremely costly alternatives. The club's membership was

not large, its funds were limited to say the least, and there was precious little chance of a successful appeal against the decision. Hence, the Committee had a difficult choice to make, not least of which was the club's very existence. The continuance of the club and its future were in the hands of the General Committee of the day.

The alternative site was Wong Nai Chung Gap, which was 'literally a valley that earlier had been declared a landfill site for future development - either for housing or as recreational space... Dumping had been going on for some years prior to the Government's offer at which time it was difficult to envisage the site as being suitable for a cricket ground with clubhouse and other sporting facilities. The area had yet to be properly levelled and filled with topsoil and turf.'

As an aside, one should record that it had also been the site of one of the final battles against the Japanese at Christmas 1941.

George Rowe had become president of HKCC in 1968 and brought all his administrative skills to bear. He also had a deep commitment to the club and the colony, having been brought up there - a picture of him as a schoolboy at HKCC in 1926 is in the HKCC book: even more significantly, he had been interned during the war, suffering all the privations of the Japanese at Stanley. He was a colonial civil servant of the front rank, a man who brought a grittiness from his Manchester background, allied to a perceptive intelligence and a reluctance to fold easily - many succumbed in Stanley, but not him.

George Rowe went around the table asking each member of the general committee for their view - the first two respondents apparently said the offer from the government was impractical and that the club should therefore simply wind itself up. Fellow Straggler Stuart Barnes spoke next and said that the committee must ensure the club continued, starting afresh in a new home, if necessary, just with a simple 'mat-shed' pavilion, making it more of a country club. Rowe continued gathering opinions around the table - only one other member of the nine-strong committee was in favour of continuation, Geoffrey Bradshaw, who was later, in 1971, also to become a Straggler.

As an experienced civil servant, Rowe realized that if he were to put the matter to a vote at that meeting, the majority would be in favour of winding up the club. He also knew that his own view expressed at that time might indeed provoke this quick, negative resolution, so he wisely kept his own counsel; he 'prudently decided', as the account by Alan Bailey relates, 'to defer the decision until the next Committee meeting the following month'.

> This familiar piece of civil service procrastination continued for several months until, coincidentally, three of the most vociferous of the Committee's 'anti-lobby' simultaneously departed on leave. At the next monthly meeting George called for a vote which resulted in a grudging agreement to go to the membership with a presentation of the Government's offer for consideration at an early EGM.

Much work was then done behind the scenes looking at the options to fund the new development. The initial government support was small, a grant of HK$75,000 and a loan for the same amount, and it was clear the members would have to find ways of raising the millions needed. After careful and thorough preparation, in June 1972, Rowe rose to make his pitch at an EGM across the road in the Hong Kong Club, which outlined the government's proposals regarding the land, displayed a professional set of drawings for a new clubhouse, laid out detailed costings and examined options for funding.

After much negotiation, the government had agreed to extend the Chater Road lease by a few years to enable the club to prepare the Wong Nai Chung site, and to offer a further loan of $1 million towards the cost of a clubhouse (at an interest rate of 7.25 per cent, repayable by the end of the new twenty-one-year lease at 'the Gap'!). The additional capital cost the club would need to fund was estimated at $3.8 million, to be raised by a $20-a-month building levy on members' bills, a $1,000 refundable debenture and the sale of new subscriber and corporate memberships – which were enthusiastically taken up by the major 'hongs' and other companies whose employees had happily enjoyed the Chater Road bars for many decades.

According to one account, 'in the space of less than half an hour, Rowe lifted the gloom as members present responded enthusiastically to the impressive colour drawings of the architect's plans for the new facilities. It was his stirring speech which finally removed the nagging doubts about the feasibility of such a step and which provided the springboard and impetus for the club to regain its direction.'

ONE ARM BOWLS A LITTLE

His major objective achieved, Rowe retired and handed over the HKCC presidency to Sir Denys Roberts, who finally signed the lease on the new ground in February 1973 and was to oversee the closing matches at Chater Road in early May 1975, where a bunch of 'Australian Superstars', including Simpson, Harvey, Grimmett, Lindwall and Davidson, were flown in by Cathay Pacific to give Chater Road a proper send-off. It helped that the marketing director of Cathay Pacific, Keith Sillett, was an Australian. Harold Larwood, the famous English 'bodyline' bowler who had retired in Sydney, also came. The great Sir Donald Bradman sent a letter expressing his regrets.

Stuart Barnes continued as secretary of HKCC until 1975 and the first Straggler vs. HKCC game was played at Wong Nai Chong Gap in April 1976, a season-ending event: Sir Denys played for HKCC, and his side won by 2 wickets. The fixture has continued almost every year since, occasionally rained off, usually a season opener or closer, sometimes supplemented with a second game against Kowloon Cricket Club. In 2010, the Hong Kong Stragglers managed three games, against HKCC, Kowloon and the Crusaders, a touring team from Melbourne, Australia. In the KCC fixture, Mike Gatting, former England skipper, turned out for Stragglers, contributing an elegant 14 in a 5-wicket win. Stuart Barnes, Rod Eddington, the author, Phil McDuell, Martin Sabine and, for the last decade, Mark Winstanley have proved able guardians of the Straggler presence in Hong Kong. Other prominent players have included Cambridge Blues Ian Hodgson and James Barrington, Oxford Blues David Brettell and Jonathan Orders, and the TV personality Mark Austin, all of whom worked in the territory at one time or other.

Meanwhile, HKCC has continued to build and improve its facilities since 1975 and is one of the premier clubs in Hong Kong, offering members a myriad of sporting, dining and recreational facilities. The president after Sir Denys, Terry Smith, then a forty-two-year-old architect, not only instituted a cleverly designed expansion of the facilities but also renewed the Constitution: his successor, Rodney Miles, titled chairman rather than the more honorific president, continued to invest the club resources very well and oversaw a fantastic 150th Anniversary, which featured a triangular tournament between HKCC and both 'MCCs', the second being Melbourne Cricket Club, with which HKCC has close ties.

THREE STRAGGLERS RESCUE THE HONG KONG CRICKET CLUB

Miles and his successors have ensured the strong cricketing tradition remains at its heart, even with the majority of members now local Hong Kong people of every community. To avoid the fate of Craigengower Cricket Club in Hong Kong, where the pitch in 1976 was almost overnight converted to tennis courts and lawn bowls, cricketing members at HKCC have five votes each at AGMs. Both Smith and Miles became Stragglers, enthusiastically participating in the annual games even at an age when standing on the balcony instead, gin in hand, would be quite acceptable!

The thousands of people who have played cricket, tennis or bowls on the HKCC turf, which was painstakingly transported from Chater Road (with a slice also sent to Lord's to underpin the relationship between the clubs), will have no idea of those very uncertain moments in the HKCC's history when it seemed a cricketing institution older than all the English counties except three (Sussex, Nottinghamshire and Surrey) might be closed. Thanks to George Rowe's tactical management of the general committee, ably backed up by the positive Stuart Barnes and Geoffrey Bradshaw, the closure was averted and a better club than anyone could have imagined has emerged at Wong Nai Chung Gap.

HKCC has played the Stragglers in the UK as well, on its tours of 2004 and 2008. In recognition of the close relationship between the clubs, in 2005 the Stragglers of Asia were granted affiliate membership of HKCC, enabling any visiting Stragglers to use the HKCC, which three Stragglers had done so much to preserve.

Curiously, the old ground at Chater Road, so coveted by the Urban Council and other civic-minded individuals, was initially used as a temporary playground and then a construction site for the new Mass Transit Railway in the later seventies; it was then reinvented as a not particularly beautiful urban garden, which relatively few people use today as a shortcut between buildings. Occasionally, late at night, figures dressed in white appear and attempt to hit balls into the Bank of China building.

Chapter Seven
THE EIGHTIES AND THE 'BIRTH OF THE MODERN STRAGGLERS'

IN 1982, the more extrovert and effervescent Bertie Joel took over as president from Paul van der Gucht. Joel was a talented pre-war club cricketer, who started playing in 1929 and scored thirty-five centuries in the next ten seasons, playing the best standard of non-county cricket and, on occasion, turning out for the Surrey Second XI. During the war, he helped form the London Auxiliary Ambulance Service and was then financial adviser to the Shah of Iran and, later, a magistrate in India, more than adequately qualifying him as a Straggler in 1956. In business he was successful, owning Kemp's Directory until he sold it in 1974 and devoted himself to cricket and charity.

ONE ARM BOWLS A LITTLE

He was heavily involved in the Club Cricket Conference and founded a midweek 'Bertie Joel' Cup with the participation of 200 clubs, which is still played for, in a smaller form, today. Prominent throughout London and regional cricket, he was on the committee of the Stragglers from 1964 to 1979 and was an obvious candidate to be president in due course, a role he performed from 1982 to 1988.

As a wealthy man and something of a *bon viveur*, he brought a focus on social events as well as a high standard of cricket: the minutes note that £64 had been spent on two cocktail parties in 1964, seen as an outrageous amount (almost £2,000 in 2024 value), and Joel had also proposed the revival of the annual dinner. Joel on the cricketing side was no pushover: he made a complaint, as match manager of the Dragonflies game at Hurlingham in the previous year, about member G.B. Eastmore: 'Eastmore was guilty of dishonest practices and bad gamesmanship when keeping wicket for the club.'

For that era, these were tough accusations and, if true, certainly not in keeping with the traditions of the Stragglers. Eastmore himself complained of 'unpleasant incidents' previously, and there was clearly a spat of some kind, even though Eastmore had caught two and stumped two of the 7 wickets the Stragglers had taken against the Dragonflies. He was a member of long standing, having joined in 1951, when he was at the Deohall Tea Estate in Assam – indeed, he was nominated as the club's area representative in Assam. Having heard Eastmore's account, and Joel's comments, the committee resolved that 'Match Managers be asked to choose their captains with care and to stamp out any attempts at gamesmanship and other such evils'. They also wrote to Eastmore 'to suggest that he might care to resign his membership if he still feels aggrieved'.

The issue clearly rumbled on for some time and the denouement came in the 1971 committee meeting, when Eastmore was removed from membership as, it transpired, his subscription had been outstanding for six years.

Memories of Bertie Joel are strong – Phil McDuell remembers him showing up to Straggler games in the eighties in a Rolls-Royce, dispensing fish and chips from the boot. Peter Marno recalls his large house on the Bishops Avenue, Hampstead, and also having to write, as chairman, to Joel to dissuade him from making executive decisions that, as president, he should not be doing, including trying to select the Straggler XI to face the Cross Arrows.

THE EIGHTIES AND THE 'BIRTH OF THE MODERN STRAGGLERS'

March 1981 saw the retirement of Kit Cowgill as honorary secretary, having served since late 1953, the best part of thirty years. His retirement was marked at an occasion recorded by the newsletter:

> A small gathering of Stragglers attended a luncheon at the Oriental Club to say 'Good-bye' to Kit and Amy. Naturally it was a sad occasion; but fortified with plenty of gin and, later, with enormous glasses of port and kummel, it ended as a delightful and convivial occasion.

Sadly, Kit died within a few months and King-Martin commented:

> He ran the Club virtually unaided. He found time to travel long distances to score or operate the board. He was a much loved man with a kind and gentle personality, with quiet unassuming ways and a delightful sense of fun.

What had been forgotten by 1981 was just how effective a cricketer Cowgill was – on his debut against the Ironsides in 1937 he scored a 50 and took 8 wickets. Chiefly a bowler, in a career that stretched to 1961, he took 153 wickets in 76 games. The last 53, as it happens, have full bowling analysis in the score cards and an average of 18.13 runs. His batting average was only 17 but he scored runs at useful times, including 70 going in ninth. *In extremis*, he even kept wicket!

As we have seen, Kit Cowgill was also in the van of trying to open the club to non-Europeans after Indian independence. Like King-Martin, he acted as a link between the pre-war Stragglers and the modern club: a quiet man, who worked in local government for many years after his police service in India, as well as a printing business, he had the same determined devotion to the club that Maynard possessed. In an interesting vignette, which says more about the conventional mores of the time probably than the individuals concerned, Tony Sanger could never drop the formal 'Dear Cowgill' in his letters.

*

Another rather different but also key figure in the 1970s/80s, first elected in 1958, was Bob Bairamian, a personality who excites different opinions and is the single best definition of 'a complicated character'. To give some flavour of his presence, *The Times* obituary noted: 'The handshake was vigorous, the talk was knowing, and the laugh was enormous.'

The son of Sir Vahe Bairamian, the chief justice in the colony of Sierra Leone and an appeal judge in Nigeria, his mother was the head of the English school in Nicosia, Cyprus, which is where Bob was born. He always said that his father was the only Armenian ever to have been knighted. A talented classicist, Bob won a hockey Blue at Cambridge and arrived as the assistant headmaster at Holmewood House, a well-established prep school for – at that time – boys aged seven to thirteen, on the edge of Tunbridge Wells, Kent. Not long after, the then-headmaster, John Collings, died; so, at the age of twenty-four, Bairamian was appointed to the position. He took to it like the proverbial duck to water and quickly established Holmewood House as the school to beat on the local circuit, both academically and in sports. He had an insatiable urge to win and attracted young masters who shared his ambition – unfortunately, this led to some questionable practices.

Academically, Holmewood boys won an unnaturally high number of scholarships to public schools, it seemed, perhaps due to the quality of the teaching: Bairamian certainly took great care of his young charges, by all accounts. However, in those more innocent days, the senior schools would send the scholarship question papers by post a couple of days before the examinations, which were of course not subject to strict invigilation, since most of them involved a handful of boys applying for scholarships (separate to the general 'Common Entrance' papers) – simply put, most of the public schools trusted the prep schools to do the right thing. Eventually, there was more than a suspicion around the circuit that Holmewood was opening the papers prematurely and giving some advance notice to their boys of the questions therein.

In cricketing terms, Bairamian established himself quickly in the Straggler ranks, taking wickets with his off-spinners that would turn and bounce on a helpful wicket, also scoring an unbeaten 146 at the Nevill Ground, Tunbridge Wells, in 1959, and importing his irrepressible verve and enthusiasm. Birth in Cyprus and residence in West Africa was accepted as qualification enough,

THE EIGHTIES AND THE 'BIRTH OF THE MODERN STRAGGLERS'

and his enthusiasm and commitment to cricket saw him invited to join the committee in 1961, by which time he had already offered to supply the balls for the club.

He was indeed a complicated character. His relationship with women seemed never settled until he married his fourth wife in 1986, Ros, who sadly predeceased him by five years – and his relationship with money was also patchy. He ran Bluemantle's Cricket Week at the Nevill for many years: returning one year from Asia, as a Bluemantle of some years' standing, the author bought a sweater and tie that were on offer for £40. On enquiring of Bob whom the cheque should be made out to, the response was: 'Just leave it blank, old boy.'

A rather darker story emerged in *The Spectator* shortly after his death, when the columnist Charles Moore wrote of a large loan that Bairamian had taken from an acquaintance of Moore's, 'because the parents had been late with the fees': needless to relate, no repayment was ever forthcoming, and the individual had apparently lost a large proportion of his life savings.

Bairamian was actually Straggler treasurer for many years, from 1973 to 1986, and while there is no evidence of impropriety, incoming chairman Peter Marno remembers a conversation with him:

Marno: How much money do we have in the Club, Bob?
Bairamian: How much do you want us to have, Peter?
Marno: Well, how do you pay people?
Bairamian: I write them a cheque. . .

It seemed that Straggler funds were co-mingled with Bob's own and there was no clear accounting – an activity in which Johnny King-Martin as previous chairman had, it seems, little interest. Marno immediately saw the problem and had no hesitation in accepting Bairamian's offer to step aside.

Bob Bairamian surely had his faults, but for those who played with him he remains an unforgettable character, of great charm, a very quick wit and single-minded determination, whose influence on many others – and especially the Stragglers and the Bluemantle's – was overwhelmingly positive. He was also one of the pioneers of bringing foreign boys to English schools – it was a rare Holmewood XV that didn't have a fast Ghanaian winger! As someone who, one suspects, had suffered more than his share of discrimination when younger, he knew what was right.

Few people had a keener desire to win and if this involved some dark arts in terms of sharp comments on the field, or clever negotiation of playing conditions, then so be it. He was also the father of two sons, one of whom, Rupert, played for many years with the Stragglers and for two decades served the club with distinction as a committee member. The younger is Justin, who gave a memorable tribute at Bob's funeral that described his enthusiasm, generosity and fun as a family man. As a fellow Bluemantle and Straggler has said: 'My life was the richer for knowing him.'

*

The Straggler AGM in 1982 marked a significant moment in the club's history, held at the Star Tavern, Belgravia. A new clause in the rules of the club was instituted:

> The committee is empowered to elect properly proposed and seconded candidates who do not fulfil the conditions of paragraph 8 above [the 'east of Suez' rule] in order to keep up a sufficient playing membership.

While this change could be interpreted as progressive, reflecting a potential openness to candidates beyond the club's traditional demographic, it is important to note that the primary motivation was practical rather than ideological. The amendment aimed to address concerns over declining numbers in the playing membership, ensuring the club could sustain its fixture schedule. It was not, at this stage, an active effort to embrace diversity, though such an outcome was an indirect consequence; following Shiv Datt's election in 1969, gradually the Stragglers, through their very name, began to attract non-white members.

Future chairman Jack Hyde Blake described this meeting as 'the birth of the modern Stragglers' and certainly dropping the geographical qualification was an important move: it allowed the club the flexibility to recruit sufficient members to grow the fixture card into the second golden period of the late 1980s and 1990s.

THE EIGHTIES AND THE 'BIRTH OF THE MODERN STRAGGLERS'

A successful dinner at the Savoy was held, mistakenly described in the newsletter as the 'first ever Annual Dinner' (there had been at least ten through the years) – it was, though, unique in being at the Savoy, as the venue moved to Simpson's from 1983 onwards. Guest speakers were Ivor Terrell, Tony Cozier and Peter May. Richard Heard, one of the outstanding players of the 1970s and 1980s, appropriately scooped the draw prize of £100, and David Gallyer, another stalwart, the second prize of £50.

The Sri Lanka Tour was the highlight of 1982/83, with the games starting on 29 December 1982 and running through to 17 January, a total of eleven, of which the club won five and lost five, with the first a draw. Quite early on, after four games with a victory yet to be registered and after the Stragglers were bowled out for 65 against Ambalangoda, the concerned captain, Bryan Hamblin, brought the team together and asked: 'Any ideas?' Jonathan Orders recalls Keith Holgate, an unconventional character, immediately suggesting that there should be a change in captain. Holgate subsequently left the tour early, people thinking Hamblin had sacked him – in fact, it was just Holgate's schedule!

Holgate was a man of many parts – rumoured to possess what some wags called a 'mobile sight screen' of two identical white Mercedes sedans, only one of which was taxed and legal. He was a tourist of the old school, fearsomely competitive on the field, the first to offer drinks at the bar and one of the more likely to return to the accommodation early in the following morning.

In Sri Lanka, according to King-Martin's account,

> David Fursdon was the cricketer of the tour, playing in all the matches and batting and bowling superbly. Richard Gracey took the most wickets. Mark Benson won the last match with a fine 100 and Hugh Morris and Jonny Orders both scored three 50s. The only snag was that their Test players turned out in force in the second and third matches before we were really acclimatized. We had a very keen side with everybody wanting to play in all games, except possibly after a day at Hikkabuwa, where palm-lined beaches, topless girls and fantastic surf provided a possible alternative!

One might question whether there truly were topless sunbathers in conservative Sri Lanka or if the story has been embellished over time.

It was probably the strongest team the Stragglers had ever fielded – full of Blues like Hamblin, Fursdon, Orders, plus the soon-to-be England batsman Mark Benson, Shiv Datt (who flew down from India) and capable side acts such as Holgate and others. It helped that the committee and the club were able to assist with the costs of some players.

Back in the UK, 1982 was a difficult year in terms of win/lose ratio, but the spirit in the club was high. The prestigious Cross Arrows fixture began in 1978 and has seen a number of Straggler victories over the years. Twenty-one games were played in the UK and ten in Germany, plus a three-match tour there from the UK.

In 1983, Peter Marno, Shiv Datt and Roger Layden made centuries for the club, while Julian Tutt managed two in BAOR – where again nine fixtures were played. Major John Eden of the Gunners finished a very successful four years as BAOR secretary and Tony Skipper took over until the cessation of Straggler fixtures in Germany a decade later, as the British military presence was withdrawn.

The following year, 1984, saw a poor return in terms of wins among some outstanding individual performances – Mike Milton scored 200 not out against the Old Wellingtonians Cricketer Cup side and David Budge took 7 wickets and scored 60 against the Infantry. Meanwhile, the mercurial Keith Holgate scored a century at Hurlingham and Brian Davenport a century against the Royal Navy CC. A tour to Jersey was again undertaken, but the side was a weaker one than in 1977 owing to several cry-offs – the key bowler, Nigel Creffield, damaged his knee after only four balls of his opening over and all three games were lost.

The annual dinner in October saw Johnny King-Martin step down as the first full-time chairman; it was, for him, 'a sad and very moving occasion for I had been directly involved in Club matters since 1970, having been elected a member in 1939'. Peter Marno became chairman at the age of forty-two, John Cook honorary secretary and Martin Beer match secretary.

In the newsletter covering the 1985 season, it was noted that 'the first season under "new management" has come and gone and the change has taken place with little fuss', a tribute to the new committee members, all ex-soldiers of course. In June, the 60th Anniversary was celebrated with a dinner and disco at Lt. Gen. Sir Geoffrey Howlett's residence in Aldershot, an idea of which was conveyed in the same newsletter:

THE EIGHTIES AND THE 'BIRTH OF THE MODERN STRAGGLERS'

it was rather like attending a country house dinner and dance in days of yore (how sorry I feel for you young people and what you missed!) . . . a gracious residence, a marquee in the grounds, super dinner and wines galore . . . Come 2 a.m. the Parachute Regiment waiters encouraged further tippling with 'Come on, Sir, this bottle has got to be finished'. Yet, there was still another to be finished!

Shortly afterwards, Howlett was promoted to full General and moved to be Commander-in-Chief Allied Forces Northern Europe based in Norway, sadly removing the possibility of further Straggler hospitality in the short term!

Another significant development in 1985 was the first appearance of the Straggler 100 Club, where members were encouraged to fund a prize draw with quarterly prizes - 60 per cent of the 'take' being reserved for club funds. This was the initiative of Jack Hyde Blake, who was on the committee and beginning to establish himself as a passionate Straggler. Over the years since, the 100 Club, rebranded as 'Patiala Club', has made a great contribution to the finances of the club, funding its own kit purchases (for resale to members) and avoiding annual deficits from the costs of putting on cricket.

On the playing side, Mike Milton made another century against the Old Wellingtonians and there were many fine bowling performances, including F.M.C. Stock's' 5 wickets for 9 runs against Barclays Bank on tour. Steve Flanagan took 6 for 26 against the Royal Engineers, and G. Potton 6 for 24 in Berlin. A fifteen-year-old Graham Thorpe turned up to play for Stragglers against Reed's Choughs and mentioned that he was mainly a batsman, but also bowled. Skipper Peter Marno gave him a longish spell of 14 overs, which went for 43 runs and no wickets, as Reed's Choughs scored 208 for 8 declared. Stragglers overhauled this with 212 for 4, Thorpe listed at No. 9 - making Marno possibly one of the few captains to leave a future England player (100 Tests!) as a 'Did Not Bat'. Of course, everyone in the club was shocked and saddened at Thorpe's early demise in 2024.

In 1986, Bob Bairamian, retired as treasurer by Peter Marno as described above, was presented with a piece of cut glass at the dinner. Mike Milton scored 623 runs in 6 innings, then emigrated to Kenya!

In 1987, side-raising was a problem, the familiar refrain, and in response a cricket sub-committee was formed under Martin Beer and the question posed:

ONE ARM BOWLS A LITTLE

'Are we expanding our fixture list too fast?' Jack Hyde Blake organized the dinner at the Naval and Military Club, which reflected on a generally poor season for results, with only five wins from twenty-six completed matches 'including 3 narrow defeats'. A planned tour to Denmark was cancelled due to lack of sufficient interest.

Again, some individuals did well - young Andrew Hartley, son of honorary treasurer Geoff Hartley (who had been elected in 1983 and scored some significant runs for the club before taking up umpiring), scored two centuries and Mark Banham another. Hartley junior was to go on to score 3,986 runs for the club at a very respectable average of 34, putting him seventh in the list of Straggler batsmen.

Annual subscriptions were raised to £10.

In 1988, the year started badly with the death in March of Straggler member Major Hugh Lindsay, a former Equerry to the Queen and close friend of Charles, Prince of Wales, now of course King Charles III. Lindsay was thirty-four, a classic Cavalry officer from the 9th/12th Royal Lancers. He was elected in 1985, 'an aggressive right hand early bat', and had learned his cricket at Millfield: 'His cricketing ability and great charm were all that one wished for in a Straggler', one tribute recalled. Although he was not a Straggler long, he went on the Berlin Tour in 1986 and initiated the fixture against the Royal Household at Windsor. Batting, he never failed completely and his 73 against the Cross Arrows at Lord's in 1985 is well remembered by those who were there, in addition to his energetic fielding in the deep.

On a banal and slightly spooky note, in October and November 1987 and February 1988, he had won the 100 Club draw - more frequently than anyone else before or since.

The circumstances of his death remain controversial - the party at Klosters, including the prince, were skiing off-piste and there was an avalanche warning in place - but the real tragedy was that his wife, Sarah, was seven months' pregnant. Such was his impact on the club in his short time with the Stragglers that a 'Hugh Lindsay Trophy' was instituted for the 'best young cricketer of the year' and has been awarded in almost every year since. Chairman Peter Marno was the initiator, and the actual trophy was a cricket ball hollowed out to act as a match holder, mounted on a wooden base with a silver area on which to inscribe winners' names, and a much-appreciated award it has been

THE EIGHTIES AND THE 'BIRTH OF THE MODERN STRAGGLERS'

– even if one winner managed to lose it during his tenure!

The first winner was Rupert Bairamian, and the trophy was presented by Sarah Lindsay at the Cross Arrows game on the Nursery Ground at Lord's. It has continued to be an important award for the club, given in most years but occasionally not when no suitable candidate has emerged. Generally, the committee awards it to a player who has contributed consistently through the season under review and previous years too – and the intent is to reward youth and enthusiasm, although sometimes the age of the winner has crept over thirty-five! More recently, the rules have been relaxed to allow repeat winners – and two members have won it twice, Tony Hooper and Jonathan Parker, excellent cricketers who continue to represent the club frequently.

A working party consisting of John Cook, Geoff Hartley, Jolyon Griffiths and Jack Hyde Blake was put together in November 1986 to make recommendations for improvements to 'the General & Finance administration of the Club', which they did in January of 1987, resulting in a tighter definition of 'rules' and earnest determination to collect subscriptions more rigorously (a familiar refrain).

In July 1988, an unexpected letter was received by the Stragglers from Martin Maynard in Bath, only son of the Founder: he had been a Straggler himself, playing in the early fifties as a young man. His letter was on another subject:

> For a number of years in the late 1940s and early 1950s the Committee of the Stragglers used to have their meetings in my parents' flat in London . . . on the last occasion that it happened your committee presented my mother with a pair of gravy/sauce boats to show their appreciation of the way she had fed and watered them over the years. She was surprised, delighted, and certainly used them. Alas, due to changing times and habits, I do not. Nor have I anyone to bequeath them to. Due to the threat of burglars, one doesn't display things now and I don't care for the thought of disposing of them for my own personal gain.
>
> It occurred to me that it could be appropriate to return them whence they came i.e. to your committee.

ONE ARM BOWLS A LITTLE

After some description of the items, which are 10 ounces of Sheffield silver made by James Dixon and Sons in 1946-47, Maynard concludes:

> Were you to take them on, there would be no question of my benefiting in any way, nor would I want any say in what you did with them. And I should be delighted to deliver them in person. What do you think!

The offer was accepted with alacrity by the committee and Maynard was invited to the dinner in October to present the sauce boats back to the club, receiving the grateful thanks of the president, Bertie Joel, and other members of the committee.

The 'Maynard sauce boats' were left in the hands of Jack Hyde Blake, who in 1991 had them valued by Mappin and Webb, 'for insurance purposes', at the not-inconsiderable sum of £360.

As the decade closed, the Stragglers recruited another key non-white individual who was to contribute hugely to the club over the following years, both on the field and off it. Ramesh Sethi was born in Kenya and became a Kenyan international player thanks to his own talent and application, and some encouragement from Major Hugh Collins OBE at the Rift Valley Sports Club in Nakuru, Kenya. As Ramesh says, when you travel two hours and 100 miles each way to Nairobi in a taxi to play cricket, you don't surrender your wicket easily. For the Stragglers, he was to play 127 innings and was not out in 50 of them - a high number, which he modestly put down to his match-managing and going in towards the end of the innings so that others got a full game: those of us who know Ramesh rather credit his phenomenal eye and classic technique!

Ramesh and his wife, Shiel, came to the UK when he became the cricket coach at Ellesmere College in Shropshire, coming across the Stragglers almost by chance at Lord's when he was invited to join Jack Hyde Blake, the chairman we meet below, and Geoff Hartley for lunch. He knew Hartley through his sons, who were at Wrekin College, on the Ellesmere circuit of fixtures.

Apart from playing around seventeen matches a year for the Stragglers as a fine batsman and metronomic bowler (scoring 3,664 runs, averaging 47.6 and taking 109 wickets at 23 runs apiece), Ramesh was gunned into service

THE EIGHTIES AND THE 'BIRTH OF THE MODERN STRAGGLERS'

as the overseas tours expert by Jack Hyde Blake. He was given no choice - Hyde Blake decided he was the man and appointed him in public during an AGM at Lord's, leaving Ramesh no opportunity to refuse!

Sethi moved on from Ellesmere to become the coach at Harrow in 1988, where he stayed until 2004, full-time, and then looked after the under-16s for a further seven years. As the professional coach, Ramesh enabled a large number of Harrovians to reach their potential as cricketers, not least Sam Northeast, one of the most successful county run-scorers of his era - although he never quite made it to a Test cap - and Nick Compton, who was unfortunate not to play more than fifteen Tests for England. More significantly for the Stragglers, another of his protégés is the oft-mentioned Robert Pollock-Hill.

The 1980s closed with the death in October of a senior Straggler from the 1930s - Lt. Col. Charles Aston, who had joined in 1933 as an ex-Authentic and scored an unbeaten 100 (at No. 7!) in the Straggler game against Old St Edward's in 1932. Born in 1893, he had already played a significant part in the First World War as an Arabist, speaking the language flawlessly and persuading Arab sheikhs to help prevent the Germans reaching Middle Eastern oilfields. During this campaign, he took a 'remarkably unflattering' view of Lawrence of Arabia, according to one obituary.

Aston spent the bulk of the inter-war years in Mesopotamia (which became Iraq) and rose to become chief political adviser in Iraq and a CBE. His *Daily Telegraph* obituary (later edited for *Wisden* 1990) noted that he was 'a founder member of the oddly-named but distinguished cricket side, the Stragglers of Asia, which required of its members that they should have served six years east of Suez' - just a couple of errors there! A better extract is this:

> It was Aston's habit to drive around the desert in Buicks, in which he carried a bag of cement and supplies of dates: he explained that a mixture of the two provided a sealing solution of just the right consistency to repair the damage done to his motor-cars by rough terrain and enemy bullets.

One of the old breed.

Chapter Eight
INTO THE NINETIES AND MORE CRICKET THAN EVER

THE EARLY NINETIES saw another changing of the guard. Bertie Joel handed over the presidency to the recently retired General Howlett in 1989 and, after six years of progress, Peter Marno stepped down as chairman, to be succeeded by Jack Hyde Blake. Under Peter's considerate but firm leadership, the club had grown to playing over forty fixtures a year against a mix of military (e.g., Royal Artillery, BAOR, Sandhurst, Royal Engineers, Royal Marines, Infantry, the Royal Navy Club), schools or Old Boys' teams (Old Wellingtonians, Old Westminster's, The King's School Canterbury, and Eastbourne, of course) and fellow wandering clubs (e.g., Berkshire Gents, South Oxfordshire Amateurs, Band of Brothers, Grannies).

A critical figure for the Stragglers through the eighties and nineties, Jack Hyde Blake had joined in 1974 at the age of thirty-eight: he is described in the register as educated at Bloxham, a member of the Berkshire Gentlemen and a 'Minor County Triallist' (the latter being probably something of a fib!), a right-handed No. 3/4 bat, slow right-arm off-spinner, 'fields in the covers'. He was elected from the BAOR section, where he was a civilian employed on the fringes of the Army. His record with the Stragglers as a player is distinctly modest – he scored 840 runs at an average of 12.3 from 72 innings, with one half-century. For reasons unknown, the Stragglers were to become a passion for him. At the earliest opportunity he virtually invited himself on to the committee in the early eighties, after returning to the UK, by posing a question at the AGM – 'How are committee members selected?'

On the committee from 1984, he demanded high standards and, having served five years as the social member, during which he oversaw some very good dinners at Simpson's and elsewhere, he was elected as chairman. Peter Marno, the outgoing chairman in 1989, was by no means in favour of Hyde Blake's candidature – he knew that Hyde Blake's rather overbearing character could upset people and there was at least one other wandering club that was not interested in having him as a member. Peter, on calling round the committee members to suggest some other name, was surprised to learn that Jack had already been canvassing!

Whatever his demeanour, the Stragglers were lucky to find a man who, while not in the front rank of their cricketers by any stretch of the imagination, was passionate about the club. It is no coincidence that the period of Hyde Blake's chairmanship is the one for which most written records remain, and he was prepared to give his all to the club when the exigencies of business allowed. His occupation was running 'Connaught Career Services', which aimed to place individuals in new jobs – unlike modern headhunters, whose clients are companies looking for talent, Hyde Blake's clients were individuals looking for a change; as a self-employed man, he had the spare time necessary to devote to Straggler affairs. He was a member of the Carlton Club and also prominent in the Forty Club, probably the largest of the wandering clans, founded specifically for over-forty players.

Behind what could be a rather intimidating exterior to a young member lay a sharp negotiator who was prepared to use all his contacts and powers of persuasion for the good of the Stragglers; while some people thought he could be a bully, Marno concurs that Hyde Blake was effective.

INTO THE NINETIES AND MORE CRICKET THAN EVER

As chairman, he was to visit many Stragglers matches and put across his views on the team and tactics to the match manager of the day - perfectly politely but quite firmly where he detected deficiencies, which raised the hackles of some to the extent that they dropped out from managing games. He had his focus on 'standards' and would repeat this endlessly - one must acknowledge that it had the desired effect though: standards were raised, and the club's fixture list grew even stronger. He took an interest in young players and a cadre of talented cricketers joined the club on his watch.

Eventually, after six years of chairmanship, Jack was gently eased aside in one of those lovely bloodless coups that club organizations can achieve - 'kicked upstairs', as he put it, to become a vice president and take over the archives of the club. He was still to take intense interest in the fortunes of the Stragglers, remained close to the committee 'in charge of publications', and had no qualms in raising points to the attention of the executive if he felt that something was slipping, especially in the printed materials such as the fixture card.

A few years later, he ran into current committee member James Allsop in the Carlton Club and questioned why the Straggler dinner had slipped away from Simpson's to a far humbler curry house in the Strand - 'Do it properly or not at all' was his message, inevitably. The issue was that the cost was becoming unaffordable, and the turnout of younger members had been suffering. As it happens, a 'proper' black tie dinner was reinstated from 2010 on, at the instigation of the then-committee and with the help of Simon Collins, honorary secretary, and member at the East India Club: this was originally just for the committee, now open to all.

Jack Hyde Blake retired to the Algarve in 2004 and handed over the archive to the present author. When the Stragglers put together a team to play in the Algarve Sixes in 2007, Jack appeared to watch both days and very kindly invited the team to the villa where he and his charming Dutch wife, Marie-Rose, had made their home in Portugal.

In 1990, the annual dinner moved to Hyde Blake's preferred venue of Simpson's in the Strand and a pre-season party was held in a wine bar. Five centuries included two from Mike Milton, back from Kenya, and one from the recently retired chairman, Marno. Phil King and Billy King-Harman took 18 wickets each - King to receive the Hugh Lindsay trophy.

After a gap of six years the Eastbourne College fixture was revived, although the club had played the Eastbourne Eclectics (their Common Room) in the interim.

Once again, General Sir Geoffrey helped organize a tour of Berlin in August with two games against the touring Sandhurst side and one against the GOC's XI. Stragglers were undefeated and a great time was had by all, it seems. 'The 29 tourists, including 8 family and friends, all had ample opportunities to observe the changing scene in the city (all called it "sightseeing", including those who habitually missed breakfast).' The changing scene was of course the reunification of Germany and Berlin, barely a year old - yet again the Stragglers were close to historically important events.

At one point in the tour, the wives and girlfriends were asked to 'talk among yourselves' while the men went to one of the many Berlin nightclubs offering naked performances: General Sir Geoffrey was happy to lead the way but immediately ordered 'everyone out!' when he spotted a camera being wielded by another punter. It was not the kind of establishment a General Officer of the British Army should be seen in!

Nineteen ninety-one was the first season of fifty fixtures - in preparation, Billy King-Harman organized once-a-week nets at Lord's for those keen. Meantime, the hard-working secretary, John Cook, and treasurer, Geoff Hartley, organized an overhaul of the membership list - a regular refrain for the Stragglers. Nearly eighty members were removed for lack of replies and 420 confirmed. Nine matches were won and seventeen lost, another poor season, but again Howlett came up trumps with 'splendid hospitality' at his home for the West Country Tour.

In early 1992, the decision was made to organize a tour to Hong Kong, where there was still a reasonable presence of the British forces, a Straggler team playing annual matches at HKCC and a powerful local representative in the figure of Rod Eddington, the incoming chief executive of Cathay Pacific Airways. Originating in Western Australia, Eddington was a Rhodes Scholar at Oxford and had completed a doctorate in nuclear physics. He had played plenty of matches for the university and became a Straggler when he went on the BAOR Tour in 1977: he took on the Stragglers responsibility in Hong

INTO THE NINETIES AND MORE CRICKET THAN EVER

Kong, sponsoring it as the Captain of Cricket at HKCC. Back in London, the Hong Kong Tour committee commenced work, led by Ramesh Sethi.

As a season, 1992 produced a much better balance of results, with a century from Jolyon Griffiths against the Maori Club. Phil McDuell took 7 for 82 against the South Oxfordshire Amateurs, always a strong side. Largely on the initiative of Geoff Hartley, a Midlands Tour materialized, with the first two-day match for nearly twenty years - against the Staffordshire Gentlemen, his other main club, at Swynnerton Park. Andrew Hartley scored 132 in a lost cause: curiously, only 13 wickets fell over two days! The following day, Stragglers were 14 for 5 chasing the Gentleman of Shropshire's 241 and lost. Laurie Lee (not the famous writer!), originally elected at the age of fifty in 1965, making him seventy-six or so in 1992, apparently fielded keenly - he had kindly agreed to be honorary secretary as a temporary appointment, which also involved filling in if a man short!

In November 1993, the Straggler party set off for Hong Kong and a fantastic tour resulted. Apart from the slight surprise of a stop in Zurich on what they thought was a non-stop Cathay Pacific flight, as the tour report related, all went very well. The team were accommodated in a hotel in Causeway Bay, within easy reach of central Hong Kong, the HKCC, and even closer reach of Joe Bananas and sundry other watering establishments in Wan Chai. Having got used to the price of beers in the local bars (Hong Kong enjoying a boom time in the years leading up to 1997), the Stragglers threw themselves into all the hospitality that Rod Eddington, the HKCC and Forces teams had laid on. With five wins and two losses, the results were good, accompanied by several fine individual performances, Chris Nield taking 9 for 58 against British Forces, and Jono Enderby, Jolyon Griffiths and Richard Sawney all scoring centuries.

A close-fought and very competitive game at Wong Nai Chong Gap between the UK side and the Hong Kong chapter of the Stragglers saw the UK squeezing home by two wickets, largely thanks to the magisterial 84 from Shiv Datt remarked on earlier. Ramesh Sethi employed all his wiles as a skipper, encouraging useful bowling performances from his brother Harsh (2 for 25), Nield again (3 for 41) and taking 2 wickets himself; on the home side, Rod Eddington equally threw himself into the game, scoring a very useful 24 not out at No. 10, a fifty partnership with the author rescuing the

HK Stragglers from 146 for 8 to 206 for 9 declared. Rod then took 4 for 49 off 11 overs of canny left-arm spin. Jack Hyde Blake pulled rank as chairman and finished off his playing career for the UK Stragglers with 12 runs at No. 5. It was a very happy day followed by a long session in HKCC's top bar, where surely George Rowe was looking on with approval.

The close of the tour saw the Stragglers throw a drinks reception in the officers' mess of HMS *Tamar*, the HQ for British Forces, where they were able to thank all those who had contributed to their happy stay. One tourist, the young Ben Hall, was so impressed with Hong Kong that he stayed for five years, landing a job with First Pacific Davies, a property firm: the wise men at HKCC had seen his formidable ability as a big-hitting batsman and swift opening bowler, not least when he scored 68 off 23 balls with six sixes in the game against them. Ben quickly played representative cricket for the full colony side.

Nineteen ninety-four saw Shiv Datt play 17 innings, the most of any player, and move into 3,000+ runs for the club - bettered only by three military men, General Withall, Martin Beer and Peter Salisbury. Meantime, the second 'non-European' member, Ramesh Sethi, was beginning to make considerable contributions both batting and bowling and as a captain. As a 'professional' cricketer, in the sense that he made his living as a coach, Ramesh had the sharpest of cricketing brains and, even when not blessed with the greatest of teams, he would extract optimal performances. A number of other players with South Asian or East African origins joined the club in the 1990s, two of the finest being Sye Razvi and Lawrence Fernandes, two individuals who were quickly to follow Datt in establishing 'non-European' names at the head of the Straggler cricketing records: Raghu Patel was another, like Fernandes introduced by Sethi, a brilliant wicket-keeper and hard-hitting batsman.

Sye went on to head the Batting Honours Board in 1999 and then again in each year from 2004 to 2007, eventually overtaking Shiv Datt's record aggregate for the club and becoming the first Straggler to score over 7,000 runs. He remains the sole person to exceed 1,000 runs in a season for the club, in 2004 at an average of nearly 48. He was almost lost to the Stragglers as, after his first game when he scored a century, no one told him that he needed to apply directly to the match managers for further fixtures! This is the common practice in wandering cricket, if not in the hard-nosed world of London club cricket, in which Sye was schooled. As a result, a couple of years went by before Sye reappeared.

Lawrence Fernandes fulfilled a similar record bowling his teasing leg spin and googlies: heading the Bowling Honours Board on four occasions, he took 52 wickets in 1999. He was also a fine fielder, with the safest hands Ramesh Sethi had ever seen, high praise indeed, and he had in younger days been a destructive batsman. He came with the East African team to tour the UK and play MCC at Lord's in 1972. In honour of Lawrence, who unexpectedly died in April 2019, the Stragglers dedicated an annual fielding prize in his name in 2020, the first winner being Matt Shales. Fernandes's son, Raphael, continued in Straggler ranks, again bowling leg breaks and googlies.

Early in 1994, General Sir Geoffrey Howlett decided to hand over the presidency after his three-year term to Lt. Col. John Stephenson CBE, the recently retired secretary of the MCC. It was typical of Sir Geoffrey's unselfish approach that, having found an eminently suitable successor, he should step down after only one term as president.

A tricky issue raised its head in 1995, where, with Martin Beer's wish to relinquish being match secretary, a youngish member applied for the job. This character was a very popular and likeable individual and a club cricketer of exceptional ability - however, he had a problem in that he was something of a kleptomaniac! He had in fact admitted to theft in court and received a sentence of being bound over for one year and to repay the money he had taken from a romantic partner. There had also been unproven rumours that money in cricket club changing rooms had gone missing when he was playing. In an admirable gesture, his proposer and friend wrote to the chairman at some length and laid out the facts, which led to a different match secretary appointment. Again, the story illustrates that a club like the Stragglers will attract all kinds of individuals, the true characteristics of whom may take some time to appear - and equally clubs rely on people of character to speak up when necessary.

In the past several decades, only one person has had to be ejected from the Stragglers and that was not the individual above. Instead, it was another very talented cricketer, who indulged just a little too much, too often - most famously giving abuse to a world-renowned Sri Lankan Test cricketer encountered by chance while on tour, implying that his bowling action was not fair! Since the remarks were made in the company of several other Sri Lankan players, the Stragglers on hand had to exercise swift damage control and extract the errant member with appropriate apologies. He was later rude to the chairman of the East India Club, at a Straggler annual dinner, and then drank too much at an Adastrians game (the Royal Air Force side), raising the ire of the match manager, Shiv Datt, whose genial approach to cricket does not encompass inane giggling and drunk slow bowlers on the field. As Straggler chairman, Peter Marno gave the member two opportunities to explain himself in writing before, reluctantly, cancelling his membership.

Energetic chairman as he was, sometimes Jack Hyde Blake's thick-skinned belief in his own opinion missed a nuance or two. In August 1995, the president, Lt. Col. John Stephenson, wrote to him saying that he would miss the annual dinner in November that year because of his daughter's wedding. He also took the opportunity to pen some other views about the role of president, 'particularly in relation to that of the Chairman':

> Having now been President for a year I find the position has little meaning. I am expected to attend meetings, social events, the Annual Dinner and the AGM, but have no authority with any of them. You take the chair while I just sit insignificantly wherever I can find a spare seat.
>
> In the near future may we have a chat about the responsibilities of the President and Chairman, because I am no longer prepared to be a total non-entity.

The upshot was that the two had a conversation during the Straggler/Cross Arrows game at Lord's, at which Stephenson got the impression the members of the club were so disappointed to miss him at the dinner that he felt obliged to write to Hyde Blake, with copies for the rest of the committee, offering to resign. Hyde Blake at once responded, opening by saying: 'I am afraid your recollection of our conversation at Lord's must have been affected by a very convivial lunch session that we had in the excellent new Cricket School.'

In fact, on the balance of probabilities, it was Hyde Blake who had been affected more by the convivial lunch and overstepped the mark with Stephenson in expressing the members' supposed views. (On the wider question of the role of president and chairman, Hyde Blake kicked this into the long grass, delegating it to a working party under the chairmanship of Geoffrey Hartley.)

At the next committee, the exchange of letters was discussed, and an odd resolution passed, with no mention of the wedding, nor that the date had been unavoidably changed due to the bridegroom's service in Bosnia - a reason that, for most Stragglers, whether military or not, would have excused any absence.

> The Committee understands and accepts the President's wish to be with his family on the night of the annual dinner and are pleased that he wishes to continue as President of the Stragglers of Asia.

Throughout the saga, one's sympathies lay with Stephenson - for Hyde Blake not to realize early on that a daughter's wedding took precedence over a club dinner was obtuse.

As mentioned, John Stephenson wanted to do more as president than he was possibly allowed to by the club's constitution. He exerted his influence in obtaining three excellent new fixtures for the Stragglers - first, the game against I Zingari, the oldest of the wandering clubs and almost a parallel universe with its internal hierarchy of Freemen, Full-Play Members, Half-Play Members and Si Benes (suffice to say that their 'History' is rather different to that of the Stragglers!); second, a fixture against the Pilgrims at Wormsley, Sir Paul Getty's purpose-built cricket ground in the Chiltern Hills; and third, it is hard to think he was not involved in obtaining the game against MCC, first played in 1996. He also invited a host of eminent speakers for the Straggler dinners while he was president, including John Emburey, the veteran English off-spinner, Sir Denis Thatcher, husband of the former prime minister Margaret Thatcher, and the prominent cricketing personalities and journalists Henry Blofeld and Christopher Martin-Jenkins: largely as a result, dinner attendance at one point reached 150.

But he was also cautious not to become too ambitious. Shiv Datt recalls returning from India, having built excellent relationships with the Punjab Cricket Association (PCA). Stephenson himself had a good rapport with Mr Indrajit Singh Bindra, president of the PCA, who had served on the

ONE ARM BOWLS A LITTLE

International Cricket Council at the same time. At committee in 2000, Shiv Datt suggested that the Stragglers could build close links with the PCA - potentially helping their young cricketers when they came to the UK, in return for assistance with future India tours for the club. In response, Stephenson was at first pensive, then dismissive: 'we are a British wandering club, and I cannot support such a suggestion, and would consider my position if it is progressed'.

His reasons for this decision may have been several, but perhaps the possibility existed, in the back of his mind, that a growing association with the PCA might expose the Stragglers to the influence of greater monetary support and detract from the spirit of wandering cricket.

In retrospect, it was a lost opportunity for the club - however, ranked against the vast number of positive benefits that John Stephenson as president brought to the club, over many fields, it is a minor disappointment. Stephenson had not served in India (although his military career had taken him to numerous other countries) so possibly was unaware of the depth of the Straggler connection with India.

More happily, with Shiv Datt's intervention again, Jack Hyde Blake revived the connection with the royal house of Patiala while renaming the Straggler's 100 Club to the Patiala Club in 1996. His Highness Maharajah Amarinder Singh of Patiala was invited to become an Honorary Life Member 'to renew your family connection' and enquiries were made as to whether playing at Chail in the 2000 Tour would be possible.

The Maharajah's reply was generous in every respect, including pointing out that a photo from 1923 that Jack had sent out was not what it seemed:

> The photograph on your brochure has definitely been taken at Chail but does not include my grandfather. The person with his arm raised holding a ball is the great Cricketer Ranjit Singh Ji of Navanagar, who was ADC to my grandfather, after whom he started the 'Ranji Trophy', the county cricket of India.

The connection was going to pay dividends as the Stragglers organized their 75th Anniversary Tour to India in 2000.

INTO THE NINETIES AND MORE CRICKET THAN EVER

Closer to home, after some lobbying from the president, the MCC in the person of John Jameson (Assistant Secretary Cricket and former Test player) offered a fixture for 1996, a game that has continued since. The conditions for playing MCC, as hundreds of clubs and schools do each year, are clear and expensive.

I should like to point out that MCC out-matches are accepted in [sic] the condition that the opposition undertake to supply the following:

a) both umpires
b) a new ball for both innings
c) meals for the MCC team
d) details of scores and bowling analyses, and
e) a ground for the fixture

Despite these conditions, the standard for all would-be opponents of the great club, the Stragglers accepted.

Also in August 1995, a gracious letter was received from Major General Bill Withall CB, whose position as the top run-scorer in Straggler history (with 4,267) had just been usurped by Martin Beer.

'Records are meant to be beaten', the General wrote, 'and I can't think of a more worthy Straggler to do it. I shall most certainly write to congratulate him.'

Of course, Bill Withall was too much of a gentleman to mention that whereas his runs had accumulated at an average of 43.8, Martin Beer's average was 28.5 - valuable batsman as he was!

As fixture and match secretary, Martin Beer was a great helpmate to both Peter Marno and Jack Hyde Blake in running the club - he was also, partly in his own interest, of course, the 'Keeper of the Records', which involved much meticulous and detailed study of an increasing number of score cards! He was extremely well versed in Straggler lore, having joined as a Lieutenant aged thirty-one in 1968. He had played for the Army and was valued by the club as an opening bat, fielding in the covers when not called on to keep wicket.

ONE ARM BOWLS A LITTLE

Indeed, for Beer with Hyde Blake, on both sides there is more than a hint that the relationship was of subordinate and boss. They were two different characters – Beer a straight-talking, guileless, slightly diffident, and kind-hearted ex-soldier (by 1995) who was far more interested in cricket and family than ego. He fulfilled his administrative tasks for many years, not only arranging the club's programme for the year but then following up with individual match managers, ensuring full sides were fielded, umpires arranged, scorers sought and a myriad of other duties that a wandering club requires – in all of these, he hardly put a foot wrong and, as one opponent commented, 'in a world where every club had a key man, Martin Beer was the Stragglers'.

Beer tried to resign from one of his jobs in September 1995.

'After much thought', he wrote to Hyde Blake, 'I realize that the level of my off-the-field cricketing activities is jeopardizing too many of my professional and family affairs.'

It was to be some time before the load could be shifted.

A disquieting event occurred when a candidate played at Epsom in July: the match manager felt obliged to send a lengthy missive:

> It is sad to report that XX's behaviour falls far below the standard that one would expect of a Straggler. During the above match, his own performance was no more than average. Whilst bowling however, his vociferous criticism of fellow team mates fielding was both offensive, lacking in sensitivity and hypocritical as his own fielding was particularly dreadful.
>
> Although I did not see it, I understand from the umpire and some team members that he was smoking whilst we were in the field . . . at lunch, as we were leaving the field, XX made it clear to me that he felt he should have bowled and that my captaincy of the game to date left a great deal to be desired . . . during lunch, XX declined to sit with his team mates.

Strange behaviour indeed and completely opposite to the normal courtesies and conventions of wandering cricket, where teams naturally vary from game to game and individuals expect that they will occasionally be let down by team-mates dropping catches or playing poorly. As for smoking on the field and criticizing the skipper, it is no wonder that a report was submitted! The individual was not elected.

With the expansion of fixtures to over fifty a year by 1991, Straggler sides became more and more diverse: the serving and retired officers remained in evidence, joined by increasing numbers of non-military cricketers across the spectrum of society – schoolteachers, accountants, beer salesmen, IT programmers, postmen, students – and others of no discernible income! Notions of racial or social-class-based exclusivity completely disappeared; and while Stragglers of today are worried, like most of the cricket world, by the seemingly increasing 'elitism' of the game (largely due to the lack of opportunity for boys and girls in state education), the club encourages anyone to join who has the right attitude to the game and team-mates – unlike Mr XX above!

As ever, in the mid- to late-nineties (or, more accurately, since 1925!), raising a side was often a challenge: one match manager studied the membership list seeking potential players in close proximity to his match in Dorset in 1996. He had a reply from Shaftesbury:

> I received your cri-de-coeur about the Stragglers game against the Signals at Bovingdon next Sunday . . . I'm afraid I can't help for two reasons.
>
> 1. I last played cricket in 1987 when I was 70 (nine years ago).
> 2. I shall not be in Dorset next Sunday . . .

Mr J.M. Dean continued:

> My Stragglers days began in 1948 when Henry Christian was so dominating as a left hand bowler, and lasted some 15 years, during school summer holidays. So, I enjoy my annual envelope of Straggler literature, but I can't offer you succor on this occasion.

One veteran who was attracted back to Straggler cricket was the Test cricketer Roy Swetman, last seen in 1967. With his son playing decent club cricket, Swetman reappeared with young Rupert in 1995 for Stragglers against South Oxfordshire Amateurs at Bloxham School, scoring 74. At St Edward's a couple of weeks later, he compiled 69 and, while he was never to match those innings again, he played a further nine games in this 'second innings'. His son remembers his father always had a soft spot for the Stragglers and enjoyed wearing the colours and contributing to the standards of the team: certainly, the club was fortunate to have such a distinguished player.

A much less positive incident in 1996 was the discussion at the committee on 3 October about the election of a member. Here again there was controversy about a 'non-European' and it takes one back to previous committee deliberations about whether to admit them at all.

The individual had played eight matches to qualify in the season (more than any candidate since 1939), with one black mark against him because he had unfortunately had to pull out of the Eastbourne game at short notice after a family bereavement. The match manager was Rupert Bairamian, who felt negatively about the incident and said the letter of apology showed 'a lack of appropriate remorse'. One comment apparently led to another and after the meeting no other than Shiv Datt wrote a stern three-page letter to Hyde Blake, on behalf of Ramesh Sethi as well (although Ramesh for medical reasons was absent):

> [We] are both extremely dismayed by the Committee's decision and the manner in which it was influenced...
>
> In the conduct of this matter last night both Ramesh and I feel this adverse influencing of the Committee was a gross travesty...
>
> We find it extremely distressing that the seed of doubt can be sown in the minds of the Committee members on the basis of 'Hearsay' which cannot be substantiated by concrete evidence.

The chairman's reply copied the president, John Stephenson, and suggested an informal meeting with Sethi and Datt before the next committee. This never happened.

In the meantime, Martin Beer, the straightest of men as noted, wrote to Toby Berridge, the secretary:

> I was very puzzled to hear that [the individual] was not elected at the Committee meeting . . . I have found him to be a very nice man and useful cricketer, dedicated to playing for Stragglers . . .

Beer notes that the rejection may have hinged on the non-appearance at Eastbourne, where the individual had tried contacting Bairamian. Beer notes:

> I myself tried to contact this match manager on several occasions during the weeks leading up to the match, by all postal and telephonic means at my disposal, and failed. How could a new candidate be expected to succeed where a committee member fails? If records are accurate, the same MM was absent from three consecutive committee meetings prior to the match concerned, each time without explanation/apology.

Another senior Straggler was also concerned enough to write to Berridge:

> I was dismayed to hear that . . . was not voted in as a member at the last committee meeting. I understand that the reasons were that he failed to turn up at the Eastbourne game (I was playing) and failed to contact Rupert (the MM) before or after the match. The facts are as follows:
>
> 1. Rupert was in the middle of a house/flat move and his company had gone into liquidation. He had NO contact numbers whatsoever.
> 2. Rupert left a message at my offices a few days before the game saying 'Hope you're ok for the game, call me if you have a problem'. He didn't leave a contact number.

The letter continues:

> After various conversations with people last year, I get the feeling that this overreaction to his behaviour is part of a hidden agenda that is borne by a few (I hope) Stragglers. Basically, his face doesn't fit. The fact it's brown may have something to do with it.

ONE ARM BOWLS A LITTLE

> If his exclusion from the Stragglers is a fait accompli and irreversible, my enthusiasm in being part of the club has taken a major dent.

The incident rumbled on with various discussions at committee about whether it was right that a candidate could be elected by majority vote, or whether it had to be unanimous – frankly, it was disappointing that it did not get resolved at once. Eventually, the individual was elected the following year, bringing to a close an unpleasant tale that had raised again the spectre of racism in the Straggler history. He went on to have a good amount of playing success and took part in two major tours with the club.

Meanwhile, Jack Hyde Blake had already signalled that he would be stepping down as chairman at the end of 1996. John Stephenson had sounded out Geoffrey Hartley, who had already been appointed to chair a '2000 Working Party', which would review the status of the club and its readiness for the new millennium. Hartley was a more consensual character, less likely to harm feelings and, with two sons playing great cricket for the club, someone who had the ear of the youth and understood that brusque authority, albeit backed up with intense feeling for the Stragglers, was not necessarily the right way to approach the younger generation in an amateur club.

A little later, Hyde Blake became prominent in the running of the Forty 'XL' Club. He became, at one point, chairman of their executive committee, and was happy to pronounce in 2002:

> I can confirm that the rumour that the XL Club is contemplating introducing ladies' cricket to play against schoolgirls is unfounded.

No one could accuse Jack Hyde Blake of being ahead of his time. As it happens, at the time of writing in 2024, women's cricket is the fastest-growing area of the sport, the Forty Club is now open to both men and women and the Stragglers are aiming to establish their own team. This history unabashedly deals with the Straggler record on issues of race: similarly, sexism is also an inevitable weakness of the club through the 100 years, as can be seen in several anecdotes, but in this respect the Straggler story is less exceptional, and less worthy of particular highlight – again, individuals adapt to societal changes at individual pace. Suffice to say that the current president, Tim Lerwill, has a vision that the Stragglers be in the forefront of this latest development in the wonderful game.

Geoff Hartley was a warm-hearted and generous man with a bluff charm that captured the attention of all: born in Burnley, and growing up in Walsall, he played plenty of rugby and cricket when young and joined his father's engineering company after National Service in the Staffordshire Regiment.

He became a Straggler at the late age of fifty but still scored 1,413 runs and introduced his two talented sons to the club as well. 'Given a little encouragement, he would offer younger players priceless, thoughtful advice, always encouraging and delivered with a warm smile and a mischievous twinkle in his eye.'

His contribution to the Stragglers over the years as a player, committee member and then chairman was immeasurable. Around the time he assumed the chairmanship, he originated the idea of a festival of wandering cricket and involved the publisher of *The Cricketer*, Ben Brocklehurst, in a scheme that, after careful planning, produced a marvellous festival in 2000, based at Oxford, where twenty-eight clubs convened, playing fifty-six matches.

After the success of Hong Kong, Ramesh Sethi started planning a South African Tour, which came to fruition early in 1997: the focus became, after research, the Western Cape, and a strong party of players and supporters flew down. Umer Rashid, an England Under-19 player, was part of the group, subsidized by the club, and the team included Sethi, Shiv Datt, Sam Chapman, one of the club's best all-rounders, Jono Enderby, probably the best wicket-keeper-batsman to have been a Straggler (after Swetman!), and Robert Tindall, ex-Cambridge and Northants. David Fursdon, Keith Holgate, Peter Marsh and Peter Fielding were very skilful support, while Brian Woodbridge and Mike Halliwell provided some more experienced advice along the way!

In terms of diversity, the 1997 Tour laid firmly to rest the 'non-European' question of the Stragglers of Asia: Padhani, Sethi, Rashid, Awan, Patel, Barot and Datt played among Fielding, Botell, Fincham, Hartley and the rest. The captaincy was rotated game by game and a thoroughly enjoyable two-week tour ended with a balanced playing record of won five and lost five. For the last game, the best Straggler team took on a 'Western Province' side and bowled them out for 220 in 40 overs, Umer taking five for fifty-one and achieving a direct-hit run-out against an 'ambling' opener, according to the match report: unfortunately, despite receiving 66 overs back and Enderby, Datt and Tindall carefully accumulating runs at the top of the order, spinners Soloman and Narramore ground the middle order out, bowling over twenty overs each, left-armer Narramore taking 4 for 19 off 22 overs and Solomon 5 for 90 off 25.1 overs. The visitors ended on 165, 55 short.

The tour report, written by Richard Merricks, concluded:

> The tour was a huge success – to win half the games was an achievement in itself, but vastly more important, the team spirit and unselfishness engendered from upwards of twenty two players . . . speaks volumes not only for their character and attitude, but also the desire to uphold the high standards of the Stragglers of Asia.

Ramesh had put together a super management team, which included Tony Lycett as tour treasurer and Chris Hartley as day-to-day manager, with his father, Geoff, splitting the umpiring with Mike Bottell. Chris Nield, unfortunately not able to go, ran a pre-payment scheme.

Umer Rashid contributed much to the playing success of the tour, taking 24 wickets and scoring 319 runs at an average of nearly 80, and it was a tragedy when he drowned in Grenada on a pre-season tour with Sussex CCC in April 2002.

Another of the tourists, Asif Padhani, went on to score over 2,451 runs for the club, becoming a frequent participant in the successful sides of the early 2000s: an elegant opening or middle-order batsman and occasional wrist-spinner, he brought a keen will to win and eloquent banter on the field.

*

With the South African games included, 1997 saw a record sixty-seven fixtures attempted by the Stragglers, although sixteen were cancelled before play started, mainly due to rain, a couple due to side-raising issues. The number of wins was ahead of losses and no fewer than eleven centuries were scored, two each by Luke Stoughton and Rupert Swetman – who combined to put on 228 for the first wicket against Old Amplefordians in August, allowing the Stragglers to chase down 250 for the loss of only Luke's wicket. This was one of the games that saw the refreshed Roy Swetman partnering with his son Rupert, in the second phase of Roy's Straggler career.

For the second year running Ramesh Sethi was at the top of the run-scorers, accompanied this time by Luke Stoughton, both with 511.

A sad postscript to the season was the death of a Straggler, Charlie Morpeth, a thirty-seven-year-old diplomat on secondment from the Foreign and Commonwealth Office, working in the Office of the High Representative in Bosnia, who was killed along with eleven others on 17 September when a Ukrainian helicopter crashed in dense fog on a mountainside. In an eerie coincidence with the crash that killed prominent Straggler Reginald Lagden during the war, the four crew members survived. Morpeth had joined the Stragglers when in the army as a young officer with the Highlanders.

*

Early 1998 saw another tour, this time to Cyprus, where a Straggler, Colonel Peter Cook, was heading up the British garrison. Thanks to Peter and his brother, John Cook, the arrangements were relatively simple and a tour party with a mix of experience and youth played four games over the course of six days, winning two and losing two. They were all low-scoring matches, the highest innings of 154 for 8 in a narrow victory over the RAF, thanks largely to Sye Razvi's undefeated captain's innings of 66. The best bowling was Peter Fielding's 5 for 42 against the ESBA XI.

The game against the Pilgrims at Wormsley saw the Stragglers at 95 for 7, rescued by two talented all-rounders, Sam Chapman and Patrick Latham, who put on 100 before the declaration came. In reply, the Pilgrims finished at 195 for 7, Keyte with 54 and Carleton-Smith (a future head of the Army) with 27 just failing to overhaul the Stragglers.

Against the Cross Arrows, Sam Chapman took his 100th wicket for the club at the superb average of 18. Meanwhile, the top batsman for the year was Tony Hooper with 373 runs at an average of 62.2, who deservedly collected the Hugh Lindsay Award.

Hooper was a Cambridge Blue in 1987 (scoring 87 at Lord's) and 1992 and was selected for the combined Oxford and Cambridge side that played the Pakistanis in the latter year, before taking a doctorate in chemistry and following a career in research. He played a total of twenty-three first-class games and is among the very best players the Stragglers have fielded over the past few decades, still scoring a heap of runs in his fifties and taking wickets with intelligent medium pace that moves both ways. He has an unquenchable zest for the game and is understandably annoyed at being described as a 'former cricketer' on Wikipedia!

Nineteen ninety-nine saw another successful year in the win/loss ratio (W20, L14), spurred on perhaps by a victory over I Zingari in May, where the evergreen Shiv Datt scored an unbeaten 100 and poor Jono Enderby was hit between the eyes first ball when keeping, requiring ten stitches; earlier, he had been out first ball batting!

A weekend tour to Perigord in south-west France was well supported, thanks to Geoffrey Hartley and Duncan Kilgour, an ex-Hong Kong Straggler who had retired from the judicial service in the colony: a 'senior' team in age ensured three victories were recorded! Tim Lerwill, Sye Razvi and John Cook were some of the younger tourists, while Geoff Downman came out of a fifteen-year retirement, only to pull a hamstring and require a runner!

Richard Sawney scored centuries against the Pilgrims (130 not out) and Royal Artillery (136 not out), while Sye Razvi scored one at Hurlingham. Tony Hooper was in the runs again with a century against Dorset Rangers, and Jonathan Hall (brother of Ben) hit 105 not out against Reed's Choughs. This was incidentally the twentieth fixture at Reed's since it had been revived in 1980 after two years, following the Hawkey incident; all had been ably managed by Peter Marno, and supervised from the school by John Savage, who very sadly died at sixty-nine in early 2000 - the Stragglers, together with the Choughs and Peter Jones's XI, presented a bench. His son, Paddy Savage, a batsman of great skill, continues to be involved today in the club, as honorary secretary.

No fewer than ten centuries were scored by Stragglers, plus a couple by guests. The standout bowler was Lawrence Fernandes, who took 52 wickets in 1999, taking him up to 122.

Umpire Derek Miles retired in 1999, having run the umpires' panel for the club over many years.

INTO THE NINETIES AND MORE CRICKET THAN EVER

The newsletter noted:

Derek's nickname 'Deadly' derives from the feeling of dread experienced by batsmen on the receiving end of his unfavourable decisions as his hand trembles inside the robes of office, the trigger finger emerges and describes a perfect semi-circle outwards and sideways from his thigh to its zenith two feet above the crown of his head, thus completing an action parallel in perfection to the bowling action of Maurice Tate in his pomp.

His wife, Maureen, often accompanied him to games and strolled around the boundary as he officiated. On one occasion, at Pangbourne, a firmly hit six was looping up in her direction and she neither saw the ball nor reacted to the frantic shouts of the fielders. Fortunately, the ball just missed her and ended up inside the Waitrose shopping bag she was carrying in her hand!

The 1999 annual dinner was one to remember – at the East India Club, thanks to the president, with over 100 attending. The Hurlingham Club and the Band of Brothers made up tables and the speakers were Field Marshal Lord Bramall, the Earl of Stockton and Peter Baxter of the broadcasting world. Tony Hooper won the Hugh Lindsay Trophy and Sye Razvi the batting (his aggregate of 765 runs beat General Bill Withall's record for a season, which had stood since 1967); the bowling went to Lawrence Fernandes with his 52 wickets. Only the legendary Henry Christian, with 56 and then 70 wickets in 1947 and 1948, had ever done better.

There was a note of caution in the report: 'The dinner . . . was enjoyed by one and all and the bar extension was very popular. However, on the night our club lost money, which it can ill afford to do.'

A painting of the club's game at the Hurlingham Club on 28 June 1998 by Jim Russell was presented to the Hurlingham's chairman and a subsequent print run was sold to Straggler members without much success. As of 2024, copies are still available at nominal cost.

Chapter Nine
INTO THE NOUGHTIES
STRAGGLERS RETURN TO INDIA

THE NEW MILLENNIUM and 75th Anniversary of the club kicked off with the tour to India, departing on 3 March, with fifty-seven members and supporters. The tour committee of Shiv Datt, Ramesh Sethi and Chris Nield had done a fantastic job, with the help of Devraj Jadeja in India, and the programme was a challenging tour of the Punjab and Delhi. A total of ten games were played, three won and seven lost; additionally, a ceremonial fixture was held up at the Maharajah's ground in Chail.

In the game at the Patiala palace against his eleven, the current Maharajah, Amarinder Singh (also democratically elected chief minister of Punjab), had laid on a pair of ex-Test players, Bishan Bedi and Mushtaq Mohammad, to face the Stragglers, plus Yuvraj Singh, who was selected for India later that year - needless to say, and despite the age of some of those, his side were victorious by 6 wickets.

ONE ARM BOWLS A LITTLE

> The game had some wonderful moments – a fine innings by Ramesh Sethi, a nice little stand by two of Their Highnesses, some wonderful stroke play from the young Sohdi, and inevitable victory for the Maharajah's XI, sealed with the mightiest six most of the visitors had ever seen. Tea, speeches, and presentations followed, as kites circled slowly above the trees and the towers of Patiala. News of India's surprise victory in the first one day international against South Africa did no harm at all to the 'unmistakable air of gaiety' (thus the *Chandigarh Herald* the following day), that had dominated the whole occasion. Players eventually retired to bathe and change in the Victorian splendors of the Patiala Circuit House before an evening of feasting, speeches, and more dancing at the Maharajah's Palace.

Richard Butler, sometime Straggler and keen Invalid, was one of the tour scribes, writing an account for the 2001 Straggler newsletter, from which the above extract comes. What he does not mention is that he was bowling when the Maharajah came in to bat, and promptly had His Highness plumb LBW first ball and duly appealed - fortunately the umpire Squadron Leader Brian Canniford, who was a fine judge of the situation, immediately pronounced it 'not out'.

Butler's report continued:

> During the day at Patiala, dire warnings were heard that the famous mountain cricket ground at Chail was covered in snow, which, in the sweltering Patiala afternoon, was hard to contemplate. But the next stage of the journey revealed a different, cooler India – a protracted climb to the hill station at Shimla, with its timbered cottages and English Church . . . evocations of another age. This provided a base for a successful game against the Lawrence School at Sanawar and a take-off point for the high spot of the trip – a return to the hilltop ground at Chail.
>
> Chail, reached after another long, winding bus journey through some spectacular scenery, is now the site of an academy for sons of servicemen, and the tourists were greeted by most of the school. The boys, it seemed, had been looking forward to the visit for many months, and there were only a couple of false starts before, under Tim

INTO THE NOUGHTIES: STRAGGLERS RETURN TO INDIA

Coombe's firm direction, they were performing a very creditable Mexican Wave. Because of exams, it was not possible for the school First XI to turn out, and instead an inter-Stragglers game was to be staged to mark the return to the historic ground. So on the hilltop, as hail fell and snow threatened, there was played one of the more extraordinary games in the Club's history. Many sweaters took the field, but the Indian gods soon relented and the whole ceremony took place in bright sunshine. The encouragement of the schoolboys was deafening, but equally felt was the quieter presence of the ghosts of Captain Sanger, Vernon Maynard and all the others who had played there before and formed the nucleus of what was to become the Stragglers of Asia. Eagles circled above and snow-covered caps of the Himalayas were visible beyond the tree-lined boundary.

The cricket back in Delhi included games against the Mohan Meakin Brewery, a strong Indian Army side, the British High Commission, the Delhi Blues and the Delhi District Cricket Association. Every playing member of the party was involved on the last two days, where two sides were put out on each day.

As Butler concluded:

This was the trip of a lifetime, meticulously planned and expertly organized. It was a total success, and at the end of it all there was a real feeling that, by this return, to the club's roots, the special character of the Stragglers had been re-established.

*

A number of non-playing initiatives came out of the tour, including the 'Chail Fund', which was to promote cricket at the Chail Military Academy, the school for children of serving 'other ranks' (not officers) in the Indian Army. The funds were used to repair the pitch, lay a new artificial wicket and defray the costs of sending cricket kit up to the school – all to revive it as a cricketing venue. The Punjab Cricket Association promised its support and the Maharajah's Tigers XI played up there over the following years. In fact, the Straggler support acted as a catalyst to encourage the authorities to budget more funds for sports at the four 'King George V' military schools, of which Chail was one. By 2006, Shiv Datt could report to the committee that further funds were not required.

*

At the Eastbourne College fixture a special 75th birthday party was held, with an excellent lunch, using the famous Maynard sauce boats, and an anniversary bench was presented to the college by the club vice president, Jack Hyde Blake. The headmaster, Charlie Bush, was warm and immensely supportive, being appointed an Honorary Member of the Stragglers; afterwards twenty Stragglers and guests dined at the Lansdowne Hotel. Since Maynard had brought the first Stragglers, the college has always been welcoming, particularly when Nigel Wheeler was running the cricket there, as he did for over twenty years.

The other highlight of the 2000 summer was the Oxford Festival of Wandering Cricket:

> This long awaited festival – the brainchild of chairman Geoff Hartley – was a great success judged both by the quality of the cricket, the behaviour on the field and, most importantly, the friendship off it. The overriding goal of celebrating the contribution of wandering cricket to our main summer sport was achieved and, such was the acknowledged success, that Lord MacLaurin not only suggested that it should take place every five years, but that it should be sponsored!

About twenty Stragglers attended the dinner at Keble College and MacLaurin's speech was rather longer than it needed to be, according to one account, with some dipping into political themes towards the end; Christopher Martin-Jenkins spoke next, and according to one commentator it was a rather 'bog standard' speech, not adapted to the occasion sufficiently.

Unfortunately, the Brocklehurst family, proprietors of *The Cricketer*, who had organized the festival, were, it seems, exhausted by the enterprise and also, it was thought, out of pocket, so it has not been repeated. Perhaps it marked the apogee of wandering cricket as an activity.

INTO THE NOUGHTIES: STRAGGLERS RETURN TO INDIA

Stragglers themselves played Stanley CC from South Africa on the Monday, narrowly losing by 11 runs, not helped by having only nine players (!), then won against De Flamingo's from the Netherlands, the Grannies and the Flycatchers. Shiv Datt, James Heardman, Rory Hills and Tony Hooper all made significant contributions, while Tim Coombe scored 104 not out against the Grannies and Rupert Bairamian 79. Nigel Sawrey-Cookson, a Hong Kong Straggler and captain with Cathay Pacific Airways, scored 118 against the Flycatchers, with Jonathan Hall on 92 not out when the declaration came.

For the season, in 20 innings, Tony Hooper broke the record for most runs with 927 at an average of 58, including two centuries and six fifties. He also took 15 wickets and caught 6 catches.

The annual dinner saw seventy-five members attending the East India Club and again Tony Hooper and Lawrence Fernandes were among the winners – Hooper made sure Sye's record for most runs in a season was short-lived, with 927 in 20 innings at an average of 58: he also took 15 wickets. Lawrence won the bowling again.

Laurie Lee, vice president, passed away; Jack Hyde Blake recalled in a funeral address that Laurie had turned up for the Hong Kong Tour resplendent in a new blazer and with a brand-new bat – aged seventy-nine! Elected at fifty, Laurie was an eternal enthusiast and happy to serve as honorary secretary at short notice in his late seventies; he was careful to encourage new Stragglers and do what he could to contribute in the games he played in advanced age (usually because someone had pulled out).

Additionally, Derek Miles of umpiring fame died – he was dedicated not just to cricket, apparently once umpiring thirty-one matches in July, but also refereed over 3,800 football games – fellow umpire and Straggler John Desmond made an address at his funeral, inevitably including Derek's unique 'out' signal: 'It starts, rather like a salute, indeed as a greeting, unfortunately does not stop at the horizontal, but goes on to perpendicular.'

*

The AGM of 2001 saw some discussion about the MCC fixture among the twenty-four members attending – initially, the thought had been to withdraw the fixture owing to 'lack of funds', but the game continues to be played every second year and the Stragglers take much care to give the fixture appropriate support.

The summer was a less frenetic one than its predecessor and out of forty-six matches, thirteen were won and sixteen lost, with eleven drawn. Sam Chapman was the highest run-scorer with 395 and took, in a tie with Lawrence Fernandes, the most wickets, 15.

For the Eastbourne College game, Devraj Jadeja had prepared a new trophy. Devraj, who had been one of the leading lights in the 2000 Tour to India, was a Straggler for many years in the noughties and handled most of the arrangements for the second India Tour in 2007, which encompassed visits to the royal palaces in Jaipur and Udaipur, places with which he was entirely familiar. The 'Patiala Bowl' was presented by Devraj, 'to be played for between Eastbourne College and the Stragglers of Asia Cricket Club. Presented by the family of HH Ranjitsinhji Jam Sahib of Navanagar.'

In 2001, the college won decisively by 138 runs!

An intention to tour Argentina was announced and Simon Prodger, who had gone out as part of an MCC team there, wrote a piece for the Straggler newsletter, extolling its virtues; unfortunately, given the general economic recession of the time, plus the run-up to the Gulf War, the tour, scheduled for February 2003, had to be cancelled.

The 2002 season was very successful result-wise, fifteen wins against only six losses – the outstanding innings was by Tony Hooper, scoring 166 chasing down the 291 scored by the Adastrians. Richard Nuttall, a Hong Kong Straggler, scored a century against the Band of Brothers, never an easy game, while Robert Tindall starred in the 8-wicket victory over I Zingari with 130 not out. Tim Taylor, son of Richard Taylor, who sired no fewer than four Straggler players, scored 100 against the Grannies in a losing cause. Tony Hooper added another sparkling century to his name with 151 not out against the Berkshire Gents, in a first-wicket stand of 226 with Sye Razvi. Martin Beer was captaining the Gents, who were crushed by 141 runs! Other highlights were bowling the Hogs out for 44 and then the Somerset Stragglers for 86.

On the downside, nine fixtures were cancelled or abandoned due to weather, and three were lost due to side-raising problems on the Straggler end.

More positively, Rupert Bairamian organized a happy five-night sojourn in Oporto, where the side beat the Invalids and the Oporto Club in between

INTO THE NOUGHTIES: STRAGGLERS RETURN TO INDIA

a couple of days sampling the local produce: Rupert was in the wine trade and arranged tours of the port wine 'factors' house (shades of the Calcutta East India Company 'factors').

At 2003's AGM, after an unprecedented term of nine years, Lt. Col. John Stephenson handed over the presidency to Maj. Gen. Stephen Carr-Smith, a distinguished Royal Signals officer who had been a Straggler since 1964: he promptly enrolled his sons in the club too. Meanwhile, Geoff Hartley handed over to Peter Marno as chairman – it was Peter's second stint as chairman and the club was to benefit once more from his level-headed, tactful and measured management of the committee.

The year 2003 was another steady season, just behind on the win/lose ratio – Ed Giddins, the England Test bowler, appeared for the Bluemantle's at the Nevill, Tunbridge Wells; he took 5 for 53 off 18 overs, but Tony Hooper again batted brilliantly, scoring 125, ably backed up by Patrick Latham's 57, although 250 was not enough. The day before, fifties from Hooper and Latham had helped the Stragglers overcome MCC by 5 wickets at Ascott Park. Sye Razvi, unusually, did not bat but contributed three catches: with 576 runs in the season he headed the averages, above Hooper with 431, but Hooper led the bowling with 24 wickets – another fine year for him.

In October, the club, under the stewardship of Simon Prodger, chairman and secretary of the Club Cricket Conference and one of the organizers, took part in a six-a-side tournament in Tangiers, Morocco, involving eight wandering clubs and two local teams. A useful squad of Prodger, Tony Hooper, Tim Taylor, Duncan Garnsworthy, Ollie Lerwill, Ramesh Sethi, Ed Fulbrook and Jeremy Paul won two and lost three. Sometime Bluemantle Ed Giddins and Norman Cowans appeared for one of the teams that the Stragglers beat!

Simon Prodger played top-quality league cricket for St Albans: partly through position but largely thanks to his gregarious personality, he had a wide range of contacts overseas, especially in East Africa, and introduced some talented Tanzanians to the Stragglers, as well as initiating the fixture against the Kenya Kongonis (his other wandering club) at the historic Sheffield Park ground in Sussex. He also induced the Kent and England spinner Min Patel to play for the club on a couple of occasions. His own record for the club is impressive, 1,701 runs at an average of 42 with four centuries: it was devastating for all when he died in 2023 at only sixty-three.

ONE ARM BOWLS A LITTLE

It was an important year for the election of new members - Robert Pollock-Hill, James Allsop, Jonathan Parker and Simon Collins, who were all to become stalwarts of the club over the next twenty years, joined. In addition, Karen Stephenson, as widow of Colonel John, who had died in June 2003 shortly after standing down as president, became an Honorary Member, following in the tradition of Amy Cowgill, widow of Kit, who was an HM from 1985 until her death in 2000. Heather Lee, widow of Laurie, was also accorded this honour - proof that the club was not as sexist as it seemed.

Another loss was John Desmond, at the early age of sixty-four: after finishing playing around the time he became a Straggler in 1980, Desmond was an umpire at a high level and a frequent Straggler in that capacity. He also chaired the cricket sub-committee of the club for several years, when Jack Hyde Blake was chairman. The meetings were invariably at the Albertine Wine Bar and the first item on the agenda was to taste and approve the wine to accompany discussions - and usually the minutes would comment on the standard. He went on the 2000 India Tour with Catherine, his delightful wife, and was a great influence in the club, as the newsletter put it: 'He was a loyal member who got on with everyone he met, having a no-nonsense approach, knowing what he was about and where he wanted to go. Above all, he was a true gentleman and will be sadly missed.'

In early 2004, the Stragglers went back to Sri Lanka, with a party of over forty people. It was a good team, involving Hooper, Razvi and Parker, among others, but inevitably quite hard going - all matches were limited-overs format, and the Stragglers only beat the Tea Planters XI (surely some ghosts helping there) at Nuwara Eliya, an evocative venue of old, and Jetwing in Colombo, under the famed Duckworth/Lewis method (the formula used to nominate winners in rain-affected matches), as a tropical downpour brought proceedings to a close prematurely. The other five games were lost: 'A mixture of quality batting and top-class spin bowling proved to be the Stragglers' downfall.'

Highlights were playing on the Test ground at Kandy, lots of sightseeing to places such as the Temple of the Tooth, one of the holiest places in the Buddhist world, and the elephant orphanage at Pinnawala. Ironically, the chairman lost a number of his teeth wicket-keeping in a later game at Colombo - Jamie Bebb ably assumed the keeping duties. The fines committee did its job, and a good sum was sent to one of the (human) orphanages in the war-ravaged north of the island. The tour report made mention of the 'death-defying tuk tuk rides', a comment that was to resonate even more during the next Straggler foray to the subcontinent.

The 2004 season in England was a patchy one with some remarkable games. The Band of Brothers fixture had moved to Torry Hill, the home at the time of Robin Leigh-Pemberton, the ex-governor of the Bank of England, Lord Kingsdown. Rather hard to find in the pre-Google Maps days, it is an Elysian field, surrounded by a country-house park of the old style, sheep chomping among the oaks and beech trees. The BB batted first, and Stragglers found wickets hard to get – the declaration came at 291 for 1, the sole wicket a stumping by the author, two centuries scored by Goodwin and Pyke for the BB.

However, cricket is cricket, and the Stragglers replied in style, led by James Allsop and Sye Razvi, after Shiv Datt had got out unusually early. With 116 and 105 respectively, they did the hard yards, and the club won by six wickets (both sides only had ten men).

It was only after the game concluded with four centuries scored that someone thought to measure the pitch – and sure enough, the whole square was found to be a yard too long, a freak occurrence and quite beyond the experience of anyone present! No wonder batting was a little easier than normal and wickets hard to come by!

Ed Giddins appeared once more for Bluemantle's as Bob Bairamian oversaw proceedings from the pavilion in his usual style – while a Straggler of some renown, there was no mistaking his loyalties during Nevill Week! Sye Razvi scored an elegant century and Latham and Walsh took the key wickets with support from Pollock-Hill.

Razvi ended the year with 1,003 runs from 24 innings – a stunning record, at an average of 48, two centuries and six fifties. Meanwhile, Robert Pollock-Hill for the first time won the bowling award, with 22 wickets at an average of 22. In Hong Kong, Martin Sabine, the Hong Kong secretary, scored 109 not out as the club just failed to hunt down the 280 required, with two wickets in hand.

The year was to end with the awful Boxing Day tsunami, which affected Sri Lanka very much – as it happened, Ramesh Sethi was back at the Galle ground with his Harrow School team and was within moments of disaster: fortunately, the teams were yet to take the field and managed to climb the pavilion to safety on the roof. One boy's father was lost, sadly. In the months following, the club donated in excess of £1,000 to the disaster funds.

The 2005 AGM chaired by Peter Marno saw the retirements of a number of committee members: Chris Nield, the honorary treasurer, stood down after eleven years, during which he managed the finances of the club with efficiency, good humour, prudence and intelligence – one particular contribution was his advance savings schemes for tourists. It was all a far cry from the earlier days! Another stalwart, John Cook, stood down as vice chairman and chairman of the Cricket Committee, to be replaced by Tim Lerwill, recently awarded an OBE for planning, coordinating and running the 60th Anniversary of D-Day commemorations. A formidable sportsman, Lerwill had played first-class cricket for Hampshire and captained the Army side as well as playing for the Combined Services and Hong Kong; he was also a fine rugby player, representing England at U19 and U23 level and playing for a number of clubs including Rosslyn Park, Bath and Paris. John Cook remained as fixture secretary.

The biggest loss was Martin Beer, who finally 'wriggled away from the post of Secretary – he tried to do so last year but he proved to be irreplaceable!' Tim Coombe was nominated to replace him.

Martin Beer had been the administrative rock of the club for many years, as mentioned above, and a vital support to the various chairmen he had served under. It was a profound shock to the club and completely unexpected when he died suddenly early in the 2005 season, shortly after the Malta Tour. At his funeral, John Cook, who had been a friend for over forty years, gave the eulogy in front of a packed church of 300 people at Arborfield, the home of Martin's erstwhile corps, the Royal Electrical and Mechanical Engineers. In part, this read:

> Martin was of course passionate about his cricket and reluctant to take holidays during the season. Sally (his wife) tells the story of how on one occasion she persuaded him to go away to Wales during the summer. While there he spotted a cricket match and said he would wander down to have a look; he soon returned to say that one team was a man

INTO THE NOUGHTIES: STRAGGLERS RETURN TO INDIA

short, and he had offered to play. Sally said, 'But you don't have any kit', to which Martin replied, 'You haven't checked the boot properly!'

In the tributes that I have seen about Martin themes which recur are his kindness, energy, sense of fair play and the fact that he was a great team man and a true gentleman. I would add that he was also generous – usually being the first at the bar to buy a round.

A large group of Stragglers attended the funeral, together with a cohort from Eversley, his home club, where he had contributed much over the years: as a send-off, the coffin left the church between an avenue of upturned bats held by members of the two clubs.

The short tour to Malta was ably arranged by Ramesh Sethi, a tour master of immense experience by now, and the club played and lost three games, two to the schoolboy sides of Harrow and St Paul's, and the local Marsa Cricket Club. The weather was dreadful, and the game against Harrow was played in drizzle the whole afternoon. Razvi and Sam Chapman scored runs while Pollock-Hill bowled well on a diet of vodka, not helped by being Mike Swift's roommate – Swift scored 3, 3, 6 in his 3 innings, unsurprisingly as, on tour without his Malaysian partner, Vian, he hit the casinos and bars with abandon. Roger Whittaker was a genial umpire, fined harshly for officiating in a wet coat.

The summer saw fourteen wins and fourteen losses out of forty-one fixtures, with Razvi again leading the batting (653 runs) and Robert Pollock-Hill the bowling, with 27 wickets. Charlie Dawson was the Hugh Lindsay Awardee – a bustling opening fast bowler and big hitter, he worked in Sye Razvi's fashion boutique business, which resulted in the odd acerbic comment between the two on the cricket field! Somehow, the trophy disappeared during Charlie's retention of it.

The following year, 2006, was a high-water mark for the Stragglers, to rank with the best years of the mid-nineties. Thirty-nine fixtures were scheduled, of which thirty-three were played, and no fewer than nineteen won and six lost, the best performance on record in terms of win/loss ratio: victories against I Zingari, the Army U25 XI, Hurlingham (with a Razvi century), Butterflies (ditto), the Somerset Stragglers (after being 46 for 8) and the Cross Arrows at Lord's were some of the highlights. Tim Lerwill with the cricket sub-committee did a fantastic job, and runs were plenty in a generally dry summer.

ONE ARM BOWLS A LITTLE

One great find was a pair of Zimbabweans who were spending some time in England, courtesy of Trinity School in Croydon, Mark Ferrao and Grant Beresford-Miller: Eyre Maunsell, the school bursar, found them and encouraged them to play for the Stragglers as candidates. Both good cricketers, Ferrao was at least the equal of the best all-rounders to have represented Stragglers in modern times, on a par with a Tony Hooper, Jonathan Parker or Sam Chapman. Grant was a useful leg-spinner (comparatively unusual for the Stragglers) and an excellent fielder. Sadly, after just a couple of seasons we lost Ferrao to the girl of his dreams back in Cape Town.

Another keen young candidate building a reputation was Matt Shales, who scored an unbeaten century against the Bluemantle's in a hard-fought draw that saw the Stragglers finish 11 runs short with 8 wickets down: a very good batting line-up failed to fire except for Matt and Keith Young.

In September, there was a memorial match in memory of Martin Beer at Eversley: a bench was presented to the club in the presence of his widow, Sally, and two daughters, with a full complement of Stragglers present, including the president and chairman.

Winter 2007 saw the club's second tour to India. A good party of forty-three tourists, including fifteen players, thirteen gentlemen spectators and fifteen ladies, set off on a Virgin Atlantic flight to New Delhi: the author was working at the airline at the time, enabling the lowest possible fare. Ramesh Sethi and treasurer Ghanshyam Patel had also arranged a golf fund-raising event back in early 2006 and nearly £4,000 was raised from this and a raffle, the money to help young Stragglers who might need some financial help with the tour. A pre-tour get-together was arranged on Straggler Mike Halliwell's floating restaurant, *The English Maid*, moored alongside the Albert Embankment, on a chilly evening in February. At the event the first souvenirs of the tour were distributed, pens and ties. Kuljinder Bahia, owner of the fast-growing travel firm Southall Travel, was a generous sponsor of the tour kit and elected an Honorary Member of the club in recognition.

The participants were a cross-section of the Stragglers and included the president and his wife, the chairman and his, Richard Lambourne, as assistant tour manager, and Peter Cattrall, a Straggler of old, with his wife, Amanda, General Bill Withall's daughter.

INTO THE NOUGHTIES: STRAGGLERS RETURN TO INDIA

Devraj Jadeja had very much taken the lead in the planning of the tour, acting as travel agent and fixture arranger.

The first game saw two ex-Test players, Manoj Prabhakar and Vivek Razdan, in the Delhi Cricket Veterans team at the Feroz Shah Kotla Test Stadium (now the Arun Jaitley Stadium) in Delhi, and the club were unlucky not to get closer to beating their 233 total in 40 overs, after a sterling partnership of 102 in 15 overs between Jonathan Parker and Ian Perry. The hospitality was fantastic, free drinks and a sumptuous buffet for lunch.

The itinerary was demanding, as it always is in India, and the standard of cricket was inevitably very high. No better illustration than Agra, where after a 04.30 a.m. alarm call to see the Taj Mahal at sunrise, the team went to a bare and uneven Agra Cricket Club for a twenty-five-over game: bundled out for 129, the side were well beaten by nine wickets, once the Agra team had turned up - unfortunately, they had forgotten about the fixture, but their captain, the local chief of police, unsurprisingly managed to find a competitive eleven very quickly. Christened the 'Stragglers' by the match commentator, Jonathan Parker and Nick Trueman were the only batsmen into double figures, with 56 and 22 respectively. With a couple of India 'A' team players, the result was never in doubt.

On to Jaipur by bus, into the 'Hotel Royal Orchid' (not quite the standard of its Thai cousins) and non-cricketers were first up for a tour of the Amber Palace and the 'pink city'. The Rajasthan Cricket Association stadium was beautifully appointed with a bowling-green outfield and flat, true wicket. Again, a Ranji Trophy player or two meant a loss, although the spinners Pat Patel, Moustafa Rajabali and Pollock-Hill meant the margin of victory was only three wickets.

Udaipur was next and here the Stragglers suffered a grievous accident, courtesy of a careless tuk-tuk or 'motorized rickshaw' driver. With the Sunday game abandoned due to weather (which had already curtailed Saturday's), many of the party went up to the Monsoon Palace, from which a good view of Udaipur and its famous lake can be seen. Regrettably, on the way down, the vehicle in which Chris Pitt and Sir Roger Hearn, two of our gentlemen tourists/umpires, were travelling lost its balance and crashed on to its side. Chris Pitt escaped with a battered arm and face, but Sir Roger suffered major spinal injuries. Devraj Jadeja had a direct line to his friend the Crown

Prince of Udaipur and medical help was very swiftly deployed. A very experienced spinal surgeon was on hand at the American Hospital and the best possible care given, with Sir Roger flying home as a medical evacuation after a few days' observation.

Stephen Carr-Smith and Peter Marno marshalled the response to this dreadful accident, with the able and vital assistance of Ramesh and Devraj: Richard Lambourne very selflessly volunteered to stay in Udaipur until Sir Roger was evacuated and it was a chastened party that boarded the flight to Mumbai. The president reported that Sir Roger was keen the tour should proceed and so it did, with a fresh awareness of the hazards of travelling to exotic lands.

Mumbai saw another loss to the Cricket Club of India side at the Test stadium of Brabourne, the venue founded by the Maharajah of Patiala as mentioned above, where the team played after some Yorkshire and Essex players on a pre-season jolly. The hospitality, as everywhere, was magnificent and the Stragglers were fortunate in having Chatrapal Singh, Devraj's father, entertain both teams to a fabulous meal and drinks in one of CCI's function rooms. Each member was presented with a crystal memento of the tour, and many went on from there.

A further loss came at the Bombay Gymkhana, next to the vast 'maidan' or central park of Mumbai, filled with almost overlapping cricket matches, despite runs from Razvi and Nick Trueman taking the team past 200 for the first time: the day was most notable for a few words from the great Indian batsman and captain Sunil Gavaskar, who is a friend of tourist Pat Patel. Gavaskar was presented with a Straggler tie and kindly noted the importance of club cricket tours in improving relations and understanding between countries.

The final game was at the Police Gymkhana, where a President's XI assembled by Devraj, including three of the tourists, took on the club, who won for the first time on tour – Alex Garman, Parker and Razvi in the runs. The game was notable for being the first day/night game the Stragglers had ever played, finishing under the lights alongside a busy Marine Drive, looking out to the darkness of the Arabian Sea.

Martin Foulds, a left-hand middle-order bat recruited via the Law Society, came into his own fielding for the President's XI, sprinting along the boundary

INTO THE NOUGHTIES: STRAGGLERS RETURN TO INDIA

in front of a substantial crowd whose cheers spurred him to unexpected heights of athleticism!

In all, without being the historic pilgrimage that the 2000 Tour had been, since the club did not go to Chail or into the Patiala domain, 2007 was full of the most touristic parts of India (Delhi, Rajasthan, Mumbai), and great cricket played on - except for Agra - excellent grounds. As Peter Marno was to note:

> The truth is we were faced with too strong an opposition on every occasion. Every side that we played had current Ranji Trophy players, and some even contained the odd ex-Indian Test player. Nevertheless, those Stragglers who played put in a spirited performance and there was no loss of face – and we did play on several magnificent and first class grounds.

One slightly sour note was that the nightly fines committee had collected the rupee-equivalent sum of £447, which the tour organizer had promised to keep safe, but despite Ramesh Sethi's follow-up in future months, the money never arrived.

The 2007 season was rain-affected and there were side-raising difficulties, so only twenty-eight games were completed out of the forty-three scheduled. One highlight was beating the Hampshire Hogs in the last game to be managed by the legendary Christopher Bazalgette, who had been a fixture for them over the years, and apparently their leading wicket-taker for over a quarter of a century, bowling seemingly innocuous slow-flighted off-spin, which was always an invitation to self-destruct in the huge outfield of Warnford. Bazalgette had clearly not expected to lose and complimented the Stragglers on bringing 'a very professional side' (thanks to match manager Eyre Maunsell) - key roles being played by J.P. (4 for 34) and Dr James Melhorn with 51 not out.

An India Tour reunion was held at the Reed's Choughs match in Cobham, close to Oxshott, from where a number of the non-playing tourists hailed, and, while Sir Roger was still in the Spinal Cord Injury Centre at the Royal National Orthopaedic Hospital, his girlfriend, Rachel, attended. Regrettably, he was completely paralyzed from the neck down and died two years later.

Meanwhile, three Stragglers were capped by their Service - Jonathan Parker continued to find success at Navy and then Combined Services level, while Oliver Lerwill (son of Tim) captained the Army side that won all the inter-service competitions and was the player of the T20 tournament with two 70s, one of which took just 18 balls!

Jono Enderby, the most talented gloveman since Roy Swetman in Straggler colours (not that Swetman kept at all for the club!), became the second Straggler wicket-keeper to pass 100 victims.

In September, a Straggler six made it to the International Festival for Wandering Clubs down in the Algarve, with ten UK teams and two local ones: captained by Alex Garman, the team won three and lost one game, before a tie with the Gloucestershire Gypsies secured a place in the semi-finals after much rumination by the festival committee. Sadly, Finals Day was washed out, so a semi-final plate was the reward the team took home, with James Houlgrave, a very talented seventeen-year-old from Amport, collecting the 'Most Valuable Player' award for the tournament - a fine accolade. In a sideshow throwing contest, he threw the ball further than Gary Pratt, a top first-class fielder who had famously run out Ricky Ponting as a twelfth man in the 2005 Ashes series: Pratt was not amused.

The following year, 2008, brought a change of chairman - Peter Marno stood down after his second innings of six years and Tim Lerwill took over. In his last message to the club, Peter replayed familiar themes:

> As I am writing this on 1st January it seems appropriate to suggest that we all make a resolution to put that little bit more into the Club than we take out – however that is defined! We all know our limitations and the success of a Club such as ours is to get the best out of our strengths and minimize the weaknesses – again I thank the team who have worked so hard during my tenure, and I wish the new Committee every success.

It was another year of numerous rained-off fixtures and cancellations - meaning only twenty-one were completed from a card of thirty-five. Highlights were beating the South Oxfordshire Amateurs (James Allsop was out for 99 but won the Hugh Lindsay Award for the year), the Bluemantle's, Millfield and Band of Brothers - however, the big games against IZ, Hurlingham and

INTO THE NOUGHTIES: STRAGGLERS RETURN TO INDIA

the Royal Navy XI were lost - as was the Cross Arrows fixture, by the slim margin of 1 wicket. Sye Razvi scored a couple of centuries, and Tony Hooper, Alex Garnsworthy (who won the batting prize after four years of Razvi!) and Ben Rogers one each. In a slightly truncated season, 18 wickets were enough to get Robert Pollock-Hill the bowling prize.

A tour to Argentina and Chile was in the planning stage for 2010, but by January 2009 the decision was taken to cancel it, as the effects of the global financial crisis worked through the economies of both the receiving countries and the prospective tourists! An alternative to Tanzania was briefly mooted - however, insufficient early commitments were received: three Tanzanian national players turned out for the club, including Hamisi Abdallah, the national captain. Simon Prodger had introduced them and was always looking for new talent for Stragglers, as a very well-connected club cricketer.

The last year of the noughties again saw almost a balance of wins (ten) and losses (eleven), with only three draws. James Musgrave won the batting and the Hugh Lindsay awards with 539 runs at an average of 53 - and this without counting a century he scored against the Royal Navy, where, unaccountably, the score card was lost.

Of course, Robert Pollock-Hill took the bowling award, with 22 wickets at a commendable average of 18, 5 for 78 against his other club - the Butterflies - being a highlight, and 4 for 28 at his alma mater, Harrow.

In a departure from tradition, the annual dinner moved to a new style and venue in October, with the dropping of a black-tie club dinner in favour of the recommendation of the 'dinner working group' - the 'India Club' of the Hotel Strand Continental on the Strand, a very informal and much cheaper option, to attract more of the young.

Chapter Ten
2010 ON

THE CLUB ENTERED THE NEW DECADE with confidence and legal members Robert Pollock-Hill and James Allsop were particularly energetic in helping match managers produce a full team to fulfil the fixture list of thirty-four - down from the 1990s peak, but still a healthy number for sure. For the first time, the Stragglers played three fixtures in Hong Kong, against HKCC, the Crusaders and Kowloon CC, the last of which saw Mike Gatting, late England captain, making his debut for the Stragglers and scoring an elegant 14. Wins outnumbered losses in a good season.

Also in 2010, Sye Razvi overhauled Shiv Datt's record aggregate runs, at an average above 45 and with fifteen centuries to his account, establishing himself as the most successful batsman in Straggler history. Appropriately, he achieved it at Torry Hill, scoring 49 in a narrow victory of 23 runs over the Band of Brothers, ably managed by Matt Shales. Two Stragglers were again selected for their service sides, Jonathan Parker for the Royal Navy and Steve Booth for the Army team. 'J.P.' has continued to be a stalwart of the Stragglers through the following years, bowling fast (or perhaps a little slower than fast-medium these days!) and batting destructively, while pursuing his career as a Royal Navy officer.

ONE ARM BOWLS A LITTLE

The club also noted the appearance of members Gus Kennedy (Cambridge) and Jonathan Ludwick (Oxford) in the varsity match, as well as Hamisi Abdallah and Khalil Rhemtulla in the Tanzania National XI. The Oxbridge pair were both to do postgraduate studies at the 'other place' and each win Blues for both! On a less serious theme, the club entered a team in the 14th Golden Oldies World Cricket Festival at Harrogate, sponsored by Theakston Brewery. A variety of experienced Stragglers made it to play in a composite team with some new-found friends/guests, and Tim Lerwill as chairman made the trek north too - Tim Coombe, Ian Perry, Richard Taylor, Ed Fulbrook, Nino Trapani. In a festival for over-forties, one of Richard's sons, Tim, made an appearance too - 'co-opted from his camping holiday and brilliantly impersonating a 40 year old'.

For 2010, Joe Reid won the batting award with 285 runs, and Pollock-Hill had another great season, with 39 wickets at an average of only 11. Tom Shrives was given the Hugh Lindsay Trophy.

The following year, 2011, was a relatively poorer season for results with seven wins and ten losses from the thirty-one fixtures scheduled: having given the Army Development XI some good games in the past, 2010 saw a crushing defeat and 2011 was not much better - the Army scoring 425 for 7 off fifty overs: despite a Musgrove century, Stragglers finished 220 runs short! In a year of mixed fortunes, Tim Lerwill, the chairman, distinguished himself by scoring the most runs (264) while J.P.'s 19 wickets earned him the bowling prize. In its wisdom, the committee decided not to award the Hugh Lindsay Trophy, a repeat of the 2001 season.

In 2012, Major General Stephen Carr-Smith handed over the club to Colonel Billy King-Harman, a Straggler since 1969, who had had an interesting military career followed by fourteen years as City Marshal to the Lord Mayor of London, for which he was awarded the CBE. A threatening fast bowler in his youth, King-Harman had played Straggler cricket intermittently over no fewer than six decades and had been on several tours, notably using his photographic skills to record India 2000 and Cyprus in detail. His finest playing moment had been a return of 8 wickets for 88 runs against the Gentlemen of Leicestershire in 1990.

The club was already resolving to reduce the number of fixtures in order to guard against an increasing trend of cancellation due to side-raising difficulties - especially for mid-week games - but a contributing factor was the commitments of the armed forces for the Diamond Jubilee celebrations and then the London Olympics, which meant that the usual armed services fixtures were cancelled. As the world recovered from the global financial crisis, the ability of people to take days off work for cricket or to spend precious family days on the pitch seemed to diminish – a trend felt by other wandering clubs. In the event, no match was cancelled in 2012 due to Straggler difficulties in raising a side, but the Grannies and Cryptics had to scratch.

In the event, the weather intervened and only fifteen fixtures were played, albeit with a healthy win/loss ratio of seven to three, with three drawn and two abandoned. The talented Simon Prodger scored a century against the Butterflies in a game filled with controversy, not least because, with Stragglers poised for victory, the opposition skipper claimed a catch off a hit that Stragglers believed was clearly a six, based on what had been allowed earlier in terms of boundaries. Elsewhere, the Stragglers were generously accommodated at Arundel by the Sussex Martlets, who were 34 for 4 when rain stopped play. A Stragglers guest, George Brooksbank, had coaxed life enough out of the usual Arundel 'road' to dismiss three and send one unfortunate batsman to hospital via a top edge. (This was Merlin Swire, scion of the aviation, shipping and property conglomerate in Hong Kong, who had scored an elegant fifty against the Stragglers the year before.)

Pollock-Hill reclaimed the bowling award, and Prodger won the batting with the rather paltry total of 152 runs – somehow, very few players appeared frequently enough to challenge him!

Twenty-eight scheduled fixtures in 2013 saw twenty actually played, with no fewer than seven cancelled due to side-raising difficulties, either from the club (two occasions), mutually (three) or the opposition (two). Some of these difficulties were self-inflicted – for instance, scheduling the Band of Brothers game on a Saturday when both sides had traditionally relied on a healthy number of league players.

One bright spot for the summer was Ian Salter joining and hitting 166 in a high-scoring game at Reed's, where the margin of victory was 7 runs after Stragglers compiled 334. Jonathan Parker scored his maiden century for the club, Tony Hooper his thirteenth and James Musgrave 123 at the Nevill.

*

The following year, 2014, was another season where the number of fixtures on the card was severely undercut by those actually played (twenty-eight against seventeen). Eight were won and nine lost: six fixtures were blighted by inability to raise a team, three on the Straggler side. Two members scored centuries, Matt Shales and Ian Salter, while Charles Lamprecht took 5 wickets in an innings, as did candidate Ed Burton. For the second year running, Ian Salter took the batting prize and Andy Duff took the bowling, on the strength of a better average for his 7 wickets than the regular winner, Pollock-Hill, had for his 7! Matt Shales won the Hugh Lindsay Trophy, having scored a century and become match secretary on the committee.

One sombre note was Tim Lerwill's match report after the Eastbourne game, which saw a weak Straggler team bowled out for 56 before lunch and obliged to play a T20 to make use of a beautiful day.

> At the end, I handed the Patiala Bowl back to the winning Captain, Jason, and left Eastbourne sad that all the effort to find players and call in favours had come to naught and with serious concern for the future of wandering cricket. The one positive to hold on to was that the College did play a game on a most wonderful day tailor made for cricket. The fixture must continue, and our playing members must be attracted to visit such a venue – to see our silver and history and understand where the club started if for no other reason.

This sentiment proved to be a low point as 2015 was a much brighter season – helped by seventeen sides being turned out on schedule by the Stragglers: even though the win/loss balance was five to ten, there were a number of very close defeats and plenty of highlights to celebrate. From the 2016 handbook, cricketing retirements of three Stragglers were noted - Simon Prodger scored 1,701 runs at an average of 42, while also capturing 19 wickets at 28. Tony Alderton took 58 wickets at 15 and became famous for removing the England Test batsman Ed Smith twice in successive years against Hurlingham. 'Wild Bill' Kincaid, otherwise known as Brigadier Bill Kincaid, Royal Artillery (Ret'd), finished with a tally of 247 wickets (the third-highest in club history) at a very respectable average of 24. A deceptively gentle leg-spinner, Bill rarely bowled without taking at least a wicket or two, often a stumping or a catch in the covers. He played for over forty years for the Stragglers, with a habit of fielding in hockey shin pads, and initiated the game against his home club, Sunbury, in 1981.

For the year, the chairman was too modest to record his own feat in winning the bowling prize with 12 wickets. Joe Cavanagh won the batting prize with 290 runs at an average of 41 and took home the Hugh Lindsay Trophy.

*

Just nineteen fixtures were planned for 2016, of which four were cancelled by the opposition not being able to raise a side, and one rained off. Four wins and eight losses meant an unsatisfying season from the results: Joe Cavanagh again headed the batting with 350 runs, while Tim Calder took 11 wickets to take the bowling honours. Tom Vila was awarded the Hugh Lindsay Trophy.

Off the field, the club lost Jack Hyde Blake, who had been such an important figure in leading the club to the zenith of sixty-plus fixtures in the 1990s; Jimmy Hilditch, a regular supporter; and, unexpectedly, Bill Kincaid, who had just volunteered to become fixture secretary.

Tim Lerwill stood down as chairman, handing over to Joe Cavanagh, who had retired as a young Brigadier after a stellar career, which included command of a Rifles Battalion in Helmand Province, Afghanistan, for which he received the award of a DSO.

There was a recurrence of side-raising difficulties in 2017, with three games being cancelled by the club. Of the rest, four were won and eight lost, with two drawn. With 206 runs, club stalwart James Allsop took the batting award, while a candidate, D. Conway, captured 12 wickets for the bowling prize. Tony Hooper was recognized for his enormous playing and match-managing contributions with the Hugh Lindsay Award for the second time (the first being in 1999).

Early in 2018, one of the more unusual Stragglers of modern times sadly passed away in Kuala Lumpur, Malaysia, of throat cancer. Mike Swift was a longtime resident of Hong Kong, where he was brought up, his father a professor at the University of Hong Kong: he spoke fluent Cantonese and after school joined the film business as well as developing his cricket at HKCC. A stylish batsman and swing bowler, Mike's best suit was probably his fielding at cover, where he was fleet of foot, had quick hands and a very flat throw to dismiss many an unwary batsman. Having played a few games for and against the Stragglers in Hong Kong, he came to the UK in 2002 and commenced a short but exciting career, playing forty-nine matches overall, scoring over 1,000 runs, including one century, and taking 43 wickets – more significantly, if anyone deserved the sobriquet 'good tourist', Mike did, going to Sri Lanka in 2004 and Malta in 2007.

Robert Pollock-Hill tells the story:

> His laid-back, almost horizontal demeanour, hid a keen competitive streak which he showed in Sri Lanka during the tour party's visit to the Rock Fortress at Sigiriya. He and a fellow tourist decided to run to the summit (rather than walk) up the steep and narrow staircase in the blazing midday sun – to the evident alarm of the tour guide, and the German tour party ahead of us. The Germans were forced to take evasive action as the pair – supported by some of the younger members of the Straggler party, hared up the side of the cliff, barrelling past the tourists and almost sending more than one off the side of the cliff.

Mike's flamboyance on the field was matched by his performances off it. After the Stragglers annual dinner in 2004 and several drinks in a nightclub or two, Robert found himself at around 2.30 a.m. tasked with ensuring Mike got back to his hotel, the excitement and refreshment of the evening having taken its toll on him. He convinced Rob he was staying at the Savoy, and upon arrival Mike laid his head on the reception desk and went to sleep while Rob attempted to obtain his room key. The reception porter did not have any record of Mike having a room while Mike, in intermittent moments of consciousness, said he did and kept saying 'Room 446'. After a further ten minutes of unsuccessfully negotiating with the porter to give Mike his room key, Mike finally awoke with a jolt and a look at the porter and then at Rob:

'Where are we?'

'We are at the Savoy,' Rob replied, 'and trying to get you a room key. Are you sure you are in 446?'

'Yes, definitely 446. Oh, now I remember, I am staying at the Ritz Carlton . . .'

2010 ON

Mike's stint in the UK was driven by ownership of some upmarket pubs and hotels in the Midlands, but it is fair to say that what he did exactly was a mystery: what was not was his beautiful Malaysian companion and a top-of-the-range Mercedes.

A singular man, ever restless, he returned to Malaysia, ended the relationship in favour of another lady and began trading in aviation fuel and who knows what. Even though in his forties by the time he came to the UK, all will recall his enthusiasm for Straggler cricket, his zest for life and abundant charm. He left a few loose ends, business-wise and with his relationships, but was almost the archetypal modern Straggler in his approach to the game.

Speaking of touring, after many false starts over eleven years since the 2007 India visit, especially the aborted trip to Argentina in 2010 where deposits had been taken, the activity was finally renewed in 2018, with a tour to the Dordogne, south-west France, which the chairman, Joe Cavanagh, described as follows:

> The tour was memorable for excellent accommodation and victuals; the loyal, patient support of the travelling wives and the Suckling family and friends; our president filming proceedings from the boundary and sometimes inside; the variable but generally trustworthy artificial tracks; the bouncy plasticized match balls preferred by the local teams (in pink given the absence of sightscreens); the hard, 'no fear' cricket played by our opposition . . .

Three games were played, against SW Bordeaux Invitation XI, Damazan CC and Eymet - all lost, but with a lot of style and *élan*. Vinny O'Neill, a retired colonel from the same elite regiment as Joe, turned up on his Triumph motorbike! The president bowled an excellent spell at Eymet, conceding a mere 6 runs an over when the rest of the Straggler attack went for over 11, the damage done by Mohammad Adnan, who scored a double century in the allotted thirty overs!

A season of nineteen games with only four wins and eleven losses was brightened by beating the Cross Arrows at Lord's; Jonathan Parker scoring a century and having taken his hundredth wicket joined Ramesh Sethi, Tony Hooper and Sam Chapman as the only Stragglers to complete the double of 1,000 runs and 100 wickets. Another highlight was the I Zingari Australia game, where the away team brought some very talented teenagers and the game was played in 'wonderful spirit', 'notwithstanding the erratic nature of some of the Stragglers' dismissals . . .'

For the season, the evergreen Tony Hooper took both the batting and bowling honours, with 270 runs and 12 wickets.

There was little change in the club's fortunes in 2019, but some narrow defeats were partly to blame – by 1, 6 and 14 runs, the latter against MCC, who were given a scare. For the season Joe Cavanagh led the way, with 265 runs batting, and Tom Vila took 19 wickets to win the bowling. Ian Salter was deservedly given the Hugh Lindsay Award 'for his matches played, for playing on through the season despite a difficult, painful injury, and most conspicuously for his introduction of some superb guests and candidates to the club'.

Ed Fulbrook, a Straggler of some note, sadly passed on in 2019. A member since 1982, he was a veteran of over 100 matches and several tours: Hong Kong, South Africa, Oporto and the Dordogne. Not a batsman of the highest rank, he could survive in difficult situations and the author recalls batting out with him for over an hour to draw at Tunbridge Wells; a big man, he could also swipe boundaries to good effect when necessary – ending with 1,756 runs from 105 innings. Heavier than many, he was the archetypal first slip and reliable there. Professionally, he worked in a host of different jobs and even started ventures on his own before finding the ideal occupation as a sales representative for a brewery – he spent twenty-five years in that line, and later was in direct marketing, making significant contributions to the Worshipful Company of Marketors.

And then came COVID . . . cricket, of course, took a back seat as the country, indeed the world, faced a pernicious pandemic that would take hundreds of thousands of lives prematurely and lead to almost wartime conditions in terms of the way of life for millions. Government restrictions meant no cricket was permissible until late in the 2020 season, with six games played by the Stragglers. Highlights were a return to Wormsley to play Sir John Paul Getty's XI and a great win at Armoury House against the HAC, strong opponents always. A young cohort of Stragglers, including Jonny McDuell, who won the Hugh Lindsay Award as his father had done before him, chased down 218, George Humphreys and Adam Abbott finishing the chase expertly when the run rate became difficult. Jonny headed the batting for the foreshortened season, with 180 runs at 36, while Rob Pollock-Hill returned to the top of the bowling board, with 8 wickets at 19 – the tenth time he won the bowling award, the first being back in 2004.

At the annual dinner, the president, Billy King-Harman, had some salutary words for the club, occasioned by the evidence of alleged racist behaviour at Yorkshire County Cricket Club and the lengthy enquiries into it.

> What cricket is going through at present at the county level – and perhaps national level – is a tragedy as well as a disgrace. The inevitable inquiries will make interesting reading, and I do hope that the ECB, counties and clubs around the country come out at the other end suitably chastened but with a will to ensure it never happens again.
>
> What is clear is that much of the behaviour should never have been tolerated in the first place and would demand a red card or dismissal from our club were it to surface here.
>
> Looking around the room, I am always delighted to see some of our club members with Asian, African, and Caribbean connections. Scan through our excellent handbook and you will find dozens more going back two or three generations. Some fled the country of their birth because their very existence was in jeopardy and sadly that scenario could still play out today.
>
> The quality and longevity of the contribution to our club by all our members with a Commonwealth background and their families has ensured the survival of our club to this day – and we owe each of them a huge debt of gratitude. We must continue to learn from the past whilst planning for an enjoyable and attainable future.
>
> And talking of the future, it is imperative, when recruiting new members, that we take to heart the words of the club constitution in the handbook that:
>
> – Candidates should be like-minded cricketers regardless of sex, age, disability, ethnicity, nationality, sexual orientation, religion, or other beliefs and
> – They foster and promote the sport of cricket and the playing of it in a Corinthian manner.

Fortunately, the Stragglers had addressed their own issues many years previously and any suspicion of errant behaviour, as with the case in the nineties, had been called out by the younger, more liberal-thinking membership.

Off the field, the club lost several of its key figures, including Geoff Hartley, past chairman, who died at eighty-seven after a long period of ill health. He had been a 'generous and warm-hearted' spirit as Straggler chairman and originator of the Festival of Wandering Cricket in 2000. While not the most prolific batsman, he had brought immense wisdom, wit and warmth. Taking over as chairman from the dictatorial, if effective, Jack Hyde Blake, Hartley was less prescriptive and the atmosphere of games he attended was more relaxed than previously. His two sons, Andrew and Christopher, became very valuable players and contributed much to the Stragglers.

The cricket author and journalist Michael Henderson (*That Will be England Gone*) wrote of Geoffrey in *The Cricketer* that he was a 'stalwart of the Staffordshire Gents and Stragglers of Asia, two of the travelling bands which give cricket much of its flavour. We are invited to titter now at striped blazers by those who want to make cricket a game of the urban young, where the past is painted black. Yet they played their part of the pageant and must be numbered.'

> Geoffrey, who spent his later years in Cheltenham, was one of the people who spring most readily to mind when I hear that much-abused phrase, the spirit of cricket. Always present at the Lord's Test, perched in the Upper Tavern Stand, he was fair, reasonable, and tolerant: qualities that some of us associate with a cricket lover of his vintage. 'I never knew anybody,' said a mutual friend, 'who felt so comfortable with so many people.' Farewell, Geoffrey. You played a fine innings.

Major General Bill Withall, another Straggler giant, also passed on in 2020, at ninety-two. A cricketer of great quality, who played for the Army and MCC, he held the Straggler record for most runs scored for some years, as related above, and was a soldier of considerable ability, rising to head the Army Air Corps. A talented pilot, he was happy to have Stragglers as his passengers when appropriate!

While he had started his cricket bowling fast-medium at Ealing Cricket Club with Eddie Ingram and Eddie Thompson, both of whom went on to play county cricket at Middlesex, Withall joined the Army in 1950 and converted himself into an opening bat: he scored over 3,000 runs for the Royal Engineers and continued playing during postings in Hong Kong and India, where he attended the Indian National Defence College by choice, demonstrating his adventurous character.

Shiv Datt recalled that:

> To Bill, cricket was as much a matter of form as of content. It was not enough to score a ton, or to take a catch, or throw a ball, as to the manner in which it was done; it had to be done with style, allied to an immense and irrepressible sense of fun. He laughed a lot, and it was infectious. He earned the nickname Nudger from his habit of stealing quick singles early in his innings – just a gentle push into the in-field and a clear, firm summons for the run. I learned early, when batting with him, that his shout of 'Come One' was as much a command to run as it was an invitation to negotiate whether to run at all.

In the field, Shiv recalls a catch by Withall at backward short leg:

> As much due to reflex as to instinct, Bill dived to his left and the ball stuck in his hands. True to 'as much a matter of form as of content', he rolled over again, and then again, before rising with a triumphant grin from ear to ear. It cost him a lot of beer at the bar later. He was as generous a man as he was a cricketer and gentleman.

Importantly, Bill Withall was 'colour-blind' in the best sense, and, as we saw above, it was Withall who introduced Shiv Datt to the club, in 1969, and precipitated the full opening of the Stragglers of Asia to all, regardless of origin.

Another loss in 2020 was Rupert Bairamian, son of Bob, who died in Sydney, where he had moved with his Australian wife and son. Rupert had been a Straggler since 1981, when he joined aged nineteen: a talented Eastbournian, he was an effective opener and occasional bowler, ending with 2,542 runs from 100 innings, putting him twelfth in the list of Straggler batsmen. Unflashy as a batsman, he knew that accumulation could be as effective as stylish stroke play, sticking to Boycott's dictum that 'you can't score runs in the pavilion'. He inherited some of the bravado of his father and would be happy to destabilize the opposing batsman's frame of mind, if possible, when trying his leg spin or 'whippies', as one team-mate remembers them! Bowling for Bluemantle's, one Straggler hit him hard over the boundary at the Nevill and the retort was: 'That's a bit unnecessary, isn't it?' The game was indeed rained off shortly after.

More often he was the team's comedian and also, being in the wine trade, happy to dispense learned advice on what to drink. Many Stragglers will always remember Bairamian senior holding court in the Nevill pavilion, slurping quantities of white wine, while Rupert batted or captained with humour on the pitch below.

Rupert was a kind soul and wandering cricket was at the centre of his life before marriage, as he played for the Bluemantle's, the Band of Brothers, the Grannies, Moose CC, the Yellowhammers, the Old Eastbournians and numerous other sides. In his younger years, playing four or five games a week was nothing unusual. For Stragglers, he played an important role on the committee for twenty years and, while demurring to become one of the officers of the club, his contribution to managing matches and raising sides, as well as running social occasions, had been immense. He also held the distinction of being the first winner of the Hugh Lindsay Trophy in 1988. His death faraway in Australia, still in his fifties and only two years after his father, was a shock to all.

*

A further loss was Colonel John Cook, who as we have seen played an important part in the club's administration during the 1980s and 1990s: he was a Straggler for fifty years, joining in 1970 after playing in the Berlin game. He went on to score 1,426 runs at an average of 18 but more significantly was the first Straggler wicket-keeper to reach 100 victims, before he retired from playing in 2004, at age sixty-five. A playing member of the MCC, as well as a host of other clubs, his proudest moment was scoring a century at Lord's in 1968, for MCC vs. Henfield. As an officer in the Royal Army Ordnance Corps, he served in Oman, Singapore, BAOR, Nigeria, Australia and Papua New

2010 ON

Guinea, a long and varied career that he followed with much voluntary work with NGOs and the Church. Described as 'steely of heart but mild of manner' in his Straggler obituary, he was one of those men whose influence was often underestimated.

*

Twenty twenty-one was a rather more normal season - although still played under COVID conditions, with a ban on catering being the most obvious loss. Out of seventeen games, the club only won three, lacking batting in a number of high-scoring matches - none more so than a mismatch at Aldershot against the Army. Carmichael and Wiseman both scored big centuries (168 not out and 153 respectively) as the home side piled up 479 in 50 overs. Only Mark Banham, a Straggler fast bowler of yore (and England Over-60s cap), managed ten overs for a very respectable 41 runs, while guest Nick Fisher was second-best, going at a mere 7 an over! The eventual margin of defeat, by 371 runs, was inevitably a record!

Probably the best single aspect of the season was Conor Brown's batting: in his last year before marriage, he scored three fifties and 365 runs in total at an average of 30 - deservedly taking the Hugh Lindsay Award for the year - not just for batting, but for his able match managing, captaincy and quality fielding. Robert Pollock-Hill took his eleventh bowling award with 25 wickets, including an outstanding 8 for 114 against Hurlingham - unfortunately in a losing cause - and 5 for 88 against South Oxfordshire Amateurs, never an easy game.

Matt Suckling scored the only century of the year, in a tight win against Northchurch to close the season, where veteran Mark Hunt received a nasty blow from a hard-hit drive while bowling, which he said he really should have caught! Another veteran, Phil McDuell, passed 2,000 career runs for the club.

At the dinner following the season, Billy King-Harman, standing down as president, was thanked for his service by Chairman Joe Cavanagh: a Straggler since 1969, King-Harman had enhanced the prestige of the Stragglers and proved a great sounding board for the chairman and committee, as well as supporting the club at every opportunity, as he has continued to do, most generously. The chairman also thanked the hard-working pair of Simon and

Brinde Collins, who had done the jobs of honorary secretary and honorary treasurer as a husband-and-wife team for over a decade, with minimal drama and calm efficiency. Brian 'Bushy' Woodbridge, a stoic support to numerous committees and chairman over a long time, latterly as vice chairman and previously an assiduous organizer of the club's annual dinners, also retired and received a presentation. Speaking collectively, Joe Cavanagh recounted:

> Of course, after such long and distinguished service it is very difficult to do justice to their contributions in just a few words, suffice to say that over several years the committee (and club) has benefited from their great wisdom, humour, tenacity, energy and imagination; the current good health of the club is due in no small part to their efforts.

In 2022, the club won seven and lost six games, more or less the perfect balance: seven fixtures were lost, among them the Gentlemen of Cambridge, scratched following the death of HM The Queen, and the traditional tussle at the HAC, for the same reason.

Chris Rogers, a new member and Wiltshire player, rose to the fore by scoring 331 runs, including a century against the Guards CC in Chelsea, while Danny Dawson topped the bowling with 22 wickets. Conor Brown won the Fernandes Fielding Prize, and the Hugh Lindsay Award went to Rogers.

A short, late-season tour to Norfolk saw a rain-affected twenty-overs victory at Thornham Cricket Club, followed by a let-down from a local club, which shall remain nameless – but the Stragglers improvised an inaugural double wicket competition that was won by Phil McDuell and Vinny O'Neill. As with all tours, the entertainment off the field more than matched that on it, despite the rain: the highlight was a drink with immediate past-president Billy King-Harman and his wife, Judi, at their home nearby.

Discussions commenced around the Centenary celebrations and what shape they should take – broadly, it was agreed that a third tour of India should be mounted, also a Centenary dinner booked at Lord's and some kind of festival game at Eastbourne College, to commemorate the first match there.

A HUNDRED YEARS NOT OUT

THE CLUB ENTERS its hundredth year with great confidence and a settled *modus operandi*, centered around twenty-five annual fixtures in England, with a calm governance overseen by Tim Lerwill as president and Joe Cavanagh as chairman. The treasurer is the former banker Phil McDuell and never have the finances been healthier; UK fixtures are expertly managed by Ian Perry and one, sometimes two, games are scheduled in Hong Kong, where Mark Winstanley has done a sterling job as Hong Kong secretary over the past decade and more. Paddy Savage, a second-generation Straggler, holds the historic post of honorary secretary, while James Allsop chairs the vital cricket sub-committee, where Matt Shales, Conor Brown, Tony Hooper and others have given sterling service ensuring that Straggler standards remain high.

The 2024 season was the most successful in the club's history in terms of win percentage: out of eighteen games played, eleven or 61 per cent were won. The only other season to come close was 2006, when nineteen out of thirty-three completed games were won – 57 per cent. Even Bluemantle's were beaten, for only the thirteenth time in seventy-three years of the fixture, as well as long-term friendly rivals the Hurlingham Club and the Guards. The Patiala Bowl played for at Eastbourne College is now in Straggler hands for the first time since 2006. Robert Pollock-Hill keeps these and other statistics in order and tracks the progression of batters and bowlers by season and by career, as well as ensuring the club's legal constitution and processes are kept up to date. He has also fulfilled a number of other vital roles over the past two decades, managing the website and chairing the cricket committee - and not least in gradually chipping away at Henry Christian's record number of wickets!

Within the individual career records, it is worth noting that the two heaviest run-scorers are named Datt and Razvi, with Fernandes the fifth-leading wicket-taker - the diversity of the Stragglers is still not reflective of the nation, possibly, but stands comparison with any other wandering side.

Gathering teams to play has never been taken for granted, since the first game when Vernon Maynard needed a schoolboy to make up the XI, but now with a pruned fixture list and WhatsApp, the chances of fielding eleven fit players is much closer to 100 per cent than it ever was. In 2024, one match manager, Charles Fidler, went from half a side a week before the game to a full complement of strong cricketers within twenty-four hours of a WhatsApp message. The recent playing success of the club helps too.

As this book goes to print, there are over thirty names on the list for the Centenary Tour of India, scheduled to depart on 14 March 2025 and play around ten fixtures in the Punjab - in Chandigarh and Patiala. Some members of the party will make a ceremonial visit to Chail, where the youthful ghosts of Maynard, Coldwell, Sanger, Mason-Mac and, not least, the Maharajah of the 1920s will surely be awaiting them.

The players going include a fine sprinkling of the young and nearly young - the two McDuell brothers, Jonny and Paddy, going with their father, Phil, Abhinav Premnath (a recent find and very competent 'keeper/batsman), Adam Abbott, Alex Asher, Debayan Dasgupta, Charles Fidler, Matt Suckling - accompanied by experience, the talented and defiantly not 'former cricketer' Tony Hooper, England Over-60s bowler Mark Banham, plus Joe Cavanagh of course - with President Tim Lerwill also available for selection! As always in India, the cricket will be tough and demanding and the hospitality overflowing.

A HUNDRED YEARS NOT OUT

The evergreen Shiv Datt has made frequent trips to represent the club as only he can and to prepare the ground with the influential individuals there.

Later in the summer, the Eastbourne College game will have a special festival atmosphere, and likewise the Broadhalfpenny Brigands game played on the hallowed turf at Hambledon in Hampshire, where many of the foundations of cricket were laid, before the advent of MCC in 1787. Then, on 7 November 2025, the Centenary dinner in the Long Room at Lord's will be held, where toasts to the Founder and Original Members will be made.

The Hong Kong section will hold their own celebration, led by Mark Winstanley with long-standing members Martin Sabine and Chris Williams to the fore, and newer ones like Eddie Middleton: over the years, the Stragglers have kept this Asian connection alive, providing a game of classic declaration cricket to enliven the Chinese New Year celebrations or sometimes, as was the case in Calcutta, Christmas. Generously, HKCC continue to support the Stragglers, perhaps subliminally aware of the part the club played in HKCC's survival! A Straggler membership is still prized in Hong Kong as a tacit recognition of a man who is a decent cricketer, a proper sportsman and good company: not all who play as candidates get over the bar!

The sixty-six games a season peak reached in 1997 seems unlikely to be repeated, unless and until artificial intelligence removes employment and provides monies for all, but the Stragglers are happy with their twenty-five games a year, a number exceeded only seven times in their first fifty years.

More than most, the Stragglers have found new recruitment challenging, as their natural hinterland, the British forces and especially the Army, has shrunk and shrunk. Unlike clubs such as the South Oxfordshire Amateurs, the Sussex Martlets and the Hampshire Hogs, there is no catchment area for Stragglers: often a relationship with a specific club has paid dividends. Playing at Pangbourne School in the nineties, where Paddy Savage was teaching and keen Straggler Keith Young drove the cricket, paid off first with the recruitment of James Allsop and Tim Hamilton, and then Conor Brown and Joe Reid a decade or so later: more recently, associations with Northchurch CC (through Tom Vila) and Old Camdenians (thanks to Ian Salter) have provided several talented young players. The intent is very much to continue attracting younger cricketers who enjoy something more than their usual league outings, and even to extend our membership across the gender and class divide as we did over the racial barrier.

The club continues to attract members representing the whole diversity of modern England - and successive administrators have ensured that the language in the annual handbook reflects the spirit, make-up and intent of the membership. There are still several serving or retired military and naval officers, including some who would have qualified under the 'east of Suez' rule, and a number of second-generation Stragglers. Of course, with the removal of that rule in the 1980s, the membership is now more eclectic and varied - many Stragglers are simply fascinated by the name and happy to contribute to a team of like-minded souls and new friends.

More importantly, the welcome that new talent receives, and the unpressured encouragement that marks the Straggler approach, ensures that individuals want to keep playing. Sadly, the two-day games of yore have been consigned to history, but the whole-day declaration games are little different from those the founders played in 1925. The games are competitive, without being overly serious - at the end of the day, a beer with the opposition is always very welcome and part of the tradition. Despite the challenges of recruitment, the club remains at the forefront of wandering cricket, whereas so many clubs have folded over the past decades - where, for instance, did the 'Gentlemen of Croydon' go?!

Reflecting on the broader social aspects of their journey over the past century, we have seen how the Stragglers, born into the complex landscape of the Indian independence movement of the 1920s and 1930s, delayed in widening their racial composition even after 1947, moving much slower than we could countenance today - principally because of the different experiences of their varied members. There is little doubt that, just as a British missionary could be outraged at the Jallianwala massacre of 1919, many of the men closest to real experience of racial integration, in the Indian Army and even the Police Service, were disappointed that their club had not moved faster. Unfortunately, for every progressive member there seems to have been a foil hindering progress - many, it seems, in the ivory towers of the managing agents of Calcutta.

It is fashionable to denigrate the representatives and servants of colonialism and empire, especially in relation to India, where the most complicated of relationships now exists between the nations - however, the real story is inevitably more nuanced and more layered and actually more interesting than the jejune assessments of the superficial commentators and one-sided historians, wherever they hail from.

The history of the Stragglers of Asia has delivered the club, founded for white colonial expatriates from India in 1925, into a fully inclusive and diverse organization for twenty-first-century England, attracting and sustaining players of all backgrounds, and proud to play against the other famous clubs of the land. The world changes and the club is fully focused on the future - determined to improve its profile among young cricketers, embracing some limited-over games among the traditional fixtures and planning a women's section.

Vernon Maynard, Alleyne Coldwell, Frank Mason-MacFarlane and Tony Sanger could never have imagined in 1925 where their wander on a hot evening around the fountains of Trafalgar Square would lead. Hopefully, they would be content to see the club they founded still playing at Eastbourne College 100 years later, their colours being worn by people of all ethnicities and tours mounted to countries as diverse as Portugal and Morocco. They might be surprised at the rise of Hong Kong as the Asian focus, the informality of the members' non-cricketing attire might shock them and certainly they would not approve of the language at times - however, we know these four men were among the more pragmatic and visionary of their ilk, and we must thank them for creating a club that has brought huge pleasure to so many cricketers from far and wide, and will continue to do so as long as the game is played.

Willy Boulter is the Archivist of the Stragglers of Asia CC, whom he first joined as a young Army officer in 1976. He is now an airline consultant, having worked in international aviation across 12 countries over 40 years, and splits his time between Kent and Yokohama. He was a History Scholar of New College, Oxford.

ACKNOWLEDGEMENTS

MY FIRST DEBT is to the Straggler committee, headed by Tim Lerwill and Joe Cavanagh, who have allowed me to write this history without interference or oversight. It is a personal account, I should stress, not an 'official history'. I have been a member since 1976, when I joined as a young Artillery officer in Germany, and have always found Stragglers, maybe because of their varied provenance, to be the friendliest of cricketers: it has been fascinating to research the origins of the club and the individuals involved, and to trace its development into the modern era.

Shiv Datt, the first 'non-European' member, has been immensely helpful with an endless store of anecdote and history, not all of which is recounted here; Peter Marno, twice chairman, added much colour and helpful advice; while Rob Pollock-Hill kindly submitted a very detailed review of the drafts, suggesting a number of corrections and improvements. Phil McDuell has been encouraging at every stage; while Ian Perry helped solidify the Northamptonshire Regimental links and set up a visit to their museum. Others such as James Allsop, Ramesh Sethi and Tony Hooper have ensured that the story is as accurate as possible, and senior members like Chris Strachan and John Quin contributed priceless memories of Calcutta and South-East Asian days. On that theme, I should specially thank the late Stuart Barnes for his extensive and invaluable contribution to the Hong Kong chapter, a story that would not have been recorded without him. It is difficult to name every Straggler who helped: you know who you are and thank you!

Others who contributed include Nick Ogden, Paddy Butler, Richard Butler, Nigel Russell and others from the wider wandering cricket community. Peter Kohli, whose father fought alongside mine in the 3rd/1st Punjab Regiment, provided encouragement from afar - his book *Raj & Norah* gives a fine perspective of the relations between British and Indian officers in the Indian Army. On a similar theme, Don Hunter helped me access important RAF records.

Much of the text was written in the library of the Tokyo Club, an institution not so far distant in ethos from the clubs of India, and a word of thanks to the impeccable staff is in order - not least for the best gin and tonics in Asia.

It was a pleasure to work with the Whitefox team, who kept me superbly on track with the project plan and intricacies of publishing. Jenni Davis and Miranda Ward were precise, perceptive and helped improve the manuscript immeasurably.

Of course, notwithstanding the help I have had from so many quarters, the errors, omissions and mistakes are my own.

Finally, a note of thanks to my wife, who has put up with more than one room's worth of scattered scorebooks, minute books, books about India, books about cricket, letters, photos and *Wisdens* - all spoiling the serenity and tidiness of a Japanese housewife's domain. The dedication is scant reward but no less sincere for that.

ACKNOWLEDGEMENTS

STRAGGLERS OF ASIA CC CAREER BATTING RECORDS - October 2024

	Name	Innings	Not outs	Runs	Highest	50s	100s	Ave.
1	Razvi S.	203	28	7121	137*	42	14	40.69
2	Datt S.D.	241	16	6524	138	8	11	29.00
3	Beer M.R.	268	38	5836	123*	5	4	25.37
4	Hooper A.M.	154	28	5419	166*	25	14	43.01
5	Salisbury P.A.	199	16	4494	152*	18	5	24.56
6	Withall W.N.J.	105	8	4267	146	NR	7	43.99
7	Hartley A.W.	133	17	3986	140*	2	7	34.36
8	Sethi R.K.	127	50	3664	103*	6	3	47.58
9	Marno P.C.S.	158	9	3385	134	5	2	22.72
10	Enderby J.C.	114	15	2892	115	4	4	29.21
11	Leigh E.B.	78	6	2632	154*	NR	6	36.56
12	Chapman S.R.	108	19	2466	105*	11	1	27.71
13	Padhani A.	96	7	2451	95	15	0	27.54
14	Coombe T.B.J.	81	9	2388	138*	6	3	33.17
15	McDuell P.J.	93	17	2327	98	9	0	30.62
16	Lerwill A.T.D.	128	14	2314	79	10	0	20.48
17	Cavanagh J.	84	11	2196	132*	3	6	30.08
18	Downman G.A.J.	99	19	2170	140*	NR	1	27.13
19	Shales M.J.W.	70	11	2148	139	13	3	36.41
20	Savage P.G.	76	9	2113	137	8	2	32.51
21	Brown C.	86	8	2081	85	12	0	26.68
22	Wilkinson G.	56	5	2020	102	NR	2	39.61
23	Allsop J.W.R.	93	15	1973	116	7	2	25.29
24	Sawney R.M.	46	4	1881	167	4	5	44.79
25	Miller P.N.	44	4	1842	119	NR	6	46.05
26	Skinner A.G.	52	10	1839	121	NR	3	43.79
27	Bairamian R.R.	59	17	1820	143	NR	3	43.33
28	Salter I.	58	2	1791	166	8	4	31.98
29	Parker J.D.	50	20	1766	132*	13	2	58.87
30	Van der Gucht P.I.	54	3	1762	204	NR	3	34.55
31	Fulbrook E.D.W.	105	20	1756	75	1	0	20.66
32	Prodger S.M.	45	5	1701	136	8	4	42.52
33	Halliwell M.J.A.	109	8	1634	74	1	0	16.18
34	Marsh P.H.	83	11	1541	80	1	0	21.40
35	Cowell C.G.	36	5	1449	123	7	3	46.74
36	Cook J.F.G.	101	22	1426	74*	1	0	18.05

ONE ARM BOWLS A LITTLE

	Name	Innings	Not outs	Runs	Highest	50s	100s	Ave.
37	Hartley G.W.	120	15	1413	68	1	0	13.46
38	Hilditch J.F.	50	6	1386	132*	NR	2	31.50
39	Young K.D.	40	9	1386	153	NR	4	44.71
40	Heard R.J.M.	86	13	1385	88	1	0	18.97
41	Berridge R.N.P.	67	5	1363	86	3	-	21.98
42	Fielding P.G.	61	12	1348	100*	7	1	27.51
43	Longfield T.	45	6	1346	117	NR	2	34.51
44	Hechle R.	47	2	1344	129	NR	3	29.87
45	Gallyer D.G.	58	3	1344	98	NR	0	24.44
46	Rowe C.J.C.	30	12	1310	138*	1	3	72.78
47	Milton M.E.	17	4	1283	200*	NR	6	98.69
48	**Musgrave J.**	**24**	**1**	**1241**	**123**	**9**	**3**	**53.96**
49	Swetman R.	33	10	1190	129	3	3	51.74
50	Blake B.E.	22	4	1190	146	NR	2	66.11
51	Anson J.W.	35	9	1186	103	NR	1	45.62
52	Hosie A.G.	33	2	1179	116	NR	1	38.03
53	Lerwill O.W.	39	1	1154	104	8	1	30.37
54	King P.	42	10	1149	115*	NR	1	35.91
55	Hall B.J.B.	26	9	1121	92	1	0	NR*
56	Cowgill J.H.C.	73	9	1097	70	5	0	17.14
57	Downman D.G.C.	23	6	1090	119	1	1	64.12
58	Stoughton L.	18	2	1058	187*	7	3	66.13
59	**Hamilton T.R.J.**	**67**	**15**	**1029**	**74**	**4**	**0**	**19.79**
60	Swift M.D.	44	6	1019	104*	4	1	26.82

Approaching 1,000 Runs	
Perry I.A.	989
Reid J.	964
Suckling M.	922

Bold type indicates a current player.

ACKNOWLEDGEMENTS

STRAGGLERS OF ASIA CC CAREER BOWLING RECORDS - 2024

	Name	Overs	Runs	Wickets	Best	Ave.
1	Christian H.K.	NR	NR	388	7 for 58	NR
2	Pollock-Hill R.D.C.R.	1721	7494	345	8 for 114	21.72
3	Kincaid J.M.W.	1601	6005	247	7 for 32	24.31
4	Heard R.J.M.	1284	3304	203	8 for 45	16.28
5	Fernandes L.	995.5	4965	195	6 for 48	25.46
6	Chapman S.R.	1037.4	3799	188	6 for 60	20.21
7	Hooper A.M.	951.2	3404	153	5 for 5	22.25
8	Cowgill J.H.C.	NR	NR	153	9 for 48	NR
9	Hughes A.A.	1017	3566	145	7 for 64	24.59
10	Neild C.D.	1013	2720	132	9 for 58	20.61
11	Cattrall P.J.	635	1874	128	6 for 36	14.64
12	Parker J.	673.4	2463	116	6 for 38	21.23
13	Hill J.M.N.	756	2463	114	7 for 37	21.61
14	Skinner A.G.	NR	NR	110	9 for 58	NR
15	Sethi R.K.	746.5	2369	109	8 for 33	23.00
16	Eden J.H.	524	1907	104	6 for 6	18.34
17	Hartley C.W.	869	3412	103	5 for 60	33.13
18	Stevens C.A.	574.2	1695	100	6 for 41	16.95
19	Fine A.M.	558	1478	90	7 for 14	16.42
20	McDuell P.J.	515.5	1891	87	7 for 82	21.74
21	Lerwill A.T.D.	414.2	2143	86	5 for 41	24.92
22	Hall B.J.B.	524.1	1882	83	4 for 42	22.67
23	Rowe C.J.C.	430	1235	82	7 for 37	15.06
24	Fursdon E.D.	406	1579	75	6 for 59	21.05
25	Bairamian R.R.	335	1937	72	6 for 54	26.90
26	Dawson C.J.A.	494.5	1684	71	4 for 15	23.71
27	Creffield N.C.	499	1744	68	5 for 50	25.65
28	Downman G.A.J.	370	1159	67	6 for 32	17.30
29	Banham M.P.	417.1	1146	65	5 for 14	17.63
30	Shore R.G.	459	1149	65	9 for 5	17.68
31	King-Harman A.W.	342	1381	65	8 for 88	21.25
32	Holgate K.C.	493	1746	65	4 for 28	26.86
33	Breen R.	417	1250	61	7 for 18	20.49
34	McDuell P. (Jnr)	192.3	865	59	7 for 51	14.66
35	Alderton A.	310	903	58	5 for 29	15.57
36	Dawson D.	282	1317	58	4 for 20	22.71

ONE ARM BOWLS A LITTLE

	Name	Overs	Runs	Wickets	Best	Ave.
37	Whyte T.	359.2	1402	58	4 for 23	24.17
38	Joyner C.S.	439	1615	58	6 for 37	27.84
39	King P.R.	374	1311	54	6 for 42	24.28
40	Vila T.	286	1346	51	5 for 22	26.39
41	Berridge T.G.C.	395.4	1585	51	5 for 36	31.07
42	Russell M.I.W.	332	919	50	5 for 54	18.38
43	Marsh P.H.	218	1400	50	4 for 60	28.00
44	Kettle R.F.	NR	NR	50	NR	NR

Bold type indicates a current playing member.

STRAGGLERS OF ASIA CC LEADERSHIP 1925-2025

	President	Chairman
1925		H.A.V. Maynard (de facto)
1934-62		Chairmen served for a single meeting, among them: Capt. (later Major) A.St.G. Coldwell, A.L. Hosie, R.B. Lagden, M. Robertson, J.R. Hechle
1962-72		T.C Longfield
1972-81	P.I. van der Gucht	Brig. J.D. King-Martin CBE, DSO, MC
1982-84	B. Joel	
1985-88	B. Joel	P.C.S. Marno
1989	Gen. Sir Geoffrey Howlett KBE, MC	P.C.S. Marno
1990-93	Gen. Sir Geoffrey Howlett KBE, MC	J.F. Hyde Blake
1994-96	Lt. Col. J.R. Stephenson CBE	J.F. Hyde Blake
1997-2002	Lt. Col. J.R. Stephenson CBE	G.W. Hartley
2003-08	Maj. Gen. S.R. Carr-Smith	P.C.S Marno
2008-12	Maj. Gen. S.R. Carr-Smith	Lt. Col. A.T.D. Lerwill OBE
2012-16	Col. A.W. King-Harman CBE	Lt. Col. A.T.D. Lerwill OBE
2016-21	Col. A.W. King-Harman CBE	Brig. J. Cavanagh DSO
2021-25	Lt. Col. A.T.D. Lerwill OBE	Brig. J. Cavanagh DSO

RELATED WORKS/ SOURCES OF INSPIRATION

Pat Barr, *The Dust in the Balance: British Women in India 1905-1945* (1989)
Mihir Bose, *A History of Indian Cricket* (1990)
Judith M. Brown, *Modern India: The Origins of an Asian Democracy* (1985)
Stephen Chalke, *Through the Remembered Gate* (2019)
Patrick French, *Liberty or Death: India's Journey to Independence and Division* (1997)
Anthony Gibson and Stephen Chalke, *Gentlemen, Gypsies and Jesters: The Wonderful World of Wandering Cricket* (2013)
David Gower, *An Endangered Species* (2013)
Ramachandra Guha, *The Commonwealth of Cricket* (2020)
Prashant Kidambi, *Cricket Country: An Indian Odyssey in the Age of Empire* (2019)
Peter R. Kohli and Shaina Kohli Russo, *Raj & Norah: A True Story of Love Lost and Found in World War II* (2021)
James Leasor, *Boarding Party: The Last Action of the Calcutta Light Horse* (1978)
Peter Oborne, *Basil D'Oliveira: Cricket and Conspiracy: The Untold Story* (2004)
Trevor Royle, *The Last Days of the Raj* (1989)
Kim A. Wagner, *Amritsar 1919: An Empire of Fear and the Making of a Massacre* (2019)
Pelham Warner, *Cricket Between Two Wars* (1942)

INDEX

Abbott, Adam 166, 174
Abdallah, Hamisi 157, 160
Abu Dhabi 83
Adastrians 91, 126, 146
Adnan, Mohammad 165
Afghan Wars 9, 27
Afghanistan 26, 52, 163
Airborne Forces 66
Albertine Wine Bar 148
Aldershot 89, 171
   Howlett's residence 112-13
Aldershot Services 65, 78
Alderton, Tony 162
   career bowling record (2024) 183
Algarve 2, 121
   International Festival for Wandering Clubs 156
Algarve Sixes 121
Allsop, James 121, 149, 156, 159, 163, 173, 175, 179
   career batting record (Oct 2024) 181
Ambalangoda 111
Ames, Les 37
Amritsar
   Jallianwala Bagh Massacre (1919) 1, 26-7, 176
Andaman Islands 32
Anderson, Sir John, Governor of Calcutta 31
anniversaries
   50th Anniversary celebrations 89-91
   60th Anniversary celebrations 112-13

75th Anniversary Tour to India (2000) 2, 84, 128, 141-4, 146
Centenary Year (2025) 2, 172, 173-6
Anson, J.W. 80
   career batting record (Oct 2024) 182
Anti-Aircraft Regiment, 34th Light 46
Argentina 146, 157, 165
Armoury House 166
Army 13, 42, 84, 159, 175
   Air Corps 168
   Army Cricket Association 89, 90
   Army Development XI 160
   Army U25 XI 151
   see also BAOR (British Army of the Rhine); Indian Army
Artillery regiment (BAOR) 77
Arundel Castle Cricket Ground 2, 161
Asher, Alex 174
Ashes 2005 156
Aston, Charles 117
Attock Oil Company, Lahore 7-8, 14
Auchinleck, Sir Claude 54
Austin, Mark 102
Australia 165-6
   Melbourne Cricket Club 102
Authentics 20-1, 40, 117

Bahia, Kuljinder 152
Bailey, Alan 99-100, 101
Bairamian, Bob 86, 90, 108-10, 113, 149, 169, 170, 181
Bairamian, Justin 110
Bairamian, Ros 109

Bairamian, Rupert 110, 115, 132, 133, 145, 146-7, 169-70
   career bowling record (2024) 181, 183
Bairamian, Sir Vahe 108
Balmer Lawrie 63
Baluch Regiment 8, 17, 44
Band of Brothers 13-14, 91, 119, 139, 146, 149, 156, 159, 161, 170
Banham, Mark 114, 171, 174
   career bowling record (2024) 183
BAOR (British Army of the Rhine) 65, 76-7, 84, 112, 119, 120, 122
   Rheindahlen 77, 92
   Rhine Army cricket festival (1976) 91-2
Barclays Bank 113
Barnes, Stuart 2, 55, 81, 96, 97, 100, 102, 103, 180
Barrington, James 102
batting records (Oct 2024) 181-3
Baxter, David 91
Baxter, Peter 139
Bazalgette, Christopher 155
Bebb, Jamie 148
Beckenham 69, 78, 79, 96
Bedi, Bishan 141
Beecher, A.W.B. 14
Beer, Martin 112, 113-14, 124, 125, 129-30, 132-3, 146, 150-1, 152
   career batting record (Oct 2024) 181
Beer, Sally 150-1, 152
Bengal
   Chamber of Commerce 40
   Cricket Association 40, 58, 87

INDEX

freedom fighters 2, 25, 29-33
and Indian independence 68
Special Constabulary 40
Volunteer Corps 29
Benson, Mark 111, 112
Beresford-Miller, Grant 152
Berkshire Gentlemen 119, 120, 146
Berlin 77, 114, 122, 170
Berridge, R.N.P.
  career batting record (Oct 2024) 182
Berridge, Toby 132-3
  career bowling record (2024) 184
BFG (British Forces Germany) 65
Bicher, Capt. 48
Bindra, Singh 127-8
Black Gunners 10, 84
Blake, B.E.
  career batting record (Oct 2024) 182
Blake, George 18-19, 23, 35, 51, 52, 55, 56
Blaker, D.J.C. 98, 99
Blofeld, Henry 127
Bluemantle's 2, 64, 79, 109, 110, 147, 149, 152, 156, 170, 173-4
Bombay (Mumbai)
  Brabourne Stadium 11, 154
  Gymkhana 154
  Quadrangular tournament 13, 37, 46, 60, 87
Booth, Steve 159
Bosnia 52
Bottell, Mike 135, 136
Boulter, Willy (the author) 102, 123-4, 149, 152
Bowling Honours Board 125
bowling records (2024) 184-5
Boycott, Geoffrey 170
Brabourne, Lord 11
Bracken, Brendan 9
Bradfield Waifs 18, 21, 28
Bradman, Sir Donald 102
Bradshaw, Geoffrey 103
Bramall, Lord 139
Branch, G.F. 14
Breen, R.
  career bowling record (2024) 183
Brentwood Martyrs 88
Brettell, David 102
British Army of the Rhine see BAOR (British Army of the Rhine)
British Empire 6, 26
British India 1-2, 11
Broadhalfpenny Brigands 175
Brocklehurst, Ben 135
Brocklehurst family 144
Brooksbank, George 161
Brown, Conor 171, 172, 173, 175
  career batting record (Oct 2024) 181
Brown, George 49
Budge, David 112
Burge, Barbara Mary Isobel 30, 31-2
Burge, Bernard Edward John 'Bobbie' 2, 27, 28-9
  assassination of 30-3, 35
Burge, John Edward 33

Burma
  destruction of the Sittang Bridge 48-9
Burmah Shell Company 17
Burton, Ed 162
Bush, Charlie 144
Butler, Paddy 180
Butler, Richard 142-3, 180
Butterflies 78, 151, 157, 161

Calcutta 2, 23, 29, 31-2, 47, 52, 95, 176
  Andrew Yule and Company 58, 74
  CCI (Cricket Club of India) 11, 154
  Mohammedan Sporting Club 25
  Special Constabulary 40
  Swimming Club 72
  University 20
Calcutta Cricket Club (CCC) 16, 23, 40, 41, 58, 59, 74
  Ballygunge 28, 71-3
  and the Hong Kong cricket club 96
  last Straggler game (1965) 95
Calder, Tim 163
Cambridge Blues 102
Cambridge Crusaders 17, 57
Cambridge tours 17, 18, 19, 20-1, 38, 64
Cambridge University 17, 26, 58, 138, 160
Cambridgeshire Regiment 42
Cameron, E. 16, 22
Cameron Highlanders 39
Canniford, Brian 142
Cantor, Darryl 86
Carlton Club 120, 121
Carr-Smith, Stephen 137, 147, 154, 160, 186
Cathay Pacific Airways 145
Cattrall, Amanda 152
Cattrall, Peter 90, 152
  career bowling record (2024) 183
Cavanagh, Joe 163, 165, 166, 171-2, 173, 174, 179, 186
  career batting record (Oct 2024) 181
CCC see Calcutta Cricket Club (CCC)
CCI (Cricket Club of India) 11, 154
Centenary Year (2025) 2, 172, 173-6
Ceylon Planters Rifle Corps 46
Chail, Simla Hills 5, 6-7, 10, 12, 174
  and the 2000 Stragglers Tour 128, 141-3
  Military Academy 143, 144
Chakraborty, Brajo Kishore 25, 32
Chalke, Stephen 60
Chamberlain, Neville 29
Chapman, Sam 135, 137, 146, 151, 152, 165
  career batting record (Oct 2024) 181
  career bowling record (2024) 183
Charles, Prince of Wales, now King Charles III 114
Chesney, Lt. Col. E.C. 8
Chile 157
China 15
  Chinese troops and the Indian army 73
  and Hong Kong 97
Christian, H.K. 62-3, 131, 139, 174
  career bowling record (2024) 183
Christie, John 28

Churchill, Winston 9, 29
City of London
  Armoury House ground 97
Club Cricket Conference 106, 147
Colchester Garrison 18
Cold War 76, 77
Coldwell, Alleyne 'Willie' 7, 8-9, 13, 14, 15, 16, 17, 18, 19, 20, 21, 23, 24, 28, 64, 74, 174, 177, 186
  and the "non-European" issue 54-5, 61
Coldwell, W.G.A. 21
Collins, Brinde 171-2
Collins, Hugh 116
Collins, John 108
Collins, Simon 121, 148, 171-2
Colony XI 97
Compton, Nick 117
Connaught Career Services 120
Conway, D. 163
Cooch Behar, Maharajah of 87
Cook, John 112, 122, 137, 138, 150-1, 170-1
  career batting record (Oct 2024) 181
Cook, Peter 137
Cooke, John 115
Cookes Rifles 17
Coombe, Tim 142-3, 150, 160
  career batting record (Oct 2024) 181
Corps Commanders XI 77
Corrie, J.C. 14
Coulthard, J.R. 35, 51, 52
COVID 166, 171
Cowans, Norman 147
Cowdrey, E.A. 17, 59
Cowdrey, Lord (Colin) 17
Cowell, C.G.
  career batting record (Oct 2024) 181
Cowgill, Amy 148
Cowgill, Kit 55-6, 61, 66, 67-8, 69, 78, 80, 86, 91, 97, 107, 148
  career batting record (Oct 2024) 182
  career bowling record (2024) 183
Cozier, Tony 111
Creffield, Nigel 112
  career bowling record (2024) 183
The Cricketer 58, 135, 144, 168
Cricketer Club 87
Cross Arrows 106, 112, 114, 115, 126, 137, 151, 157, 165
Crusaders 20-1, 102, 159
Cryptics 161
Cyprus 108, 137, 160

Dalrymple, William 11
Das, Bina 20
Dasgupta, Debayan 174
Datt, Dev 79
Datt, Shiv 79-80, 83-4, 86, 89, 91, 112, 123, 124, 126, 127, 132, 138, 145, 149, 159, 174, 179
  on Bill Withall 169
  career batting record (Oct 2024) 181
  election as Stragglers' member 80-2, 110, 169

India tours 141, 144, 175
  and the Punjab Cricket Association
    127-8
  and the South African Tour (1997)
    135, 136
Davenport, Brian 112
Davies, Peter 97
Dawson, Charlie 151
  career bowling record (2024) 183
Dawson, Danny 172
  career bowling record (2024) 183
Dean, J.M. 131
Deccan Horse 17
decolonization
  Hong Kong 97
  India 1, 59, 73-4
Delhi Blues 143
Delhi District Cricket Association 143
Delhi Durbar 6, 26
Deng Xiaoping 97
Denmark 114
Desert War 46
Desmond, Catherine 148
Desmond, John 145, 148
Devon Dumplings 18, 28
Dewar, M.B. 18
Dexter, Ted 2, 59
Diamond Jubilee 161
Dogra Regiment 17, 22
D'Oliveira, Basil 82-3
Dorset Rangers 138
Douglas, Robert 30
Downman, D.G.C.
  career batting record (Oct 2024)
    182
Downman, G.A.J.
  career batting record (Oct 2024)
    181
  career bowling record (2024) 183
Downman, Geoff 90, 138
Dragonflies 64, 86, 106
Duff, Andy 162
Dyer, Brigadier General Reginald 1,
  26-7

Ealing Cricket Club 168-9
East India Club 121, 126, 139, 145
East India Company 27
East Surrey Regiment 43-4
Eastbourne College 7, 8, 14-15, 16,
  22, 46, 47, 49, 63, 91, 119, 122, 132,
  133, 146, 162, 177
  75th birthday party for the Stragglers
    144
  Building Scheme 62
  Centenary celebrations 172, 175
  and the 'Patiala Bowl' 146, 174
Eastbourne Eclectics 122
Eastmore, G.B. 106
Eddington, Rod 102, 122-3, 123-4
Eden, John 76, 89, 92, 112
  career bowling record (2024) 183
Edrich, John 69
Elizabeth II, Queen 172
Ellesmere College, Shropshire 116, 117
Emburey, John 127
Enderby, Jono 123, 135, 136, 138, 156
  career batting record (Oct 2024)
    181

The English Maid (floating restaurant)
  152
Eritrea 84
ESBA XI 137
Evans, Richard 83
Eversley 151

Farrell, Brian 42
Fernandes Fielding Prize 172
Fernandes, Lawrence 124, 125, 138,
  139, 145, 146, 174
  career bowling record (2024) 183
Fernandes, Raphael 125
Ferrao, Mark 152
Festival of Wandering Cricket 2, 144,
  168
Fidler, Charles 174
Fielding, Peter 135, 137
  career batting record (Oct 2024)
    182
Fine, A.M.
  career bowling record (2024) 183
First World War 6, 8, 9, 27, 36, 38,
  40, 41, 48, 117
  Indian Army 11
Fisher, Nick 171
Flanagan, Steve 113
Flycatchers 145
Forster, E.M.
  A Passage to India 1
Forty Club 120
Forty 'XL' Club 134
Foulds, Martin 154-5
France
  Dordogne tour 165, 166
  Perigord tour 138
Franks, R.J.S. 80
Free Foresters 9, 13, 43, 46, 64
  BAOR section 77
Freeman, Tich 37
Frontier Force Regiment 17, 92
Fulbrook, Ed 147, 160, 166
  career batting record (Oct 2024)
    181
Fursdon, David 90, 92, 111, 112, 135
  career bowling record (2024) 183

Gallyer, David 111
  career batting record (Oct 2024)
    182
Gandhi, Mohandas 26, 27, 29, 30, 33
Gardner, H. 46
Garman, Alex 154, 156
Garnons-Williams, A.F. 14
Garnsworthy, Alex 157
Garnsworthy, Duncan 147
Gatting, Mike 102, 159
Gavaskar, Sunil 154
Gentlemen of Cambridge 172
George V, King 6
Germany
  Army 75-6, 77
  Berlin 77, 114, 122, 170
  British Forces Germany (BFG) 65
  Nazi Germany 29
  RAF 75-6, 77
  reunification 122
  Straggler fixtures 6, 77, 112
Getty, Sir Paul 127, 166

Ghosh, Nirmal Jeevan 25, 32
Giddins, Ed 147
Gibraltar 9
Gilligan, Arthur 46
Gloucestershire 87
Gloucestershire Gypsies 156
Goddard, L.J. 59-60, 61
Golden Oldies World Cricket Festival 160
Goldring, Steve 76
Gopalan, M.J. 17
Goward, E.E. 56
Gower, David 88-9
Gracey, Richard 111
Grannies 119, 145, 146, 161, 170
Grantham, Sir Alexander 98
Greece 44
Gresham School 41
Griffiths, Jolyon 115, 123
Guards CC, Chelsea 172, 174
Gucht, Paul van der 80
Gulf Wars 77, 146
Gunners 5, 112
Gurkha Division, Malaya 75, 84
Gurkha Rifles 16, 17, 96
Gurkhas in Hong Kong 96

Halifax, Lord 29
Hall, Ben 124, 138
  career batting record (Oct 2024) 182
  career bowling record (2024) 183
Hall, Jonathan 138, 145
Hall, Peter 98, 99
Halland, G.H.R. 67
Halliwell, Mike 135, 152
  career batting record (Oct 2024)
    181
Hambledon 175
Hamblin, Bryan 90, 91, 92, 111, 112
Hamilton, Tim 175
  career batting record (Oct 2024)
    182
Hammond, Wally 87
Hampshire Hogs 13, 19, 35-6, 146, 155, 175
Hardinge, Lord, viceroy of India 1
Harlequins Rugby Club 7
Harper, K.J. 45-6
Harris, Lord 40
Harrogate
  14th Golden Oldies World Cricket
    Festival 160
Harrow 157
Hartley, Andrew 114, 123, 135, 168
  career batting record (Oct 2024)
    181
Hartley, Chris 135, 136, 168
  career bowling record (2024) 183
Hartley, Geoff 114, 115, 122, 123, 127,
  134, 135, 136, 138, 144, 147, 168, 186
  career batting record (Oct 2024)
    182
Hatteea, Saeed 91
Hawkey, Richard 90, 92, 138
Heard, Richard 92, 111
  career batting record (Oct 2024)
    182
  career bowling record (2024) 183
Heardman, James 145
Hearn, Sir Roger 153-4, 155
Heath 15

INDEX

Hechle, Jim 54-5, 56, 69, 74-5, 186
Hechle, R.
  career batting record (Oct 2024) 182
Henderson, Michael 168
Hendon Police College 21
Herbert, Margaret 45
Heroys, N. 91
Hider, Ken 76, 85, 86
Hilditch, Jimmy 163
  career batting record (Oct 2024) 182
Hill, J.M.N.
  career bowling record (2024) 183
Hills, Rory 145
Hirst, George 54-5
Hitler, Adolf 9
Hodgson, Ian 102
Holgate, Keith 111, 112, 135
  career bowling record (2024) 183
Holmewood House school 108
Hong Kong 72, 161, 169
  Centenary (1951) 98
  Combined Services 74
  Craigengower Cricket Club 102
  decolonization 97
  Gurkhas 96
  HKCC (Hong Kong Cricket Club) 55, 81, 96-103, 159
    Chater Road site 97-8, 101, 102, 103
    and racial discrimination 99
    Stragglers Centenary celebration 175
    Stragglers section 2, 83, 103, 122-3, 138, 145, 149, 164, 177
    Wong Nai Chung Gap site 98, 99-103, 123-4
  Japanese occupation 98, 100
  Kowloon Cricket Club 102, 159
  Stragglers tours 2, 90, 123, 145, 166
Hooper, Tony 115, 137-8, 139, 145, 146, 147, 148, 152, 157, 161, 163, 165, 166, 173, 174, 179
  career batting record (Oct 2024) 181
  career bowling record (2024) 183
Hosie, A.G.
  career batting record (Oct 2024) 182
Hosie, A.L. 'Alec' 16, 17, 22, 41, 58, 87, 186
Houlgrave, James 156
Howard, Geoffrey 60, 66, 112-13, 122, 125, 186
Howlett, Bernard 37-8, 66
Howlett, Geoffrey 37-8, 84-5, 91, 119
Hugh Lindsay Award 114-15, 122, 137-8, 139, 151, 156, 157, 160, 162, 163, 166, 170, 171, 172
Hughes, A.A. 184
Humphreys, George 166
Hunt, Mark 171
Hunter, Don 180
Hurlingham Club 78, 106, 112, 138, 139, 151, 156-7, 162, 171, 174
Hyde Blake, Jack 92, 110, 114, 115, 116-17, 119-21, 124, 126-7, 128, 132, 134, 144, 145, 148, 163, 168, 186
  and Martin Beer 129-30
Hyde Blake, Marie-Rose 121

I Zingari 2, 46, 127, 138, 146, 151, 165-6
ICEC (Independent Commission for Equity in Cricket) 3
ICS (Indian Civil Service) 12, 13, 22, 23, 27-8, 36, 44-5, 61
IGs (Instructors in Gunnery) 92
INA (Indian National Army0 42
India 176-7
  Agra Cricket Club 153, 155
  decolonization 1, 59, 73-4
  Delhi Cricket Veterans 153
  Government of India Act (1919) 12-13
  Government of India Act (1935) 33
  home leaves for white colonial servants 13-14
  ICS (Indian Civil Service) 12, 13, 22, 23, 27-8, 36, 44-5, 61
  Indian National Defence College 169
  Jallianwala Bagh Massacre (1919) 1, 26-7, 176
  Lawrence School, Sanawar 142
  Partition of 53-4
  princely states 10-11, 12, 26, 54
  Rajasthan Cricket Association 153
  Stragglers' tours 172
    2000 2, 84, 128, 141-4, 146, 160
    2007 146, 152-5, 165
    Centenary year (2025) 2, 84, 172, 174-5
  tea companies/estates 13, 40, 72, 73, 106
  see also Chail, Simla Hills
Indian Army 6, 10, 13, 22, 44, 54, 61, 176, 180
  12th Frontier Force 84
  17th Indian Division 48
  British officers 53, 54
  and Chinese troops 73
  First World War 11
  Indian officers 12-13, 26
  Indian Reserve of Officers 46
  in Midnapore 32
  and the 'non-European' issue 83
  Punjab Frontier Force 54
  Sikh Regiment 47, 54
  Stragglers members 17, 22
  and the Stragglers' tour (2000) 143
Indian Civil Service see ICS (Indian Civil Service)
Indian cricket
  2000 Tour 7
  Centenary tour (2025) 2, 7
  Ranji Trophy competition 13, 87
Indian Freedom Movement 29
Indian independence 2, 12, 13, 25-6, 33, 53-5, 68, 82, 176
  and decolonization 73
Indian National Congress 20, 26
Indian Railways 22
Indian University Occasionals 87
Indo-Pakistan War (1965) 74
Infantry 119

Ingram, Eddie 168-9
International Cricket Council 128
International Festival for Wandering Clubs 156
Invalids 146-7
Iran 83
Iraq 26, 52, 62, 117
Ironsides 21, 41, 107
Irwin, Lord 29
Italy 9, 84
IZ 156-7

Jadeja, Devraj 141, 146, 153-4
Jallianwala Bagh massacre 1, 26-7, 176
Jameson, John 129
Japan 42-3, 47, 48, 52
Jardine Matheson 2, 96
Jersey tour 93
Jervois, Brigadier W.J. 64
Joel, Bertie 78, 80, 105-6, 119, 186
Johnston, G.S. 14
Johnstone, Conrad Powell 17-18, 56
Joyner, C.S.
  career bowling record (2024) 184

Kashmir 54, 89
Kemp's Directory 105
Kennedy, Gus 160
Kenya 116, 121
Kenya Kongonis 147
Kerr, Rait 60
Kettle, R.F. 185
'khaki election' (1945) 9
Khanna, S.K. 56-7, 59, 60, 62, 82
Kilgour, Duncan 138
Kimbolton School 79
Kimmins, B.C.H. 14, 22
Kincaid, Bill 91, 162-3
  career bowling record (2024) 183
King, Phil 122
  career batting record (Oct 2024) 182
  career bowling record (2024) 183
King, Stephen 11
King-Harman, A.W. 122, 160, 171, 172, 186
  career bowling record (2024) 183
King-Harman, Judi 172
King-Martin, Johnny 58, 66, 75, 80, 83, 84-7, 88-9, 90-1, 91-2, 107, 109, 112, 186
  newsletters 85-6
  on the Sri Lanka tour 111
King's African Rifles 18
King's Own Yorkshire Light Infantry 14, 43
King's School, Canterbury 88-9, 90, 119
Kipling, Rudyard 1, 18
Knox, General Sir Henry 64
Kohli, Peter 180
Korea 52
Kuala Lumper 75
  Selangor Club 74

Lagden, Reginald 20, 39-41, 52, 137, 186
Lahore
  Attock Oil Company 7-8, 14

189

Gymkhana 6
Lambourne, Richard 152, 154
Lamprecht, Charles 162
Lancing College 16, 46
Langdale, Simon 91
Langford, C.W. 80, 96
Larwood, Harold 102
Latham, Patrick 137, 147, 149
Lawrence of Arabia 117
Layden, Roger 112
League of Nations 11
Lee, Heather 148
Lee, Laurie 123, 145, 148
Leigh, E.B. 'Ted' 55-6, 60, 61
 career batting record (Oct 2024) 181
Leigh-Pemberton, Robin 149
Lerwill, Oliver 147, 156
 career batting record (Oct 2024) 182
Lerwill, Tim 135, 138, 150, 151, 156, 160, 162, 163, 173, 174, 179, 186
 career batting record (Oct 2024) 181
 career bowling record (2024) 183
Lincolnshire Regiment 64
Lindsay, Hugh 114
 Hugh Lindsay Trophy 114-15
Lindsay, Sarah 114, 115
Lloyd-Jones 92
London Auxiliary Ambulance Service 105
London Olympics 161
Longfield, Susan (formerly Dexter) 59
Longfield, Tom 2, 56, 57-8, 61, 69, 80, 82, 83, 86, 87, 186
 career batting record (Oct 2024) 182
Lord's 6, 39, 79, 86, 117, 122, 125, 170
 Centenary dinner for the Stragglers 175
 Cross Arrows games 63, 114, 115, 126, 151, 165
 and the Hong Kong Cricket Club 103
Ludhiana Sikhs 48
Ludwick, Jonathan 160
Lycett, Tony 136

McDuell, Jonny 166-7, 171, 174
McDuell, Paddy 174
 career bowling record (2024) 183
McDuell, Phil 102, 106, 123, 172, 173, 174, 179
 career batting record (Oct 2024) 181
 career bowling record (2024) 183
Mackenzie Lyall and Co., Calcutta 14
Mackintosh-Walker, F.R. 38-9
MacLaurin, Lord 144
McLeod, R.H. 67, 80, 81
McLeod tea company 40
McMeekin, Terence 80, 81, 89, 95-6, 96
Macmillan, Harold 59
Madras Cricket Club 17
Maharajah's Tigers XI 143
Major, Sapper 79
Malaya 42, 62, 75, 84, 96
Malaysia 72, 95
Mallinson, H.P. 22
Malta Tour 2, 150, 151, 164
Maori Club 123

Marno, Peter 88, 106, 109, 112, 113, 114, 119, 120, 122, 126, 129, 138, 147, 150, 154, 155, 156, 179, 186
 career batting record (Oct 2024) 181
Marsh, Peter 135
 career batting record (Oct 2024) 182
 career bowling record (2024) 185
Martin-Jenkins, Christopher 127, 144
Mason-MacFarlane, Frank 9-10, 13, 22, 174, 177
Maunsell, Eyre 152, 155
May, Peter 111
Maynard, Jane 66
Maynard, Martin 65, 107, 115-16
Maynard silver sauceboats 66, 115-16, 144
Maynard, Vernon 7-8, 13, 16, 17, 19, 21, 24, 51, 53, 107, 143, 144, 174, 177
 and the club colours 10
 death 66-7
 first Straggler game (Eastbourne) 14-15
 as the 'Founder' 7, 65
 and the 'non-European' issue 54-5, 56, 61
MCC 9, 13, 14, 16, 37, 46, 53, 60, 79, 88, 125, 170, 175
 and the D'Oliveira affair 82-3
 Stragglers' fixture 129, 145-6, 147, 166
Melbourne Cricket Club 102
Melhorn, Dr James 155
Merricks, Richard 136
Middleton, A.D. 22
Middleton, Eddie 175
Midlands Tour (1992) 123
Midnapore assassinations 25, 29-33
Miles, Derek 138-9, 145
Miles, Maureen 139
Miles, Rodney 102-3
Miller, P.N.
 career batting record (Oct 2024) 181
Millfield 156
Milton, Mike 112, 113, 121
 career batting record (Oct 2024) 182
Mohammad, Mushtaq 141
Montgomery, Field Marshall Bernard 22
Moore, Charles 109
Moose CC 170
Morgan, G.N.R. 52, 57, 59
Morocco 2
Morpeth, Charlie 137
Morres 15
Morris, Hugh 111
Mountbatten, Lord, Viceroy of India 53
Mukherjee, D.K. 59, 73
Musgrave, James 157, 161
 career batting record (Oct 2024) 182

Nasser, Gamal Abdel 66
Naval and Military Club 114
Naylor, G.E.M. 80
Nazi Germany 29
Nehru, J. 30, 53

Netherlands
 De Flamingo's 145
Nield, Chris 123, 136, 141, 150
 career bowling record (2024) 183
Nigeria 83, 108
Nigeria Cricket Association 65
Nigerian IX 65, 66
Norfolk
 Thornham Cricket Club 172
North Africa 44
Northamptonshire County Cricket Club 9, 64
Northamptonshire Regiment 14, 17, 21, 22, 28, 37, 38, 62, 63-4, 179
Northchurch CC 175
Northeast, Sam 117
Northern Ireland 37, 76-7
Norton, Philip 25
Norway 45
Nuttall, Richard 146

Oakham School 79
Ogden, Nick 180
Old Amplefordians 137
Old Biltonians 21
Old Camdenians 175
Old Eastbournians 170
Old Edwardians 17
Old St Edwards 117
Old Wellingtonians 112, 113, 119
Old Westminster's 119
O'Neill, Vinny 165, 172
Oporto 146-7, 166
Orders, Jonathan 102, 111, 112
Original Members (OMs) 21-2
Oxford Blues 102
Oxford tours 16, 17, 19, 20-1, 28, 64
Oxford University 16, 26, 44, 63, 138, 160

Padhani, Asif 135, 136
 career batting record (Oct 2024) 181
Pakistan 33
 Army 89
 Indo-Pakistan War (1965) 74
Pangbourne School 175
Parachute Regiment 113
Parker, Jonathan 115, 148, 152, 153, 154, 156, 159, 160, 161, 165
 career batting record (Oct 2024) 181
 career bowling record (2024) 183
Pataudi, Nawab 59
Patel, Ghanshyam 152
Patel, Min 147
Patel, Pat 153, 154
Patel, Raghu 124, 135
Patiala, Amarinder Singh, Maharaja of 128, 141-3
Patiala, Bhupinder Singh, Maharaja of 5, 7, 10-12, 13, 154
 as an Honorary Life Member 10, 61-2
Patiala Bowl 146, 162, 174
Patiala Circuit House 142
Patiala Club 113, 128

INDEX

Patiala, Rajinder Singh, Maharaja of 10
Patiala, Yuvraj of 87
Paul, Jeremy 147
PCA (Punjab Cricket Association) 127-8
Peddie, James
  assassination of 25, 29-30
Pembroke College 18
Pentangular Tournament 13
Perry, Ian 153, 160, 173, 179, 183
Peter Jones's XI 138
Philpot-Brookes, R.F.H. 38
Phipson and Co. 46
Pike, Major C.J. 96
Pilgrims 127, 137, 138
Pitt, Chris 153
Plato 28
Police College, Hendon 21
Police Service, Indian 14, 25, 32, 55, 61, 176
Pollock-Hill, Robert 117, 148, 149, 151, 153, 157, 159, 160, 161, 162, 164, 167, 171, 174, 179
  career bowling record (2024) 183
Ponting, Ricky 156
Portsmouth, United Services 17, 21, 36, 79
Potton, G. 113
Power, H.R. 56
Prabhakar, Manoj 153
Pratt, Gary 156
Premnath, Abhinav 174
Prodger, Simon 146,147, 157, 161, 162
  career batting record (Oct 2024) 181
Public Schools Club 68
Punjab Cricket Association (PCA) 127-8, 143
Punjab Regiment 17, 180
Punjab Wanderers 22, 38

Quadrangular tournament 13, 37, 46, 60, 87
Queen's Own Royal West Kent Regiment 37
Quin, John 72, 74, 95, 179

race issues 1, 3, 82, 134, 167-8
Radley College Chapel 88
Radley Rangers 87
RAF 126, 137, 180
  Germany 75-6, 77
Rajabali, Moustafa 153
Ranji Trophy 63
Ranjit Singh Ji of Navanagar 128
Ranjitsinhji, Maharajah of Navanagar 7, 12, 146
RASC Bovingdon 21
Rashid, Umer 135, 136
Razdan, Vivek 153
Razvi, Sye 124-5, 137, 138, 139, 146, 147, 148, 149, 151, 154, 157, 159, 174
  career batting record (Oct 2024) 181
Reed's Choughs 88, 91, 92, 113, 138, 155, 161
Rees, Major General 'Pete' 54

Reid, Joe 160, 175, 183
Rennie, Thomas 39
Rhemtulla, Khalil 160
Rhodes, C.K. 44-5
Rifle Brigade 27, 40
Roberts, Sir Denys 102
Robertson, Murray 16, 22, 52, 186
Robertson, S.D.G. 43
Rogers, Ben 157
Rogers, Chris 172
Rooney, F. 32
Rooseboom, SS 43
Rowe, Charles 92, 96, 97
  career batting record (Oct 2024) 182
  career bowling record (2024) 183
Rowe, George 92, 96, 99, 100-1, 101-2, 103, 124
Roy, Ram Krishna 25, 32
Royal Anglian Regiment 64
Royal Armoured Corps 43
Royal Army Ordnance Corps 170
Royal Army Service Corps 65, 66
Royal Artillery 6, 10, 14, 17, 84, 119, 138
Royal Engineers 63, 90-1, 113, 119, 150, 169
Royal Fusiliers 14, 27
Royal Garhwal Rifles 42
Royal Lancers 114
Royal Marines 56, 66, 119
Royal Naval Club 119
Royal Navy 49, 157, 159
Royal Norfolk Regiment 42
Rubie, C.B. 46-7
Russell, Jim 139
Russell, M.I.W. 185
Russell, Nigel 180

Sabine, Martin 83, 102, 149, 175
St Edward's Martyrs 21, 56-7, 69, 132
Salisbury, Peter 75-6, 85, 92, 124
  career batting record (Oct 2024) 181
Salter, Ian 161, 162, 166, 175
  career batting record (Oct 2024) 181
Sandhurst 119, 122
Sanger, Eira 10
Sanger, P.B. 'Tony' 6-7, 10, 13, 14, 22, 65, 66, 74, 75, 107, 143, 174, 177
  and the 'non-European' issue 61-2
Savage, John 92, 138
Savage, Paddy 138, 173, 175
  career batting record (Oct 2024) 181
Sawney, Richard 123, 138
  career batting record (Oct 2024) 181
Sawrey-Cookson, Nigel 145
SCC (Singapore Cricket Club) 74
Scott, Paul
  Raj Quartet 67
Seaforth Highlanders 38
Second World War 2, 9, 18, 19, 33, 35-49, 51-2, 84
  Dunkirk 9, 38, 39, 48
  Straggler deaths 36-47
Senior, A.F. Reggie 8, 14, 21, 35, 52, 54-5, 56, 61, 67
Sethi, Harsh 123, 147

Sethi, Ramesh 116-17, 123, 124, 125, 132, 135, 137, 149-50, 151, 165, 179
  career batting record (Oct 2024) 181
  career bowling record (2024) 183
  India Tours 141, 142, 152, 154, 155
  South African Tour (1997) 135-6
Sethi, Shiel 116
sexism 134-5
Shales, Matt 125, 152, 159, 162, 173
  career batting record (Oct 2024) 181
Shaw, A.A. 47
Shaw Wallace 60
Shaw Wilson and Co, Calcutta 14
Sheffield Park, Sussex 147
Sherwood Foresters 47
Sherwood, L.V.S. 2, 44
Shore, R.G.
  career bowling record (2024) 183
Shrives, Tom 160
Shropshire, Gentlemen of 123
Sierra Leone 108
Silk, Dennis 88
Sillett, Keith 102
Singapore 42-3, 62, 95
  Army members in 95-6
  Cricket Club (SCC) 74
Singh, Chatrapal 154
Singh, Yuvraj 141
Sir Roger Manwood's School 66
Skinner, Alfred Graham 63, 88
  career batting record (Oct 2024) 181
  career bowling record (2024) 183
Skipper, Tony 76, 112
Slazenger 79
Smith, Charles 25
Smith, Ed 162
Smith, Terry 102, 103
Smyth, Jackie 48-9
Somers-Cox, Major 8
Somerset Stragglers 2, 8, 14, 18, 146, 151
South Africa 2, 26, 142, 166
  the D'Oliveira affair 82-3
  Stanley Cricket Club 145
South African Tour (1997) 135-6
South Oxfordshire Amateurs 2, 119, 123, 132, 156, 171, 175
Southall Travel 152
Spectator magazine 11, 109
Sri Lanka
  Boxing Day tsunami (2004) 149-50
  tours 2, 111-12, 126, 148-9, 164
Staffordshire Gentlemen 123, 168
Staffordshire Regiment 135
Stanley Jackson, Sir Francis 19-20
Statham 59
Stephenson, John 125, 126-7, 127, 128, 132, 134, 147, 148, 186
Stephenson, Karen 148
Stevens, C.A.
  career bowling record (2024) 183
Stock, F.M.C. 113
Stockton, Earl of 139
Stockwell, General Hughie 66

191

Stoughton, Luke   137
    career batting record (Oct 2024)   182
Strachan, Chris   71-2, 179
Straggler's 100 Club   114, 128
Stragglers of Asia
    annual committee meetings   52-3
    annual dinners   19, 20, 106, 111, 112, 116, 120, 121, 126-7, 139, 145, 157, 167
    annual subscriptions   55, 115
    career batting records (Oct 2024)   181-2
    career bowling records (2024)   183-4
    club colours   10, 63
    'East of Suez' membership qualification   15-16, 52, 176
        relaxation of   74-5, 110, 176
    finances   19, 62
    founding of (Trafalgar Square meeting)   6, 9, 10, 65, 177
    governance   84
    Hong Kong section   2, 83, 103, 122-3, 138, 145, 149, 164, 175, 177
    leadership (1925-2025)   184
    membership list   23, 52, 122
    new recruitment   175-6
    non-European members   2, 12, 80-2, 110, 116-7, 123, 124-5, 167, 169
    the 'non-European' question   12, 54-5, 55-7, 58-62, 79-83, 107, 132-4, 135-6, 176
    Original Members (OMs)   21-2, 175
    Rules   19, 23, 86
    silver cup   63-4
    Straggler 100 Club   113
    Veterans List   23-4
    Working Party ('2000')   134
Suckling, Matt   171, 174, 183
Suez crisis   52, 66
Suffolk Regiment   32
Suhrawardy, Hassan   20
Sunbury   163
Sussex CCC   136
Sussex Martlets   2, 12, 161, 175
Sutcliffe   87
Sutton Valance   91
Swanton, E.W.
    The World of Cricket   78
Swetman, Roy   78, 131-2, 137, 156
Swetman, Rupert   78, 132, 135, 137
    career batting record (Oct 2024)   182

Swift, Mike   151, 163-4
    career batting record (Oct 2024)   182
Swire, Merlin   161
Swynnerton Park   123

Tangiers   147
Tank Corps   41
Tanzania   157
Tanzania National XI   160
Tate, Maurice   46
Taylor, A.O.D.   14, 15
Taylor, Richard   146, 160
Taylor, Tim   146, 147
Terrell, Ivor   111
Thatcher, Denis   127
Thatcher, Margaret   97, 127
Theakston Brewery   160
Thistle, HM Submarine   45-6
Thomas Walker & Co, Calcutta   69
Thompson, Eddie   168-9
Thorne, G.C.   42-3
Thornham Cricket Club   172
Thorpe, Graham   113
Tindall, Robert   135, 136, 146
Tokyo Club   180
Torry Hill   149, 159
trading companies   13
Trafalgar Square meeting   6, 9, 10, 65, 177
Trapani, Nino   160
Triangular Tournament   13
Trinity School, Croydon   152
Trollope, A.J.   8, 14
Trueman, Nick   59, 153
Tunbridge Wells   2, 108, 147, 166
Tutt, Julian   112

Ukraine   26
United Services Portsmouth   17, 21, 36, 79

van der Gucht, Paul   86, 87-8, 89, 91, 105, 186
    career batting record (Oct 2024)   181
Vaughan-Arbuckle   97
Veterans List   23-4
Viceroys XI   87
Victoria, Queen   26
Vietnam   26
Vila, Tom   163, 166, 175
    career bowling record (2024)   184

Warner, Sir Pelham ('Plum')   58
Warren, C.M.   41
Wavell, General   49
Webster, Harold   18
Webster, W.H.   18
Welch Regiment   47
Welchman, Roger   47
West Country tour (1991)   122
West Indies   63
West Kent   69
West, S.E.   22
Western Desert   84, 87
Western Tour   19, 20, 28, 41
Wheeler, Nigel   144
Whittaker, Roger   151
Whyte, Sir Frederick   9-10
Whyte, T.
    career bowling record (2024)   184
Wilberforce, W.B.S. 'Bill'   43-4
Wilberforce, William   44
Wilkinson, G.
    career batting record (Oct 2024)   181
Williams, Chris   175
Williams, Dennis   92
Willingdon, Lord, Viceroy of India   11, 19
Wilson, Sir James   89-90
Winstanley, Mark   102, 173, 175
Wisden Cricket Monthly   83
Withall, Bill   79, 80, 81, 89, 90, 92, 93, 124, 129, 139, 152, 168-9
    career batting record (Oct 2024)   181
Woolley, Frank   37
women as Honorary Members   148
women's cricket   134-5, 177
Woodbridge, Brian   135, 172
Wooldridge, J.H.C. 'Hugh'   41-2
Wooldridge, J.W.   41
Wooldridge, Lesley   42
Woolwich Garrison   65
Worcester College   89
Wormsley   127, 137, 166

Yamashita, General   42-3
Yellowhammers   170
Yorkshire County Cricket Club   167
Young, Keith   152, 175
    career batting record (Oct 2024)   182

www.ingramcontent.com/pod-product-compliance
Lightning Source LLC
Chambersburg PA
CBHW052043280426
43661CB00085B/104